ACKNOWLEDGEMENTS

To my wife Marian, our four children Mark, Michael, Michaela and Matthew for all the hours of my life you have permitted me to indulge in Gaelic games. To my six brothers and two sisters for their kindness and consideration towards the "baby" in the house. A special word of appreciation to my sister Mary and the Mallaghan family for opening their doors (and food cupboards) to an ever-increasing Tyrone fan base over a generation of All-Irelands dating back to the early seventies.

To the Tyrone County Board who have afforded the privilege of working with the best talents in the country at various age levels from 1991 until the present day. To Club Tyrone and all the other sponsors for their contribution to the development of our games over the years. To all the players and people who have worked alongside me with Tyrone and my club, Errigal Ciarán, helping to make the journey of the last 18 years such an enriching adventure.

Thanks to Lairdesign and Glen McArdle for their expertise in relation to the cover of this book. Thanks to Sportsfile, Kenny Curran, Jim Dunne and Cormac McAleer for permission to use photos. Thanks to Kenny Curran also for providing the statistics at the end of the book. To all at Poolbeg Press and Brian Langan in particular for helping us complete this piece of work within the time schedule. To Eoin Conroy of Byrne/Conroy Consultants for his expert guidance on every step of this particular journey.

To Michael Foley for putting this book together with the quality I have always looked for in my teams. Our journey was one of discovery. May it bring you to new places too.

To my late mum and dad,
Mary and Peter Harte,
for the inspiration they continue to be in my life.

CONTENTS

PROLOGUE

All-Ireland football semi-final, Croke Park

23 August 2009

Cork 1-13, Tyrone 0-11

IT'S THE SILENCE that hits you hardest. That inescapable, agonising silence that clings to the dressing-room walls. That silence that grabs you, choking the words in your throat. You can't speak. You can't express the disappointment sticking like a pain in your side. Cork have won. Our season is over. Our chase for two All-Irelands in a row, our shot at history. Gone. All gone.

Moments from today race through my mind: frees that weren't given, missed chances, dropped hand-passes, soaring points, flu and stomach ailments. I think of the last few weeks, the hours at home draining from night into early morning watching Cork on video. Analysing them. Thinking about them. The nights at training in Cookstown and Clogher talking to the boys, trying to strike the right tone. Beating Cork was about earning the right to play into September. That was the motto for the game. That was the statement that crystallised what this team was about. Playing into September. Playing to make history.

1

I watched the players at training, skirting around the cones during the drills. Pushing hard. We pushed them harder. "Don't cut them," I shout. "Are you going to go round the cones, or cut them by six inches? What difference can that make?" Years making those tiny differences count tell us that matches are won and lost on less.

Little incidents dotted the previous few days. Did they make a difference? Joe McMahon started the week with flu. Not good. It was never going to stop him playing, but those problems always drain a little energy by Sunday. Enda McGinley had overcome an injury to start the game at midfield. Brian Dooher has struggled between games all year, but has always found a way to get himself right in time to play. Extraordinary effort. Extraordinary man.

On Saturday morning Philip Jordan isn't well. He has a stomach bug. Another wee drain on our energies. Sunday morning Sean Cavanagh comes to see me. He's not happy.

"I didn't sleep last night at all," he says. "I'm not feeling good. I feel wrecked."

His body language isn't good. There's something wrong.

"Are you telling me there's not 70 minutes in you?" I reply.

"Aye, I don't think so."

A shock ran through me. He said he felt jaded.

I was puzzled. In 2008 Sean had been Footballer of the Year. He had played midfield for Tyrone as a 19-year-old in 2003 and won an All-Ireland medal. He had All Stars. He had coped and performed brilliantly in pressure games before. He had already placed himself among the greatest footballers of his generation. I needed to try and see things from his perspective. Apart from a few isolated flashes of brilliance, his form hadn't been great all season. Why was that?

As a player Sean had always delivered. He was an icon for us and that greatness had been rewarded in 2008. Maybe the pressure was stemming from that recognition. Did Sean feel he needed to deliver a towering performance every time he put on a Tyrone jersey? Like any other player, all we ever wanted from Sean was to give his best. What that amounted to might be different on any given day. We didn't want him to feel pressure. He had given us so much over the years, he didn't need to prove anything to anybody. We simply wanted him to be Sean.

A lot was going on in his life. He was preparing to get married in December. His commitments to the GPA and his profile made him a natural spokesperson for them. Commercial sponsors wanted more of his time. The media wanted to hear his voice. He had been suffering with a slight ankle injury all year that required regular monitoring and treatment. Had we addressed all those pressures properly during the year? Had our support structure been strong enough to share his burden?

I didn't feel Sean was letting us down. It was a shock, but it was better to share his worries rather than start the game in a negative frame of mind. This moment seemed the culmination of a year's worth of pressure and expectation leaning on him. In the end, the roof simply caved in.

I needed to make a decision. Fast. I could try and talk him round, but Sean's demeanour told me not to. That was fine. We had a squad built to withstand these losses. Sean still had something to offer us, just not from the start. I decided to hold him back and introduce him during the game. When he did come on, Sean would know he just had to empty himself for the time remaining. Plus, it would be some boost for our team.

The next hour was crucial. I found Tony Donnelly, my selector, and told him the news. We started bouncing ideas around. Sean had been a key part of our strategy to hurt Cork. He was to start at midfield, with Enda McGinley switching to centre-forward to move around and play as a utility attacker. It was all based around worrying Cork's centre-back, Graham

Canty, who we saw as Cork's spiritual leader and driving force. Instead of pushing Cork along, we wanted him to start thinking about us. About Sean. About Enda.

Now we had to think again. Tommy McGuigan had started the All-Ireland quarter-final against Kildare and made way when Enda regained fitness. He had something to prove.

We told Tommy he was starting at centre-forward, and told Enda he was reverting to midfield. We also told them to keep it quiet till we reached the dressing-rooms in Croke Park. When we got there, I broke the news to Brian Dooher. Word gradually filtered through the group. No big announcements. No fuss. Sean wasn't with us from the start, but we had jumped higher obstacles before. This was simply another.

WE WERE RATTLING HURDLES inside the first ten minutes. A blocked shot in front of our square landed in Daniel Goulding's lap. Goal. Another Cork point. Suddenly we're seven points down.

Crucial calls were going against us. Tackling without conceding a foul was an issue we had worked on all year. Before we played Cork, we increased that focus on clean, crisp tackling. Yet we were being blown time after time. All the while, it seemed Cork weren't being made subject to the same rigour.

Referees don't win and lose games for anyone, but as the game went on John Bannon's influence was increasing. After 29 minutes Alan O'Connor was sent off. Cork were down to 14 men. As it turned out, O'Connor's departure caused us more problems than it did Cork. In the last eight minutes before half-time, Cork was awarded seven frees. We got none. In any match, it's highly unlikely that the weight of frees would go so heavily against one team over that length of time. Was the referee balancing things out?

We were penalised for two pick-ups off the ground that never happened. The result of one was a point for Cork. As we approached half-time we had narrowed the gap to five points and Ryan McMenamin was getting within shooting distance again. Then, the whistle blew for the break. Ricey was incensed. We couldn't believe it. Four points in Gaelic football is always a more manageable deficit than five. Another massive moment had gone against us.

We get close in the second half, but never close enough. We're trying to run at Cork's defence, but they're packing the area in front of goal and forcing us around the sides. When we run at them, our players are getting mauled in the tackle. We look for frees. We get nothing.

We pull the deficit back to four. Owen Mulligan misses a free to make it three. Crucial. Cork pull away again to a six-point lead. Sean Cavanagh comes on and tries to open up some avenues to run into, but Cork players are blocking up every route. Graham Canty lands with his knees on Enda McGinley. A few minutes later he takes Kevin Hughes out of the game. The net result from both challenges is only a yellow card. I'd love to have Graham Canty on my team, but those incidents distilled the infuriating inconsistencies within the game that irritate me most.

Contrast John Bannon's reaction to those fouls with Pat McEnaney's reaction to an incident during our Ulster championship game with Armagh this year. Although Conor Gormley had dragged him to the ground, Ronan Clarke wriggled free and slotted a goal. Even though Ronan was fouled, Pat allowed the goal to stand and still booked Conor. Because he was already on a yellow card, a red followed and Conor was off.

Such key moments can decide entire championships. Now, a few months later in Croke Park, it seemed those inconsistencies were tipping the scales against us again. With ten minutes to go, John Miskella lands a swipe on Brian McGuigan. Another yellow card. Another key moment goes against us. Unbelievable.

It was more than that, too, though. We were getting legitimately turned over in the tackle too many times. We didn't have that bite that said, "You're not getting this ball." That desire we thought was in the team all year had been bettered. Referees and circumstances didn't help us, but Cork were better. Bottom line.

I HEAD FOR THE PRESS CONFERENCE. I am thinking about this disappointment. How will I process it? How do I convey our true emotions to the wider public after losing this game? As a team, we have never celebrated victory or endured defeat on our own. Others have travelled with us, in body and in spirit.

I think of Cormac McAnallen. Of Paul McGirr. Back in 2003, Cormac shared these rooms with us. He held the Sam Maguire Cup and crowned a glorious career with every honour the game could bless him with before he was 24. The following year he died. For a while we felt alone, but his spirit never left us.

It was the same with Paul. It was June 1997 when Paul collided with the Armagh goalkeeper during an Ulster minor championship match and scored a goal. As manager I helped carry the stretcher from the field that day. Paul was a friend of my son Mark. That evening he died from the injuries he sustained in the accident.

I remember standing in a hospital room in Omagh that evening. Francie and Rita McGirr, grieving for their son, still dressed in his Tyrone strip, suddenly taken from them during a game of football. When we lost Paul McGirr, life laid a challenge before us. Could we find the hope in this tragedy? Could our actions and our attitudes help us break the clouds that had gathered over us and threatened to shadow our lives for good?

We couldn't think of Paul as a crusade back then, but as an inspiration. Paul's passing opened us up to all sorts of new relationships and engagements with each other. You would never want it to happen that way, but that's how it was for this group, and for myself.

I look back now and see how boys became men in 1997. I think of Kevin Hughes mourning his brother's death in a car accident two months after Paul, but using football as a way to keep some perspective in his life. Years later, when we mourned Cormac and found ourselves mired in the sort of grief I feared might finally wear this group of men down, it would be Kevin Hughes who would stand up and tell the boys we simply had to move on.

Courage. It was Mark Harte angling an impossible shot over the bar to draw against Kerry in the 1997 All-Ireland minor semi-final when we had entered the last five minutes trailing by three points. It was Cormac being carried from the pitch in Parnell Park during the replay, paralysed by cramp and returning to the field to help drag Tyrone to victory in a game that redefined everything we ever thought about Kerry.

It was what these boys were prepared to give for that game, for that group. It was how they would continue to give for something that was so special to them but in a way that was inexplicable to anyone outside that group. Paul McGirr's death was a moment of sadness none of us will ever fully get over or understand, but it was also a profound moment. From then on we have always won and lost together. We have mourned together. We have recovered together.

I sit at the desk in the press conference room. A platoon of dictaphones whir. Reporters are waiting for answers. Paul and Cormac are on my mind. I can feel their presence as I speak.

"Life has given us worse knocks than losing semi-finals and we have dealt with them, so we'll deal with this too. We'll be hurt. We'll be annoyed. We'll have many regrets by all means, but they are only sporting regrets and ultimately in the real scheme of things it won't be that crucial."

After following our story for years, the reporters know the sad subtext to that sentiment. When I say it on behalf of our team, we say it with a conviction no one else could.

At the anniversary Mass for Paul a month after he died, Fr Gerard McAleer delivered the sermon. I had known Fr Gerard for many years by then. He had joined me with the minors in 1991, and had been beside me on the side-line as part of the management team on the day Paul died. In his sermon, he reflected on how Paul's character brought to mind the alphabet. A for athletic, B for brave, C for courageous, D for determined, E for energetic, and so on. There was no point in just remembering Paul; what could we learn from him? How could we honour him? The answer was left unspoken, but everyone knew what it was. We don't lie down. We go ahead.

Today was sickening. Losing hurts so much because we give our lives to this obsession, but the years sharing the same triumphs and tragedies as a team have taught us how to cope and understand. The only true defeat is when you don't bottle the learning from it. We will shoulder our hurt together tonight, but we will rise once more. Paul and Cormac have provided the light before.

It will help guide us again now.

1

THE JOYFUL MYSTERIES

A SUNDAY MORNING in April, 2009. I leave my house in Glencull before eight. Heading west for Swinford. A few weeks before, I had been met by some members of the local GAA club after Tyrone had played a league game against Mayo. They asked me to visit them. Garda Robert McCallion had been a member of the Swinford team. In March he had been struck by a car while on duty in Donegal and died from his injuries. He was 29 years of age.

I had read about his death at the time. The funeral had been a massive occasion in Swinford and prompted a profound outpouring of grief in the area. A guard of honour formed by the Garda Síochána and the GAA club lined the way to the cemetery. The club was trying to find ways to overcome the tragedy. One sad legacy of our time as a team has been our experience in dealing with tragic losses. Alongside losing Paul and Cormac, our team-mates have lost brothers and sisters, relations and friends, in equally tragic ways. We learned to absorb those blows together. If I can help others as they cross the same hurdles, I will.

I drive along through quiet country roads. Through Omagh, on towards Ederney and Kesh. Across the border near Belleek and heading towards the Ballyshannon bypass and Sligo. Imagining the trip down through Curry and Charlestown, the road broadening out as I reach the turn-off for Swinford. After a short while, I begin to whisper the Rosary to myself. It's an old habit. If I'm in the car for longer than 20 minutes, I will usually begin to work through the decades. It helps me journey to a peaceful place. It allows me to reconnect with memories of my childhood and find a spiritual calm within myself. So, in the quiet solitude of a Sunday morning with the road dissolving in front of me, I begin to pray.

The Annunciation – The Creation of Humility

WHAT DO YOU SAY to soothe people's souls? Over the years I have been invited to speak to so many groups: schools, GAA clubs, congregations at Novenas and Holy Days. My experience with Tyrone has given me a face people recognise. It's also compelled me to confront the kind of problems and challenges we never expect when we get involved in sport.

The key to everything is to respect uniqueness. That is the thread that defines my teams, and maybe my entire outlook on life. To get the most from life and other people, we must respect every individual. That is the baseline principle from which we can never go wrong.

When I was young, my mother was a wonderful listener, a counsellor to her neighbours before the title was ever even coined. My parents looked at everyone as equals. They listened to every problem and story with the same sincerity. Their wisdom was a lesson to us all at home. We must accept that every person is here for a God-given purpose, and that we cannot make judgements on one person against another. There is only one judgement we can make: is this person doing the best they can? Can we help them to do better? It's not about creating clones either. It's about helping people embrace their own uniqueness. That applies to football teams. And to life.

You have to accept that everyone is responsible for the world in which they must live, but that responsibility is also accompanied by a sense of liberation. That world we inhabit is within our control in so many ways. Wayne Dyer, a self-help advocate, once identified seven crucial words to live our lives by:

As you think, so you shall be.

That is the core philosophy I have carried on every step of this journey. Our destiny is based on how we react to life. Take that sentiment on board, and gradually we can find we have much more control of our destiny than we might once have thought.

As you think, so you shall be. Everything about that phrase appeals to me. It's comprised of seven words. The number seven has always been important to me. It was the number on the first house I ever bought with Marian, my wife. George Best wore number seven. Nobody is perfect, but many things we once thought beyond our capabilities are within reach. We simply must accept we are all people in the making. Goals and ambitions are merely signposts to guide us along a much longer, deeper journey.

The Visitation – The Love for Our Neighbour

ABOUT 60 PEOPLE were gathered in Swinford, including Garda McCallion's brother and brother-in-law, waiting to listen. Over the years I have stood in many rooms and felt the same sense of sadness. The week before Derry played Kerry in the league final this year, Conor McCusker, a brother of Derry footballer Niall McCusker from Ballinderry, was killed in an incident outside a bar in Cookstown, sending ripples through the small GAA community across south Derry. I got a call from their manager Damien Cassidy, asking for my thoughts on how to deal with that situation.

Patrick Devlin from Ardboe was a teenager when he died from a cardiac condition. His father asked me to speak at his funeral. I didn't know the family well, but if that presence helped them in any way at such a difficult time, then I felt it was the right thing to do.

A young man called Brian Óg McKeever from Derry was suffering from leukaemia. His mother had spotted a story in the paper detailing a car accident I had been involved in, in October 2008. She read that I had a rosary ring on my finger and a Padre Pio relic in my pocket at the time of the accident. While I waited for help, I simply prayed.

From that story, she felt a connection with me through my religious beliefs. She also knew Joe Brolly, and asked Joe if he could make contact with me. A few days after the accident, I received her contact details and got in touch. One evening I visited their house outside Derry city. We sat together and talked football with Brian. He was very ill then, but I remember he managed a bowl of soup on my first visit. Another night Brian Dooher and Cuthbert Donnelly, the guardian of the Sam Maguire Cup on its stays in Tyrone, called to Brian with the Cup. The next time I called, Brian had fallen into a coma. His friends were around his bed, offering support. As I spoke to him, I saw him move slightly. He was still there, still fighting. When he died I went to his wake with Brian Dooher and Cuthbert. It was a sad visit, but we were honoured to have made the connection with him.

Every trip contained its own strain of sadness. In March, Oisin McGuinness died of a heart condition while playing soccer at home in Newry in March of this year, aged 16. Christopher Coary from Derrylaughan in Tyrone was killed in a road accident in 2006. Eamon McIntyre, a teenage boy from Ballerin, County Derry, was killed in a car accident on his way to a graduation ball. I was invited by the GAA club to a special night for their under-age teams and their mentors, and to meet with Eamon's parents. When Sean Paul O'Hagan from north Antrim died in a road accident on New Year's Day, his local GAA club asked me to visit with them. Darren Price was 18 when he was killed on the road near Tyrrellspass, County Westmeath in 2006. I spoke to his team-mates about getting over their loss, too.

A team from Fermanagh came to Ballygawley so I could talk with them. I travelled to Skryne in Meath another night to address a team. People know you have experience in dealing with these traumas. They are reaching out for support and help. There have been many others through the years. Phone calls at home. Letters and cards seeking consolation. Although I'm not a professional, all I can do is share our experiences with them.

I shared the same thoughts with the people in Swinford.

Most of all, people need reassurance that feeling different emotions are acceptable. People deal with tragedy in different ways. The main message is to be there for each other. Don't make your sporting lives a crusade to remember others. If you really wish to hold these people in high regard, think of what good you can find in them and bring it into your own life. You never have to go out and win anything for somebody you really respect. You simply must do your best.

It's important to find a way to share those thoughts, too. It's also important to share the burden of grief. Keeping in touch with the family was a crucial element of the process when we lost Paul and Cormac – the odd visit, a card on anniversaries and at important times. Prayer can help keep you connected to people too. It all adds up to a sense of community, the feeling that you are not alone.

It's important to know it's okay to laugh again. Sometimes people think it's almost disrespectful to laugh, but it's what those who have passed on would expect. You live your life. Be aware of what they brought to life and take positives from that. Nothing will ever feel the same again, but that's fine. You start a different life in a different place. Ultimately, everyone will be okay.

Back in March 2006 I received a letter from a teenager in Fermanagh. Shane McAloon was part of the Devenish football team. His best friend was Damien Dolan. They had grown up together, playing football, playing on their tractors and diggers pretending to be farmers, doing all the things children do. In September 2005, Damien had been killed in a road accident. After Damien's death, I had been invited to speak with the Devenish team about ways to deal with their loss.

I put a lot of time into figuring out how to address groups, but ultimately I turn everything over to God. I don't have the answers for people. I can only search my soul for what I believe might be useful for them. These visits are an opportunity to empathise with others. That is a quality that transcends every element of life.

As a basis, I used the same concepts that helped us deal with the deaths of Paul and Cormac. You can never know how your words affect people. You hope to leave them with something to think about, maybe a route to find some consolation. What Shane wrote touched me deeply. He had struggled to find any route away from the sadness he felt, but the steps that helped us move to a new place started him on the road too.

Before Damien died, Devenish had been struggling to stay in Division One at their grade of football in Fermanagh. In the end they won their last two games and retained their status. The players visited Damien's parents. They prayed. "I always prayed," he wrote, "but I feel there is more meaning to prayer now."

He had been suspended from playing in the McRory Cup with St Michael's Enniskillen, and the loss of those games hurt him. "At the start of the school year I had said to myself: 'I am going to do this for Damien'; but I recalled your words: 'Don't do it for Damien, do it in memory of him.'" He didn't feel like he had let anybody down any more. "When life was tough," he said, "you gave me enough to keep my head up." Shane McAloon gave me as much encouragement, too.

14

The Nativity – The Birth of Spirit

I GOT TALKING to Matthew, my youngest son, recently. He is 21 this year. The little boy I once brought along with my daughter Michaela on the team bus to matches, and always among the first to reach me on the side-line in Croke Park after every big game, has grown into a man.

He has grown into a deep thinker, too. We spoke about spirituality and what it meant in our lives. I started wondering when it was I began to think about life as Matthew was. I discovered a lot through football: motivational speakers and great sports coaches all informed my thinking. But football was never divisible from the rest of my life. My mind wandered back to an evening in the mid-seventies when I lived as a student off the Falls Road in Belfast. I saw a sign for a religious meeting. The group resided under the banner of the Charismatic Movement, a vibrant religious revival that spread across the country like wildfire at the time. It was a movement designed to increase the awareness among people of the presence of God in their lives. That hall on the Falls Road was filled with people of all religious denominations – with the Troubles at their height, all were drawn by the power of Spirit.

I found those meetings inspiring and intimidating at the same time. People might begin speaking in tongues while someone else would interpret their words for the congregation. Another person might call out a passage from the Gospel entirely from memory. All the time, you were taught to praise God with your hands open and lifted towards the heavens. It opened my mind to the idea of giving thanks. I had grown up a devout Catholic and always observed the feast days and sacraments, but somewhere along the way maybe my faith had become routine. This felt like a reawakening, a reinvigoration. A true celebration of God.

I attended those meetings wherever I found myself. When I took my first job as a teacher in Kircubbin, County Down, I found a meeting hall in Portaferry out on the Ards Peninsula. When Marian and myself moved to Dungannon, meetings were held at a venue across the road from our house. One woman in Dungannon had a special gift for quoting scripture. One night she repeated a verse of scripture that stayed with me forever. It was from the Book of Romans, chapter 12, verses 7–13:

> *"So we are to use our different gifts in accordance with the grace that God has given us. If our gift is to speak God's message, we should do it according to the faith we have."*

That helped form part of my outlook on life ever since. If you're a healer, you heal. If you're a teacher, you teach. Over the years I have begun to figure out that my best role is as a communicator. So I communicate. I try and share things with people. Sometimes that brings me to corporate events. Sometimes to parish novenas. Sometimes that brings me into dressing-rooms, trying to focus players' minds on their greatest strengths and how that power can help them to get the best from themselves on the field. Sometimes it brings me into houses shrouded in grief.

The Presentation – Finding Peace in Mind and Body

LATER THAT DAY, I met with Garda McCallion's parents. We shared a pot of tea as they told stories about their son. He loved his football and his job. He travelled from his base in Letterkenny all the way home for matches and training. We talked for a half hour. They smiled and laughed a little. It's all we can do: listen, care. Simply be there.

People have sometimes asked me if these experiences are an emotional drain. I think they're a privilege. This is part of the prayer life, part of fulfilling the role your God-given talents allow you to play. It's what I learned at home as a boy, and it has always rung true.

Sharing time with the people I have met because of the experiences I endured through Paul and Cormac has changed my life. It opened my mind to a whole new avenue of thought and reflection that impacted on my spiritual life and my life in football. As you think, so you shall be. Don't let the future be defined by circumstances or fear. That simple sentiment brings us all hope and illuminates a whole new set of possibilities for all of us.

And, at the start of every year, it always brings me back to football.

2

THE SEARCH FOR DIFFERENCE

15 February 2009

THE MOOD IN OMAGH is turning sombre. Half-time. The score tells me everything I need to know: Kerry 2-8, Tyrone 0-3. We are All-Ireland champions, but Kerry are playing all the football. Standing on the line, I have been thinking my way through the problems all half. We've been doing more physical work with the players than normal for this time of year. At times we look a little heavy-legged. But there's more going on than that. Although it's only a league match, Kerry are here to leave a dent on us. We knew this was the way it would be this year. Trying to defend our All-Ireland titles in 2004 and 2006 told us that. Teams would drive harder at us. Where plenty of teams and pundits doubted our quality in 2007 and 2008, we were now in everyone's crosshairs again. All the cheers from winning the last All-Ireland had died away into memory. There was nothing left now between us and returning to the battlefield. How would we respond? Days like this could give us an idea.

We pulled the boys into the dressing-room. We asked them one question: why were we 11 points down? This wasn't a witch hunt. This was a mind search. Kerry had been allowed too much space. Too often they had been able to take their first preference shot. We needed to make them think again. We needed to swallow up the space we had allowed them. We needed to work much harder.

That has always been the basic cornerstone that has supported every team I have ever produced. They work. They don't flinch. They hound and hustle and harry. They tackle. They win the ball back. Then, they create.

We redrew the team on a board in the dressing-room and started to move players into different positions. Apart from those switches, though, the most important message was simple. All the arrows on the board pointed towards the Kerry half. Pin them back. Whatever about the circumstances of the game, every half-time was the same to me. You didn't begin the second half ahead or behind, but level with your opposition. Our aim today was to win the second half. That was achievable.

I looked around the dressing-room at the boys. An idea ran through my head. I looked over at our kit man, Mickey Moynagh.

"Have we a second set of jerseys, Mickey?"

"We do."

"Fire them out."

We needed to start fresh. The first half was gone. We'll leave the jerseys behind too, but we'll do it right. It's become a tradition that my players respectfully unfold their jerseys before every game and put them on together, as a unit. It's a way of paying tribute to what that jersey stands for, and the work we've done to uphold its traditions. We're not throwing these jerseys away because of a bad performance – on these days it's even more important to fold them and place them on the bench. I call each player up and hand him his new jersey. The players put them on in unison. It's a sign of a new start. A new beginning.

Days like this tell a little parable about the journey we have taken too. Years ago, Tyrone would have welcomed Kerry to Omagh like visiting royalty. Not any more. The welcome is still warm, but Kerry are the team seeking to leave an impression on the game.

People say our rivalry with Kerry has dominated football for the past decade. Some reckon we have degraded football only for Kerry to come and save it. Others think we have reinvented the entire game. I simply see two teams with a contrast in style, sharing the same relentless ambition to win. We can look them in the eye. There's respect, but no fear.

When we won our first All-Ireland in 2003 we went through Kerry in the All-Ireland semi-final, scored nine points in the first half, shut them down all over the field with a performance of such intensity that never gave Kerry a chance to catch their breath. Some pundits reckoned we were a disgrace. Pat Spillane, the old Kerry footballer blessed with eight All-Ireland medals, described our performance as "puke football". Blanket defence was another term destined to stick with us.

I respected where these people were coming from, but I couldn't see the logic in their point. Our performance struck me as a passage of footballing perfection. We weren't defensive. Each player worked relentlessly for every other player that day. Was that not the epitome of team? And we scored nine points in 35 minutes of football against Kerry while holding them to just two points. We couldn't have played bad, negative football and still gather that kind of tally.

But people made their own assumptions. In 2005 Kerry prepared for a war and we beat them in a game of football. In 2008 we returned with Kerry chasing three-in-a-row. We had spent all summer reshaping our team, and produced the ultimate expression of a team unit. The All-Ireland final was billed as the clash to decide the team of the decade. Our victory meant we extended the debate into 2009.

Now the country was waiting for another gunfight later in the summer. Whether it would happen or not didn't concern me. That sentiment, though, tells us about the journey we have made. It's a tribute to what we have achieved over the past decade, and a reflection on the challenges to come. You don't create that kind of legacy by thinking about it, though. We have problems in Omagh today, but I can see how we can still salvage something for ourselves.

New jerseys. We begin again.

SECOND HALF. We outscore Kerry 0-10 to 0-2 and slim the losing margin to just a goal. That's massive for us. At the end Ryan McMenamin and Marc Ó Sé are isolated on the side-line. They jostle a little. Ricey throws out a slap with the flat of his hand that catches Marc. Tyrone players are on the way. Declan O'Sullivan is steaming in but Conor Gormley blocks his way. Kerry manager Jack O'Connor is out on the field but he's not pulling his players away. He's in Colm McCullagh's face. Whatever about laying down markers, I'll not be doing it that way.

There had been an edgy feel about Kerry all day. Over the years any conversations I had with Jack O'Connor were confined to a few chats on the odd All Star trip or sharing a table at the All Stars banquet. But Jack wasn't passing the salt on Sunday.

Before the game I strolled down the line to shake his hand as the ball was being thrown in. Jack was already locked into watching the game. He shook my hand, but his mind was elsewhere. That gave me an idea about his mindset for the day. With all the commotion at the end of the game I didn't get a chance to seek him out to congratulate him on Kerry's victory, though I didn't see him making a beeline for me either.

A few nights after the Kerry match, I talk to Ryan McMenamin about the incident between him and Marc Ó Sé. The TV cameras have also captured an episode with Paul Galvin where Ricey planted a knee in a sensitive spot. It looks bad. I tell him that behaviour isn't what we're about. He's certain to be suspended and if that behaviour is impacting on the team, maybe he should think about that. He accepts culpability and apologises. Where I support him, though, is on the length of the suspension. Six weeks? It's an entirely contrived number.

There is plenty of precedent here – Paddy Campbell for Donegal against Derry a few years back and the Cork hurler Tom Kenny both received four-week bans for the same infringement Ricey committed against Galvin. Four weeks means Ricey misses the Galway game. Six weeks means he misses Galway, Westmeath, Donegal and Derry. I'm hard on Ricey about his behaviour, but I'm right behind him should he appeal the length of the sentence.

If it was four weeks and he missed that many games, fine. There's no arguing the crime. It's the punishment that's causing the problem. If Ricey is being targeted because of a perceived reputation he has, and because the incident happens to be captured on television, where's the fair play in that?

Dealing with these incidents is always a challenge. When talking to players about their behaviour, there is an equation that always has to be observed. No one is ever sent out of our dressing-room to do anything outside of the rules. We always say that to the players. This is a team game. You must behave in a way that befits the team. Sometimes players will transgress. It's like life. We can aspire to perfection, but things will get in the way. All we can do is promote what we believe to be the right thing to do. We don't condone the errors we'll make along the way, but we always try to minimise them. If our players are behaving in a way that's jeopardising our team, we point these things out, just like Ricey's incident.

Sometimes our players are accused of gamesmanship. Trash talking. It's not a practice to be encouraged, but if something is

going to happen, what would people prefer? Someone talking in your ear or putting their fist in there? It's all about balance. Nobody is coming off the pitch having played Tyrone with broken noses or cuts from that kind of behaviour. Psychologically it might annoy some people, but when I consider that punishment, I often put myself in the victim's place. Would I prefer the verbals or the punch? They could talk in my ear all day.

We can never worry about those influences, though. We can only worry about ourselves. This time of year is more about communication with the players. It's a lesson I've learned over the years. You might feel you're getting your message across, but are the players hearing the same thing as you? It's early in the year and I've got a few players on my mind. Marty Swift had to leave the panel early last year for work in America but he's been training well since he came back. He's a young lad and it's important he knows we're aware of him. He'll get more games this spring.

Our goalkeeper Jonny Curran had a few hairy moments against Kerry but made two crucial saves as well. We had planned to start him in one game out of every three during the league, but he'll be getting one in two now. Aidan Cassidy is new in the panel and played well against Dublin. He's making a big step up this year. I tell Aidan it's about a learning curve. Look around, soak it up. He's getting better, bit by bit.

I've been talking to Stephen O'Neill too. He's in such a good place again. His performance against Dublin in our first league game was a classic. It was as good an exhibition of scoring I've ever seen, and there's so much learning for everyone around him in the way he plays the game. There's no wastage in anything he does. Every pass is measured. Every movement is perfectly designed to create the space he needs. And his kicking has been immaculate.

23

But the biggest thing for me was his reaction to getting a knock against Dublin. It was another knee injury. Before he retired at the end of 2007, that was the kind of injury that was draining the enthusiasm from him. This time he's coping with it. He's positive about recovering and getting back again.

The boys are moving well. Fergal McCann's training is excellent and drawing a good response. My old friend Tony Donnelly is floating around, taking mental notes and helping set the tone. This group has always felt like a family, but the last few years have brought us even closer together.

It's not a bond simply woven through years of success, but one that sustained us through hard times and tragedy. We suffered a devastating loss in 2004 and endured injuries in 2006. I've never been able to fully figure out how deeply the death of Cormac McAnallen affected our performances in 2004, but I know the injuries ripped the heart out of our challenge in 2006. Right now, even with Kerry winning in Omagh, I sense a difference in this team. Our first game of 2009 against Dublin was a celebration of everything good about us. We moved the ball with fluency and invention. Players were imagining remarkable possibilities with the ball, and making them happen. It was a joy to watch. At the end we closed out the Dubs with a volley of scores. We had played with great artistry, but we knew how to win too.

Part of my coaching philosophy has always been to encode the awareness of the need for "difference" into my teams. One line I have always cherished is, "If you keep doing the same thing, you will continue to get the same result." That doesn't necessarily mean success. It simply means you will usually keep hitting the same levels of performance.

Difference. Every year is about bringing difference. Our core philosophies stay the same, but we always try to change the window dressing. Mickey Hughes, a former Tyrone footballer now living in Louisville, Kentucky, sent me a book recently. It is written by Rick Pitino, a basketball coach and motivational speaker. It charts his journey as a coach having accepted a ten-year $50-million dollar contract with the Boston Celtics in 1997. After that, he endured a series of personal tragedies. Results with the Celtics were modest. He lost two brothers-in-law, one in the 9/11 terrorist attack, and an infant son. The underlying theme of the entire book is how adversity can create opportunity and perspective. "Accept detour, learn from the unexpected new path you're on," he writes, "and arrive at your destination with greater wisdom and an enhanced perspective."

Read a line like that, and I wonder if Rick was following our progress through 2008. Another line of his about rules runs along these lines: if it ain't broke, break it and make it better. I can see what he means. Nothing must stay the same. Life and teams are in a constant state of alteration and flux. Accepting that and finding the awareness to change things when required is key to maintaining standards and success.

But I can't do that alone. I need Tony Donnelly and Fergal McCann. I need the Tyrone board. I need the players. I need our entire back-up team. We are all part of one body. One soul. One spirit.

Fitness tests in Belfast showed the players are fitter now than they were in February 2008. We sat them down before the season began, split them into small groups and gradually crystallised our ambitions for the coming year.

We want to win Ulster and the All-Ireland, but we want to do it in a certain way. We had won our last two All-Irelands through the back door. We need to stride through the front door this time. Our defence of the All-Ireland titles in 2004 and 2006 had been mixed, and neither had reached the expected standard. That would change.

Little things mattered. Two nights' training a week is difference. Stevie bouncing back with determination to beat his knee injury is difference. Chasing two-in-a-row is difference. I'm ready. The boys are ready. As you think, so you shall be.

That is where we always begin.

—◄o►—

I THINK ABOUT the contrast between our starting point now and a year ago. At the beginning of 2008, it felt like all the good things that had gone before had never happened. We had won that Ulster title in 2007, but in the eyes of the public – and maybe ourselves – it counted for zero. It had been a strange game. Monaghan were a decent team but we never felt in any danger of losing. In the second half we pulled eight points clear. Even though they reduced the final margin to two points, it still felt like a reasonably comfortable win. But other people saw it differently.

A few weeks later we fell apart in the All-Ireland quarter-final against Meath. A day later Monaghan ran Kerry to a point. We were Ulster champions, but technically speaking, Monaghan had actually lasted longer in the championship than we had. When the *Irish News* picked their Ulster GAA All Stars, Monaghan received seven awards. We got three. Ask anyone outside the province to name the winner of that year's Ulster championship, and there's a reasonable chance they'd answer Monaghan. As trophies went, it felt like a forgotten Ulster title.

It was another sign of the new landscape we had created for ourselves. Ulster titles were foothills now. Even All-Irelands didn't feel like Everest any more. People expected. We expected.

So where were we now? Where was our collective mentality? Did we have the resolve to reinvent ourselves again? The climb back was going to be steep. As a management team, we knew we were ready to start again. I needed to see if our players had the legs and the stomach for it too.

Some time after the Meath defeat, we arranged to meet every one of the 30-man panel. We always convened with the players at the end of every season to reflect on the year past, but this one was accompanied by an edge. Over the course of two Saturdays and a Wednesday evening, we spent a minimum of 30 minutes with each player, asking them how they felt about the year gone by and the season to come. It was a way to measure the scale of their ambition and gauge how they were thinking. We needed to transmit how committed we were to getting the team back on track.

It was an exhausting process, but an enlightening one. The emotions that the management were dealing with were mirrored in the players. There was a massive sense of frustration about how the season had ended. We might have collected two All-Ireland titles together, but it felt a long time since we had won in 2005. As a group the players have always been acutely aware of their talents and used that confidence like no other Tyrone team before them. They also knew what they wanted their legacy to be. Good teams had won two All-Irelands in the past but often disappeared into the pages of history, destined to be a footnote. If this team wanted to leave their mark, they had to begin again. And they knew it.

The year had damaged some players. They had issues with the training, with their own form, with the entire vibe around the team. A few were wondering whether they had a role any more with Tyrone. Take Martin Penrose. Martin was starting to get restless. He was convinced he had no future with Tyrone. He was getting snatches of game time during the year, but nothing like the amount he wanted. His own club were in his ear. What was the point in breaking yourself up to play with Tyrone and they won't even give you a game? They wanted him to concentrate on club football. I knew Tyrone needed Martin.

We talked. I told him exactly how I saw him. To me, Martin Penrose has the talent to be our Tommy Freeman. He has pace to burn, he can finish and if he's in the right frame of mind with the correct ball delivered in to him, he's a serious threat to any inside defender. A football season lasts a long time and forces you to clear many hurdles. Tyrone needed Martin Penrose, but Martin Penrose needed to know that. In the end, it struck the right chords with him. He stayed.

That doubt in itself reinforced a valuable lesson as a manager. We might have a high regard for some players, but unless we share that with them, how will they know? That was a crucial lesson I took from these meetings. One key skill of leadership is that ability to communicate. Once you have a vision of what you're about, then you need to convey that clearly to the people you need to be part of that vision. Sometimes you need to take the lead on things, but if you end up imposing decisions, you will always come up short.

People must identify with your vision. They need to realise they can contribute to reaching that goal. Ironically, in an era when we can communicate with people in an unprecedented variety of ways, the skill of listening is something that has been compromised and almost lost. A crucial component of creating a team is giving people our time and listening. They can learn, and you will learn. It is a lesson that is reinforced year after year.

Ryan McMenamin came in to talk. Stephen Bray had given him plenty of trouble against Meath and the year had left him feeling down. Ricey had been around a while and was lipping over 30 years of age now. He wondered if he had any more left to give. He was ready to quit.

We also knew the competitor in him would make it hard for him to let go. He was feeling down now, we said, but the winter break would help. We talked about looking ahead, leaving the past behind. He had injuries. Let them heal. We needed to challenge ourselves and stretch to new levels. To reach them, we needed him there. A few months later, he was sitting beside my wife Marian at a function. It was a few days after his club, Dromore, had lost to Crossmaglen in the Ulster club championship but Ricey had played well. "It was the best I've seen you play for a while," Marian told him. It was a simple comment, but it went deep with Ricey. It was the spark he needed and lit the route to a good place again.

We came to Stephen O'Neill. He entered the room, but before we even got down to our conversation, he cut us off at the pass.

"There's no point in wasting your time or mine," he said. "I'm quitting."

I was stunned. It was an awful moment. He was wrecked from injuries, he said. He had given Tyrone ten years' service. Now he felt he owed something to his club. After all my years working with Stevie, I knew certain things about him for sure. When he made a decision like this, there was no point in butting heads with him. He was single-minded when it came to fundamental decisions. He wouldn't be swayed, not immediately anyway. It was a terrible pity, I said, but if that's the way he felt, we had to accept that. He left the room and walked away. It seemed like the year couldn't get any worse.

Deep down, I always felt he'd come back but it promised to take time. I let him cool off that autumn, then met with him a few times. He was sticking to his decision. Once his injuries cleared up, his club was the priority now. I still felt he was too young to be retiring from inter-county football, but we couldn't wait for him either. Although Stevie's decision hadn't become public knowledge, it was only a matter of time. Of all the players to lose, Stevie was one we badly needed. It had been over two years since Peter Canavan's retirement but the team was still figuring out how to compensate for his absence. With Brian McGuigan still fighting a terrible eye injury, Stephen O'Neill was crucial to our team. But he appeared to have moved on. We had to do the same thing.

In mid-January, he publicly confirmed his retirement.

While we were asking questions of the players, I was asking questions of myself, too. I have never lacked for enthusiasm over the years, but I've always felt the need to continually review what I'm doing. In winter 2007, a mutual friend put me in touch with Caroline Currid. Caroline is a performance coach based in Sligo who was looking to add a sports team to her roster. I had a chat with her. I liked the approach she was taking. She would meet every player monthly for an individual one-hour chat. They could chat about their form, any problems they had in training or beyond the panel, where they saw themselves in the context of the team. The meetings with the players had told me the communication lines needed to be improved. Caroline could facilitate that.

It took the business of liaising directly with each player away from the management, too. We talked with Caroline directly to gauge where the players felt we were. We bounced our own thoughts around with Caroline too. Once we knew how the players were feeling about certain issues, we could act on them. It could be simple little details in training, issues in their private lives, positive and negative. But everything was being addressed without any hassle or drawn-out conversations.

After the Martin Penrose episode, I also found myself spending more time around the players. The conversations might last only 30 or 40 seconds on the training field, but they all helped. It might be something like offering congratulations on an engagement, or letting them know you'd heard they were playing well with their club, or some encouragement following a good performance. Small, innocuous things that add up to a warmer relationship. Sometimes that link can be diluted. We take certain assumptions for granted. We forget to tell players how we think of them, what their qualities are and what unique element of themselves they're bringing to the team. If we don't keep that in mind, even the most important player will be left wondering if we even know he's there. That wouldn't happen with this group again.

I also brought in the Sport Tracker Diaries I worked on for Caroline to use. The diaries are an amalgam of my philosophies on coaching and performance, combined with detailed, weekly assessments that allow the player to record their training regime. There are sections to record your daily workload, where you trained – from the pitch, to the weights room to a game, to monitor your nutrition, rest times, energy levels and your personal motivation, and also to assess your own performance, the team performance in training and to set weekly goals. It's a significant investment for players to take on, and requires them to truly reflect on their workload and the commitment they're giving. It's a big task for players, but Kilkenny used them in 2008 too, so they can't be all bad.

As we convened for our first meeting of 2008, we felt we had everything in place. Stephen was gone and the rumour mill was rumbling, but we had other business to deal with. When the main points from the meeting were collated, the message was clear. The players wanted to set standards for themselves. Demanding standards. We also knew we had lived through worse times: Paul McGirr's death in 1997, Cormac's death in 2004. The injury-ravaged season in 2006 that almost wore us all down to nothing. We had survived those and still found a way to win. Why not do it again?

The *Irish News* awards were brought up, noted and stored away. One line from a newspaper article I had read kept ringing in my head too. It claimed that Tyrone were pursuing greatness while becoming ordinary. That made my blood boil. I didn't do ordinary. Neither did these players.

The public perception was clear. Ulster titles didn't offer us any status any more. The coming year stretched out in front of us like a tightrope with no safety net. One quote in the players' diary chimed loudly for this group as the year began: Don't measure yourself by what you've accomplished, but by what you have accomplished with your ability.

2008 was about winning an All-Ireland.

As THE YEAR BEGAN, though, September seemed a long way off. We had our worst McKenna Cup campaign for six years. Darren McAnenley, a brother-in-law of Fergal McCann's, was killed in a car crash before our first league match. It left a cloud over many of us. We felt for Fergal and his family circle. When one of our group was cut, we all bled a little.

Our league form was patchy and unconvincing. After three games we had collected just a point, and the heat was coming on. We went down to Kerry and lost by three points. It could have been much worse if Packie McConnell hadn't made two excellent saves. We were probably missing eight or nine players from our championship team, but Kerry didn't mind. I'm sure Tyrone people aren't behind the door when we turn them over, either.

As it was, they had other things to vex them. The vibes on the street suggested the panel was unsettled. All the talk centred around a rift between myself and Stephen O'Neill. I found it hard to understand how people could imagine such a scenario. Stevie had been a central part of the collective conscience of every Tyrone team I had managed since 1997. He was the one alongside Brian McGuigan who had dragged me back from the edge when we lost the All-Ireland minor final that year. Now, people were saying there was trouble brewing between us.

We both worked for Martin Shortt Estate Agents at the time; therefore it had to be work-based. Rubbish. We worked in different sectors of the business for a start, so there was never even the vaguest ground for conflict.

I tried to douse the sparks. So did Stevie. But the more we denied any rift, the more convinced people seemed to become. I reiterated that the door to his return was always open, but it's harder to debunk these myths than it is to create them. It would take almost the entire year to put that one to bed.

People were tugging at loose ends surrounding the training, too. When Dromore won the Tyrone county title, Ryan McMenamin made a remark that their trainer, Ryan Porter, was the best in Ireland. When we met as a group for our first meeting of the year, a few of the players had suggested Ryan Porter should be introduced as a strength and conditioning expert alongside our trainer Fergal McCann. We took the point about strength and conditioning on board, but I felt there was a better way to approach it.

Ryan's expertise is unquestioned, but we felt his presence might overlap with Fergal's role as physical trainer. In turn, Fergal had no problem with bringing in some strength and conditioning expertise. We made contact with Queen's University, and went to meet Willie Moore in Belfast. The outside world recycled all that into some kind of feud for a few weeks, but it wasn't something we could worry about. Willie came in and did a superb job, and we got on with our business.

On the day of Cormac McAnallen's anniversary that March, we were on the road to Galway for a league game. As with every day, Cormac was in my thoughts. The team was puttering along without showing any great signs of improvement. Were some of these boys in a comfort zone? I was thinking about lads like Joe McMahon and Tommy McGuigan. They were in their mid-twenties now. I thought about what Cormac had achieved by the age of 23. If that generation of Tyrone players compared their attitude with Cormac's, what might they discover?

I picked up on the theme in the dressing-room before the game. I asked some of the younger players in the squad about when they won their All-Ireland minor medals. A lot of them had come through from the All-Ireland winning team of 2001. That made them 25 years old now. Cormac was 23 when he died, I said, decorated with every honour the game could bestow. They needed to realise they were no longer young fellas that needed taking by the hand. Only Sean Cavanagh and John Devine had come through to make a serious impact when winning the All-Ireland in 2003 and 2005. Peter Canavan and Stephen O'Neill were gone. They needed to carry that weight together, starting in Salthill.

We didn't get the right result, but the performance was our best of the year. People were recognising they needed to give more of themselves. After three difficult months, we were slowly turning the team in the right direction.

Finding more scores, though, was becoming a pressing problem. Over the previous three seasons, our forward line had been destroyed by injuries and retirements. Of the 2005 forward line, Peter Canavan and Stephen O'Neill had retired. Owen Mulligan and Brian McGuigan were tortured by injuries. We were winning enough ball out the field and putting it into the right areas, but we lacked a killer punch.

One night we played a league game against Derry in Celtic Park. Our two inside forwards, Niall Gormley and Colm McCullagh, struggled to make any dent on a physically stronger Derry defence. The solution required a gamble. We needed someone with heft, cleverness, and a cast-iron confidence in front of goal. We needed Sean Cavanagh.

It promised to be tricky. Sean had spent the winter recovering from an ankle operation. We had perched him out at wing-forward to get him some game time, but being kept away from midfield was already leaving him with questions. Moving him to full-forward was going to require some selling.

We talked it out. Even though he might have thought otherwise, I had no doubt about his ability as a midfielder. He had three All Stars to prove it. When the Brisbane Lions came to his door looking for him to switch codes to the AFL in the middle of 2005, I told him exactly what I saw in him as a footballer. He had the potential to be one of the greatest in his chosen sport. That was a level he could never reach in Australian Rules.

That was how I saw Sean Cavanagh, but this move was about more than him. This was the ultimate expression of team. We needed Sean to sacrifice his own preference for what the team required. We needed presence on the edge of the square. I promised him the flexibility to move in and out from full-forward if the need arose. This wasn't a restriction, but an expansion on what he could deliver for the team. His pace and athleticism meant starting at full-forward was an idea that could be altered depending on the demands of the game. But it was an essential change that had to be made.

He was sceptical, but he bought into the plan. There were times during matches he got frustrated and you could tell he hankered for the open prairies around midfield, but the team was taking shape around him. When Brian McGuigan returned, the flow of ball to Sean improved, and our scoring rate started to improve.

As the championship loomed we were a weakened team but players were returning gradually. Sean gave us a new element to structure our attack around. The rest of the football nation were looking at Kerry and wondering if injuries and defeat had finally taken the last puffs of wind from our sails. I reckoned there was another Ulster title there for us at least. We were getting better. And we always knew we were good enough.

We also knew Down would come charging at us in the first round. They had been talking about Tyrone in Omagh since their victory speech when they lifted the McKenna Cup in January. Looking at it coldly, it promised to be a tight game.

Down would never fear Tyrone. We had injuries and they had had us in their sights for six months. They were ready to take us down.

For the next fortnight, we shared a fresh lesson in the fine lines that separate joy and devastation. By half time in the first game, we might have had four goals and been out the gate. We were that close to looking a very good team. Instead Down raised their game and earned a draw.

The replay unfolded into a heartbreaking classic. We were 0-16 to 0-12 down as the game entered its final ten minutes, but refused to yield. Tommy McGuigan came on and brought us level with a brace of points, then ahead. Down might have dragged us into extra-time, but it didn't matter to me. I had already seen enough. Win or lose, those few minutes told me our season wasn't over.

In the end, Benny Coulter took a ball that slipped from Ryan McMenamin's hands and slotted it to the net. Down hung on to win. At the end I was devastated. Losing any match always sticks in my gut, but having played so much good football? I knew what the reaction outside the wire would be. Tyrone in decline. Time for change.

Something had happened against Down, though, that made me think differently. Tyrone weren't dead.

We were coming back to life.

3

RESURRECTION

I COULD SENSE THE ARCHERS taking aim outside. We were getting no credit for being part of two classics. How could it be deemed such a great victory for Down, and such a bad defeat for us? We were being undervalued again, but those matches had told me plenty about the true worth of this team. After the match I pulled the players together in the dressing-room.

"We're not a team that wants to be blown away or put out of existence," I said. "If we did, we had a great opportunity to do it tonight. That opportunity was at 0-16 to 0-12. We could've said, 'We've had our day, let's go home now.' We proved we weren't taking that. That suggests to me there's more in this team. We start the business of doing that now."

Backs stiffened. Heads started to lift. We offered them the week off to clear their heads and spend some time with their clubs. The players declined. They wanted to meet Monday night and train Tuesday. It reminded me of a day back in 2002, when I took an Errigal Ciarán team to play Crossmaglen in the Ulster club championship. It was at the end of a year that had seen Armagh win their first All-Ireland title, partly built on the back of Crossmaglen's mighty dominance of the club scene in Armagh, Ulster and beyond.

That day we went into the dressing-room at half-time in Crossmaglen nine points down. In my mind, though, the game was only beginning. A few moments before half-time, a Cross shot was blocked by a pair of our backs. The deflected shot might still have gone in, but our goalkeeper John Devine stretched to make the save. We were nine down, but we weren't dead.

The same feelings were running through me that night in Newry. Players were refusing to accept defeat. They were demanding more. Outside that dressing-room, the Tyrone public were already mourning the loss of another season. We felt resurrected.

That evening I got a phone call from my daughter Michaela. Over the years she has always been my greatest supporter. Every father has a special relationship with his daughter, and this was always special. She loved her football. She was with me and my Tyrone teams from the beginning, helping with little jobs at the training sessions, shredding tissues and rosary beads in the stands during matches.

She was seven years old when I started with the Tyrone minors in 1991 and has never missed a championship game since. We went to league games all over the country following Tyrone. One day we headed for Ennis to see Tyrone play Clare. On the way back we noticed a sign for Knock Airport. Slight, unintentional detour from the appointed route. We didn't see Glencull for a long time that night. When the final whistle blew on our greatest days, it was Michaela and Matthew I wanted with me. On evenings like this, we needed each other too.

"We'll be all right, won't we?" she asked. I knew she still believed in the team, but she needed to see I believed as well. At that moment, I was convinced. I could tell her everything would be all right. "We'd rather be beat by Down than Armagh anyway, Daddy," she said. "We'll be okay."

The following day was Father's Day. There was a card from Michaela at home with a message written inside. "You're always the man," it said, "no matter what." After the heartbreaking disappointment of the previous night, it brought me back to reality again. All our family is like that. I picked up my mobile and sent her a text: "Thanks for your support last night. I know you're right and God is sending us on a different route. I am really encouraged by the spirit our boys showed last night. We haven't gone away. Luv da."

Then I remembered something else: "Thanks 4 da lovely card."

Later that day I was thinking of Ryan McMenamin. He had started the year with doubts. Now he had made a mistake that handed a crucial goal to Down. Having done so many wonderful things for Tyrone over the years, he had no need to beat himself up over this. He needed to know that.

I sent him a text, told him he had nothing to worry about after years spent bailing us out. Stick with it, said the message, we're going to win the All-Ireland.

AT A TEAM MEETING that night the players split into groups to outline some thoughts on what the team needed to focus on now. The results on the flipchart were encouraging:

- Prove people wrong
- We did perform well against Down
- We have a lot more to offer
- The systems are good
- We're fighting for our own good name
- 2005 is history.

I had no fears about our structures either. Communication between every level was now excellent. Fergal's training was superb and the players were flinging themselves into the work. With players coming back from injury, the panel was starting to look stronger. The most important thing now was to communicate with them using the language of positivity.

They had reacted well to defeat against Down, but we still had to choose our words carefully. Positive language doesn't guarantee positive results, but negative language will guarantee defeats. Our videos from now on would highlight our good play. I was more vocal at training. I nudged players a little harder and commended them when they responded.

The players were more vocal too. It wasn't all effing and blinding about the opposition either. They were pushing each other to do things better, quicker. If there was a drill that involved a pass count, they'd challenge each other to top their tallies in the next one. Different people would push the right buttons: Brian Dooher, Philip Jordan, Colin Holmes, Kevin Hughes, Ricey, Packie McConnell, John Devine. The mood was perfectly pitched.

Beyond the training camp, the county was in turmoil about the team. There are plenty of supportive people out there, but the critics are never far away, even at home. All I know is, the farther I get from Tyrone, the more respect I seem to earn. It's something like the old cliché about never being a prophet in your own land. I can live with that, but sometimes you have to wonder. Those enlightened, anonymous souls that keep the *Irish News*'s "Off the Fence" column going every week were busy agitating for my removal. Martin McHugh threw his two cents on the BBC one evening. He reckoned it was time for me to step down. I had been there too long, he said. Essentially, he said, the team was the victim of same-voice syndrome.

After 11 successful years with Tyrone teams, I found that insulting. How would I have survived 11 years transmitting my message using the same voice? It told me nothing about my situation, but confirmed that Martin didn't know what was needed to last 11 years in this job. To survive, you always have to change. You might be delivering a similar message but you always needed new ideas and a new way to get that message across. Martin's theory didn't reflect on me. I wasn't that person. I wasn't stuck in a time-warp. I knew that. Crucially, the players knew that.

Others were more supportive. Peter Canavan backed me in his newspaper column. Joe Kernan said some kind things too. When the issue came up with the players in interviews, they rowed in with their endorsements of our system and quietly let me know during training that things were good too. It brought us all closer together. The team ethos was strengthening. Now we just needed to win a few games.

As THE MOTIVATIONAL SPEAKER George Zalucki defined it, commitment is doing what you said you'd do long after the mood you said it in has gone. The qualifiers were our time. All the flipcharts and dialogue wouldn't stand up to much if we didn't make some progress.

Louth first. In 2006 they had taken us to a replay in the qualifiers. Now they were happy to convey their satisfaction in drawing us again. They were looking forward to playing us.

We could see that sentiment bugged our boys. It wasn't hard to turn that itch into a rash. Louth thought they were getting a wobbly looking Tyrone with a soft centre. We drove that home all week. Was that what we were? Was Louth's perception the right one? There was only one way to sort this one. By half-time we were 1-10 to 1-0 ahead. We won the second half too.

On the way back, I witnessed another episode that amplified my instincts about where this group was heading. We stopped in the Carrickdale Hotel on the border for a meal and a recovery session for the players. While those who had played bobbed along in the pool, the rest of the players disappeared into an adjoining gym. I heard the radio pumping music. All of them were on the exercise bikes. They emptied themselves for 45 minutes on the bikes. I made a point of mentioning the work they had done at dinner. This showed we were all in for the long haul, not just the glory of getting a place on the team. This wasn't about 15 or 20: this was truly now about 30.

It set the scene. Fringe players now trained an extra night with Fergal. A few boys had started coming in with wisps of stubble on their chins. Ricey first. Then Ciaran Gourley and Martin Penrose. Owen Mulligan followed and Joe McMahon. It was a bit of fun and lightened the mood nicely, but it also gave the public something else to latch onto. While they chuckled at the Tyrone boys' beards, we could get on with improving their performance levels without the heat of the media on our backs.

The Westmeath game brought another shower of criticism, but I was happy we had made another stride forward. They had the best defensive record of any team in the National Leagues in 2008. They had two men sent off, but it made no difference to their massed defensive formation. We still had to break down 11 defenders.

We got a few frights, but we coped. Sean Cavanagh fell heavily on his neck but was okay. His brother Colm cracked his collarbone after replacing him. Dessie Dolan dragged a shot wide that might have put them in the driving seat at the end if he had goaled. Even if he had scored, I'm not so sure we would have lost. At the end, though, when I thought about it, losing to a 13-man Westmeath in Omagh might have been a hard result to defend. I was treading a fine line. We all were.

After Westmeath, the bright lights were coming into view again. Our match against Mayo brought us back to Croke Park, and again drew plenty of derision in victory. Once again, I refused to yield to the negativity. The facts seemed simple to me: Mayo had beaten us in plenty of league games and in the 2004 championship.

After years of near misses, they needed to make a statement about themselves as much as we did. Indeed, if they only beat Tyrone that would probably be enough to make their season a success.

But we grafted and scrapped and survived.

Now we faced Dublin. The following week the team was prepared publicly in the media for burial. The phone calls and chit-chat around the county had the sombre feel of someone calling after funeral arrangements. Three-in-a-row looked a *fait accompli* for Kerry.

Mick O'Dwyer and the usual cast of Golden Years greats were heralding a showdown with Dublin in September. Our boys listened to all this talk of tradition. It never wears well with them. Apportioning that kind of affection for football that happened 30 years ago has always seemed to undervalue what we're about now.

There's surely no question standards are better now than 30 years ago. Now is what it's always about, not the past. But it seemed our quarter-final with Dublin was just a sideshow on the way to a neat old-money All-Ireland final followed by a coronation in the Kingdom. We might have had other ideas, but we were happy to keep them to ourselves.

Firstly, I tried to seal off the players' minds from all the negativity out there. When we convened to study the Mayo video, I highlighted all our positive play. This had been a tough game, but we had ground it out and won. Tommy McGuigan had missed the bones of 1-5 during the game. He needed reassurance. Tony and myself told him it was okay. It was actually a sign of good things. He was pushing himself to be involved, no matter what. He was leaving his comfort zone behind. He was taking the same responsibility as he did against Down. Tommy had changed over the summer from the squad player in that dressing-room in Salthill to a major player. Others were starting to follow his example.

Dealing with Dublin didn't faze me either. If anything, I figured that after beating Mayo, Dublin wouldn't create as many individual problems for us across the field. We knew Dublin well. The second half of their Leinster final against Wexford had basically been a kicking-in game, but Dublin appeared to be already talking like All-Ireland champions. They always had teams that got reasonably close to getting over the line, but never did. That made them mentally vulnerable.

They have some fine individual players – Ciaran Whelan, Conal Keaney, Bryan Cullen, Shane Ryan, Barry Cahill, Jason Sherlock and the Brogans, but they tend to play in – individual ways. There was no discernible Dublin style of play. Individuals might do some things well in isolation, but there was no real pattern or purpose there.

We were happy if we stopped Alan Brogan and blocked up Whelan in the middle; we would be a good way down the road to victory. We knew we had a better system and ultimately a better team. We were guaranteed underdogs in front of a full house in Croke Park. If we wanted to make a statement about our rehabilitation, now was the time.

As it turned out, Brogan was gone early through injury and Dublin managed to kick away their best spell of dominance in the first 15 minutes. After that, we created something special. The rain poured down but our handling and kicking was excellent. Our finishing was marvellous. We got our match-ups right, blotted out their strengths and Dublin simply couldn't put a hand on us.

By half-time people were already describing our display as total football. After years of aspiring to produce a team of men with the character, skill and courage to achieve that level of excellence, it was a wonderful compliment.

In the middle of all this flowing football, though, the simple, understated principles that underpinned the team were visible if you looked closely. For his goal, Joe McMahon started out by taking a side-line kick near halfway. The ball went to Tommy McGuigan out near the corner of the Cusack and Davin Stands.

He was surrounded by defenders, but had the confidence and skill to make the space and time to pick a pass. He swung the ball across the goal, back to McMahon. He had followed his kick in towards goal, finding the energy and the ambition to get himself back into the game. His finish was supreme, but the goal spoke of an entire team ethic.

In the end we won by 12 points, Dublin's heaviest beating in Croke Park since the 1978 All-Ireland final against Kerry. It was a good day, but it couldn't end here. We had looked at the draw and re-imagined 2005: Dublin in the quarter-final, Armagh in the semis, maybe Kerry in the final. Instead, Wexford had rubbished the script by beating Armagh. We knew how public opinion was about to swing.

If we had beaten Dublin by 12 points, and Dublin had beaten Wexford by 23 points, went the theory, heaven knows what Tyrone might do to them. We didn't buy into that fuzzy logic. We knew Wexford posed a potentially bigger threat than Armagh. Playing Armagh would have guaranteed we were mentally steeled for the day. Wexford meant we had to drive home some messages.

I started early in the build-up to that match, and didn't let up. The country was reassessing its views on Tyrone now, but what would that victory over Dublin mean if we fell to Wexford?

Wexford had hurt us before too, beating us in the 2005 league semi-final. Failing to make that league final hurt. How would failing to make an All-Ireland final feel after everything the players had put themselves through?

Defeat would wipe everything out. To secure any credibility at all, we had to make the final. The players had to believe they were on a mental precipice. Climbing over Wexford was the only route back to safety.

I got the right response. We had looked at Wexford's defensive make-up in their matches against Down and Armagh, and noticed how their running game that hurt those teams usually emanated from defence. Armagh and Down had funnelled back when Wexford got the ball and allowed them to build up a head of steam coming forward. We were going to stop them at source, and press them in their own half. We pushed Ryan McMenamin up. He ended the match with 0-2. We hustled and hunted them down. We gave them nowhere to run. By the time they went for a more orthodox formation and opened up their game, we were eight points ahead.

The end of the match came like a surreal dream. We were in the final. You believe and you hope and you pray. You talk and you plan and you trust, but you can never be sure. We had overcome injuries and public derision. Players had been questioned, but crucially had the bravery to question themselves.

They had created a sense of team unlike anything I had ever seen before with Tyrone. After years spent creating the structure where players could nurture themselves into more rounded players and people, this assumption of personal responsibility in the face of imposing odds was perhaps the greatest expression of what I believed by the word "team".

From nowhere, we were there.

4

TWO IS NOT ENOUGH

"There are no whole truths; all truths are half-truths. It is trying to treat them as whole truths that plays the devil."

AN WHITEHEAD

THE WAY THIS GROUP of players bound themselves together into a team in the truest, most profound sense of the word was the greatest legacy of 2008. We always wanted to create a structure that would empower everybody on the team. Every team has stars that always twinkle a little brighter than the rest, but that's no reason for the others to disappear out of sight. Our injuries and retirements had forced us to take our concept of team to a new level. We had to find new players and leaders that year. Players were propelled from their comfort zones. Some were forced to reinvent themselves for the good of the team. Sean Cavanagh became a better player because of 2008, but first he had to accept that he needed to change. Not for himself, but for the team. That took time. When he made that leap, the entire team benefited.

That attitude seeped into everybody. The stars wouldn't be our only guide to winning this All-Ireland. Everyone would play their part.

That was the point about our team that so many people missed. Jack O'Connor painted a portrait of Tyrone in his book in 2007 that I certainly didn't recognise. He depicted northern football as football's nouveau riche, "flash and arrogant and full of it".

I thought it was harsh. I knew it wasn't true. Over the years I had always been at pains to defer to Kerry's achievements, while emphasising we were no world beaters. We didn't create anything new. We simply modified the game to suit the players we have and the kind of football we believed in. I would never be smug enough to say this is how football should be played. I have always maintained the opposite: football evolves over time. Kerry had their skills and they were successful. Others did the same. We didn't do any more than create another way for people to look at playing football, depending on their personnel. Calling us "nouveau riche" in our outlook was completely unfair. It's an arrogant philosophy I never would have supported or nurtured.

Still, on weeks like the All-Ireland final it was all handy fuel to keep us going. The quotes had been extensively carried in the northern media and debated up and down at the time. The idea was ingrained in the players' heads. If Jack wanted to paint a broad brushstroke about northern football, I took it as somebody who wasn't sure about what they were talking about. I see Tyrone having more in common with Galway or Mayo than some counties in Ulster. I respect his opinion, but I don't buy this idea of a northern brand. Different people use different things to motivate themselves, though, and deep inside all of us we don't like to be told we're something we're not.

The underlying theme for the three weeks before the All-Ireland final borrowed from that perception. This final was about defining our identity: who we were, what we stood for, who we wanted to become.

Little things we had done for years were magnified during that time. In 2003 we had learned the words of *Amhrán na bhFiann* and adopted it as a team song. Some of the players wouldn't have been exposed to Irish in school, so I got Michaela, who was studying Irish in college, to write out the lyrics in Irish and phonetically for the boys to sing. It seemed a good way of bucking one accepted assumption: while the boys from down south would mumble their way through an anthem in their native tongue, the Ulster team would belt it out correctly and with passion. In time, it became a song that bonded us together. We might be nouveau riche in the eyes of some, but we're all Irishmen too. That was important.

That was who we were.

What did we stand for? In this final, we were going out to make a statement for ourselves. Even though the media and the public had dismissed us during the summer, we were taking our rightful place in the All-Ireland final.

We might have been meeting one of the great footballing powers, but we have never lacked confidence against anyone. The last five years had told us what we were capable of. In Croke Park, we would be fuelled by that confidence.

All the heat was on Kerry. The world expected three-in-a-row. They were shoo-ins. We weren't supposed to even be here but in our minds, going back up the road without that cup was not an option.

Who did we want to become? We never paid too much attention to all the talk about the battle to be crowned team of the decade, but it was always there in a corner of our minds, prodding and poking at us all year. I knew if we lost, that contest was over. By extension, Kerry's status as the team of the decade would automatically diminish our achievements. We hadn't come together as a group of players and management for a decade to settle for being rated as okay. We had to be more than that.

Given the talent in our squad and the journey we had made, our average had to be above average. We were going into a final striving to become a team that would be remembered. We are not pursuing greatness while becoming ordinary. We aspired to an old adage of John Wooden's, the greatest college basketball coach America has ever produced, about competitive greatness: being at your best when your best is required. That's what we had to be for this All-Ireland final.

As we made our way through the championship, I had kept an eye on Kerry. Little things had stuck to the back of my mind. Darragh Ó Sé had been a wonderful player for many years, but I wondered if he had 70 minutes at full throttle in him any more. A few years back he named Kevin Hughes among his most difficult opponents. Watching Kevin in training over those few weeks, I could sense he was building towards a special performance. What impact might the sight of a fresh, driven Kevin Hughes sprinting onto the field after maybe 45 sapping minutes in an All-Ireland final have on Darragh? What impact would it have on our morale?

Kieran Donaghy's arrival at full-forward had given them a different dimension since we met them in 2005, but while the long ball into the big man had been effective, it had also become pretty one-dimensional. Tommy Walsh's size alongside Donaghy with Colm Cooper floating around had added another element, but it still looked a limited approach to me. Feeding Donaghy and Walsh had become Kerry's power play. Shutting down Donaghy and Walsh would seriously reduce their options. Precedent suggested they would be slow to abandon the twin towers strategy, and our own score-taking had been improving steadily. But first we needed to deal with their aerial threat. We knew we had the boys for the job.

TACTICS PLAY A HUGE PART in winning All-Ireland finals, but deeper, more inexplicable things play their role, too. Lawrence

Black is an old friend of mine. I have bought my cars from his dealership, TC Autos, in Omagh for years. Lawrence was always a solid man to deal with, and a friendship grew from that.

Lawrence is a Presbyterian and always prays at his church that Tyrone will do well. My phone always beeps with a text message from Lawrence before a big game. Back in 2003, when I became Tyrone senior manager, Lawrence called me one day to tell me a story. As a lifelong supporter of Northern Ireland's soccer team, one of his cherished possessions is a picture he had taken with Martin O'Neill at an airport. That season, he told me, Martin won three trophies. "This year," he said, "I must get my picture taken with you." Lawrence got his picture. I finished the year with the Sam Maguire Cup, the Anglo-Celt Cup from the Ulster championship and the trophy for winning the league.

During the summer of 2008 I dropped my car in for a service. I had cleaned the interior out, but as usual I still left a pile of bits and bobs behind. Over the years, Lawrence has always known where to look for the important things. This time, he found a Padre Pio relic and my rosary ring. He tucked them into an envelope and left them in the office for me to collect.

When I finally called for them, Lawrence was at a wedding in Scotland. The person at the desk called him to check where he had put the envelope. He was having a cup of coffee in a café when his phone rang. He directed the person to a drawer, and hung up. As he did, Lawrence noticed a crumpled-up piece of paper on the table. Out of curiosity, he unfolded it. It read:

Don't be discouraged. It's often the last key in the bunch that opens the lock.

When telling the story later, he said he immediately thought of me. He knew the journey the team had already taken through 2008. When he thought about it, this felt like a comforting phrase. It was a phrase of hope. He kept the piece of paper and gave it to me when he returned home.

The Tuesday after we beat Wexford in the All-Ireland semi-final, Lawrence's little motto ran through my mind again. I got a call from Francie Martin. Francie had played with Carrickmore for years and grown up in a family steeped in GAA. He didn't have any particular connection with Stephen O'Neill, but decided to get in touch with him to convince him to return to football with Tyrone. His timing couldn't have been better.

I knew that Brian Dooher had been in touch with Stephen all summer. Other boys had dropped him texts about returning. His form with his club, Clann na nGael, had been excellent and his injuries had cleared up. I had heard that he might have considered coming back before the Dublin match, but he had booked a holiday with some friends and didn't feel he could break up their plans. It was the kind of guy he was. Letting people down simply didn't apply to him.

Now Francie had news. Stevie was ready to come back. I called him when training was over. I asked him, "Is it true?"

He said it was, but with the team turning into an All-Ireland final it was surely too late now. I didn't see things that way. "Call over to my house," I said. "We could talk about it."

I rang home. Michaela answered.

"Michaela," I said, "will you put on the kettle? Someone's calling to meet me and Tony."

"All right," she replied. "Who is it?"

"Stevie."

She nearly dropped the phone.

When we got there after eleven, the whole house was up. Buzzing. As we arrived, Michael was lugging in his physiotherapy equipment from our training session. He met Stevie emerging from the shadows in our front yard.

"Well, Stevie," he said, his jaw heading for the ground.

Matthew was coming down the stairs.

"Good to see you, Stevie," he said.

"Good to see you too, Mattie."

As Michaela made tea, the three of us sat down together. We went over the pros and cons. Stephen suggested coming back in 2009. "If you're intent on coming back next year," I said, "why miss the opportunity now? Do you think on your current form you could offer something to us in an All-Ireland final that would make a difference?"

He looked at me with those eyes; solid, unstinting. Certain.

"I could," he said.

"Well, there's your answer," I replied. "Why would you not be there then?"

My logic was simple. He wasn't coming back for just one game. He was resuming his career. If it had been for just one game, I might have thought differently. But it wasn't. Stephen O'Neill was ready to come back. That was worth withstanding any criticism or questions.

We told him we needed to speak with the players, but all being well, he could return to training on Thursday night. The following evening, we broke the news to the players. After a discussion, the consensus was pretty straightforward. Get him back. In the middle of it all, Owen Mulligan crystallised the entire argument. "We're not just talking about anybody here," he said. "We're talking about somebody with the stature of Peter Canavan to this team. This is Stephen O'Neill we're talking about. We know this man for 11 years. We know what he's given to Tyrone. We know what he's about. This isn't a debate we'd have about any old player. This is Stephen O'Neill!"

It was an incredible moment. Owen didn't have a place on the team. He had been carrying a little weight all year and didn't seem as tuned in at times during the season. In terms of making the team,

Stephen's return could potentially relegate Owen down another notch. This was where the endorsement for Stephen's return needed to come from. It was definite and delivered with real conviction. I rang Stephen that night. He was in Clogher the following evening for training. A few nights later he took Justin McMahon for 1-5.

Meanwhile, I put Lawrence Black's piece of paper in my wallet. It's lived there ever since.

As FOR KERRY'S TWIN TOWERS, I had been thinking around that challenge for a few weeks. We tried a few things in some conditioned games at training. We placed a few tall players in around the goal and got our best kickers to deliver the ball in. Although he had spent all year as a wing-forward, some days we put Joe McMahon in at half-back. Other days he played the role at full-forward. Sometimes he was delivering ball in to our Walsh/Donaghy replicas.

We would make another rash of switches. In the middle of them all was the one we really wanted to watch: Joey at full-back alongside his brother Justin. The results were promising. He had the physique to match most players. He had played full-back in an All-Ireland final before, in 2005. It might have been robbing us of a beautiful ball player in attack, but my belief that preventing goals wins games overrode everything. Although Ciaran Gourley had enjoyed a decent year, he simply didn't have the physique to deal with either Walsh or Donaghy. The two McMahon boys did. I knew it was a gamble that might backfire badly if we lost, but it was one I felt compelled to take.

The other gamble was Brian McGuigan. Battling back from breaking his leg and an eye injury that almost cost him his sight had made him even more of an icon in Tyrone than his footballing ability had already done, but I was worried about his stamina. I didn't feel he had enough game time behind him to last an All-Ireland final.

Not selecting Brian McGuigan for this match would draw a negative reaction from the public and was another decision guaranteed to draw questions, but we had to consider it. Did I want Brian on for the first 25 minutes before being hauled off, or coming on for the last 25 minutes and the lift that would give the crowd and the team? To me, it was a straightforward call.

Having started the year with such uncertainty about his own future, Martin Penrose was now central to our plans. His mobility could cause Aidan O'Mahony problems at centre-forward, especially with O'Mahony probably bracing himself to face McGuigan. After years of hard work and the loyalty of the last eight months, this was the reason Martin had stayed. There were lessons in this for everyone.

Ensuring we made our plans without disrupting the rest of the team involved timing. I didn't want to break the news to Martin and Joe too far in advance in case it deflated the others. It was a heavy burden to carry. You looked at the players involved, and imagined their reaction. Delivering that kind of news to any player remains the most traumatic exercise I have to endure as manager. Doing these jobs is all about the language you use. It's not about cutting or dropping: it's about choosing others. We're not in the business of discarding people. We don't do it in a dismissive, detached way. We show that we feel for them.

Making these calls is a horrible process, but it's a practice I needed to learn along the way. I realised the need to be decisive and humane. You don't make these decisions to flex your muscles. You make them to empower others. At some stage you must realise you're responsible for the big picture. You're setting the tone for the group. Being a leader is a decision-making process on every level: committing to it and carrying out what needs to be done. Some of those decisions can be acute and painful, but they must be done. Otherwise you're no leader. It promised to be a gutting experience for Brian McGuigan and Ciaran Gourley, but there was a greater good at stake. Once more, this was about the team.

The Thursday before the game, Brian and Ciaran were the last players left in the physio's room. Brian Dooher was leaving the dressing-room when Tony and myself called him aside. We explained to Brian what we needed to do. Brian agreed to bring the lads into an adjoining dressing-room, where we would wait.

It went as well as we could have hoped. We explained our worries to Brian McGuigan about his match fitness, and our guarantee that we would need him for the final 20 minutes. He could see our point. It turned out that he had been thinking along similar lines. Ciaran's reaction was equally exemplary. He knew it was a horses for courses call, and had seen it as a possibility all week. They agreed to keep silent until Sunday. For us, it was a release. It was the last hurdle. We reckoned everything that needed saying to these boys had been said. But it hadn't.

THE WEEKEND BEFORE we had played Wexford in the semi-final, we had headed to Carton House to get away for a few days. One evening I gathered the players in a room for a talk when a tall, red-cheeked man walked in. Brian Cody.

I had known Brian through my work with SportTracker and met him over the years at various GAA events and functions. We always had a similar outlook on management. He looks for players to deliver a lot of their own solutions. He doesn't provide them with crutches to lean on. Having him in that day to speak with our players was an extraordinary moment of validation for all of us.

He told the players that Kilkenny had taken their cue from Tyrone: the work ethic, the relentless commitment, the complete respect for the concept of the team, and a constant pursuit of excellence. It was a hugely impressive statement. He was endorsing the philosophy we had lived by for 11 years. What Brian spoke about largely mirrored what we would have emphasised to the players in the past. Coming from him, though, was a magnificent endorsement of everything the team – and the entire group – believed in. It seemed to galvanise us all. Having heard this from a man like Cody, how could we ever doubt what we were about?

At that time of year, with the championship edging towards September, my mind often wanders to a place parallel to our football work. I'm looking for symbols and signs, ways to crystallise the theme of the coming weeks for the players. A few weeks before Cody visited us, I had given Marian's sister, Catherine, a rough design of a logo to work on. The idea was adapted from a line Cormac McAnallen used on his first night as captain in 2004. Great teams win more than one All-Ireland. We had already won the second All-Ireland that Cormac always craved, but I now interpreted that statement as being open-ended. Would Cormac have stopped at two? We all knew the answer to that.

Our motto into September was: *Two Is Not Enough*. We placed a small crest on our gear, and carried the sentiment into Croke Park.

After a turbulent summer, it seemed everything was easing into place. The press night was almost jolly. The players were laid-back and relaxed. We seemed to be hitting all the right notes at the right time. We were being carried into the final on a wave of real belief. Then, we were stopped with a jolt.

John Devine's father had been ill for some time but as the week before the All-Ireland final went on, he got steadily worse. By Friday night, the family had been called for. The choice to travel was John's. John Snr had always been a friendly face around Ballygawley, and took huge pride in his son's achievements with Tyrone. His father was in a coma, but his family felt he would want John to play.

The following morning, John arrived at the team bus. As we journeyed to Carton House, the news about John's father was spreading through the bus. The boys were promising to have a Cup for him in the hospital on Monday. Sadly, John Snr would never see the Sam Maguire Cup again. We had barely landed in Carton House when news came through. John Snr had died.

I gathered the Errigal boys and brought John down. We shared our sympathies and wished him well. Now he needed to say goodbye to the rest. The players were doing some light stretches on the lawn following the bus ride when John went out. I gathered them in a circle and made the announcement. They circled and shook his hand. There were tears and hugs. His second family was soaking up his grief.

When he was gone Enda McGinley sat down beside me in the hotel lobby. "That's the last piece," he said. "We can't lose now." I knew he was right. John wasn't alone on the road back to Ballygawley. They wouldn't be without him the following day either.

Once John left, we needed to set our sadness aside. On Sunday morning, we assembled for Mass. Our usual priest at Carton, Fr Liam Rigney, was in Lourdes, but Monsignor Eoin Thynne had married my niece Deborah Mallaghan, and was able to step in. I always love these Masses in an intimate setting, just the 30 players and the backroom staff, sitting tightly together in a small room, sharing a moment of spiritual solace before the raging excitement of the day took over.

And this Mass was special. Mgr Thynne gave us all a candle to bring to Communion. Each one was stamped "Tyrone: All-Ireland Final 2008". That was a wonderful touch. As an army chaplain, his sermon was singed with fire, too. He spoke about the hours before going into battle, about the need to believe in yourselves, that your preparations will be better than the oppositions, that no matter what they throw at you, you will have more.

It was magnificent stuff. I looked around at the players. Here they were, listening to a man of God telling them it was okay to put some bite into your performance today. It was like another seal of approval on our approach.

We needed all the positive affirmation we could get. I thought about our team: Joe McMahon at full-back; Martin Penrose at centre-forward; Brian McGuigan and Ciaran Gourley on the bench; Sean Cavanagh, the best midfielder in the country, moonlighting at full-forward; Stephen O'Neill back in the panel after over a year away; Kevin Hughes left on the bench for an All-Ireland final. These were gambles on a scale we hadn't tried before. Defeat would bring questions. Mgr Thynne was right. It was a day for courage.

As we had learned through the years, life rarely works out the way you want. How you react defines everything. It felt that way at the start of the final. Instead of hitting Donaghy and Walsh early on, Kerry were feeding Colm Cooper. He was doing damage. I looked back at Tony Donnelly on the side-line. It's amazing how our relationship works sometimes. I can be standing on the sideline in Croke Park with noise cascading down from the stands and people flitting around my peripheral vision, trying to intrude on my thoughts, yet all I see is 30 players and Tony. We had a quick chat about the Gooch. We decided to ride out the storm. Expectation and pressure might see Kerry crack and revert to type.

The half went on. We weren't playing particularly well, but Kerry had stopped sending ball into Cooper. We were pleasantly confused, but we still needed to find a way into the game. We looked jittery. Players were making simple errors, even Brian Dooher. Then, he gave us something special.

First, Packie McConnell made a superb save from Tommy Walsh. Martin Penrose scooped up the rebound and passed to

Joe McMahon, who fed Dooher. Having picked up the ball on his own 45-metre line he set off, brushed past three Kerry defenders and finished a 60-metre run with a sweet shot from the right wing that landed over the bar. That was the message at half-time. Don't think about what went wrong. Think about your reaction, and take Dooher's as your cue. We were one down. Kerry had made all the running. The game was ours if we could take it.

An injury to Colm McCullagh meant Stephen O'Neill was in. Apart from introducing Stevie's quality, it also opened up a few avenues for us. After a summer tethered to the small square, Sean Cavanagh could now come out to centre-forward and give us more presence around the middle. Inside a few minutes of arriving, Stevie had drawn enough Kerry defenders that Martin Penrose found himself in 30 yards of space in front of goal. It was a sign of the attention Stephen O'Neill would draw all afternoon, and the avenues that would open for others.

The key, though, was the scrappiest moment of the game. Kevin Hughes also joined the game at half-time, and won the first throw-in. From there the ball was moved in towards goal. Stevie grabbed it. Like Joe McMahon against Dublin, Kevin had followed his pass and took the return. His shot was deflected, landing in front of Tommy McGuigan. It might have grazed Tommy's shin but it crept over the line. Maybe it was lucky, but it was borne from hard work and the courage to do the right thing. Pat Riley, the old LA Lakers coach, once described attitude as the mother of luck. This was a massive moment.

Kerry hit a purple patch soon afterwards, but scoring that goal meant they could only establish a one-point lead. At that moment, though, you could sense it from them. They reckoned the hard yards had been made. Kerry were ready to strike for home.

Instead, we grabbed the match back. We sent Brian McGuigan in to control the game, as planned. He played for 25 minutes with the calm of a child kicking about in his backyard. Owen Mulligan went in and looked sharp. Kevin Hughes started taking over at centre-field. Although Stephen O'Neill might have berated himself for his performance later, all I saw was a Kerry defence stricken by the fear of God every time the ball came near him.

We were looking good with a few minutes left, but Kerry were still there. Declan O'Sullivan slipped through for a shot, Packie McConnell stretched and diverted the ball wide with his foot. People might have called it lucky after the game, but I reckon the keeper did superbly. He got out, spread himself, and gave O'Sullivan little to aim at. There was years of learning in that save, years of learning that added up to an All-Ireland title.

The end was a blur. Tony was nearby. Michaela was there. Little moments stick out. I grabbed Brian Dooher before he received the Cup, remembering how Peter Canavan finished his career in those few moments back in 2005. "Don't make any decisions now," I asked him. Brian followed his instructions as usual.

It was a day peppered with the morality tales that defined our season: Martin Penrose's emergence; Justin McMahon's transformation from a fringe player to an All Star full-back; Stevie's return; Owen Mulligan's courage in jeopardising his own hopes by pushing for Stevie's return; Joe McMahon and Tommy McGuigan becoming the players they always promised to be. A group of players became a team.

The week before the All-Ireland, Michaela had re-sent me my Father's Day message. I read the lines again. "God is sending us on a different route." He had guided us to the golden shore. No All-Ireland has tasted as sweet.

DID THAT ALL-IRELAND make us great? I'd always be careful about those labels. I would believe we are a team that did great things, but does that make us a great team? What is more significant is the transition over the years. We didn't win three All-Irelands with the same 20-odd players. We kept the panel fluid. We brought people in for a slice of the action, taught them how to win. The current generation knows what's required to win All-Irelands now as much as Peter Canavan, Gavin Devlin and Cormac McAnallen did back in 2003. Our players won't retire together, they will go in phases. Tyrone will stay strong. That's our greatest legacy.

One year rolls into the next. You enjoy the warmth of an All-Ireland win, but you learn when to leave it behind. The winter may be filled with functions and smiling interviews recalling the summer's greatest days, but in my mind it's done.

Life moves on. Football too. That day some of the McAnenly family visited us in the dressing-room. Nine months after Darren had died, Fergal could bring this Cup to them. It wasn't much, but it was something. The day after the All-Ireland final we took the Sam Maguire Cup for its annual visit to Crumlin Children's Hospital. Among the children we met there was Turlough Conefrey. Turlough was six years old and suffering from leukaemia. He was a Tyrone fan too. Brian Dooher and myself helped Turlough lift the Cup over his head. He was a lovely child with a marvellous interest in Gaelic games. All he wanted was to see the Cup and meet us. Giving him that day was the least we could do.

A few months later we took the Cup to his national school in Drumnamore, near Aughavas. Turlough lifted the Cup again. Everyone cheered. It was a wonderful day. The teachers and his schoolmates made it a special day for the school, and for Turlough. In February I got news that Turlough had lost his battle with leukaemia. I visited his house for the wake and remembered the happy days the Cup helped inspire in his last few months. That was the power of Sam.

You take the Cup to John Devine's house for his father's wake and watch John lift the Cup. For a moment a chorus of happy cheers blots out their grief. If we can use what we've done to create good, then it means we're doing more than winning trophies.

We know what's ahead. There will be more trials and crises. The whole world will want to put you down more than normal. The quest for excellence will become harder and more rewarding. The morning will come soon, blessed with new challenges, new hopes and new dreams. The spiritualist Anthony De Mello doesn't speak about life as an ending, but a continuing path to seek learning, wisdom and enlightenment. I see football in the same way. I will always burn with ambition to be the best I can be, and losing will always make me hurt like nothing else, but cups are still just signposts along the way. Building a team is a process. Every step takes you somewhere new. That is the joy and the challenge.

But the journey is all.

5

BEGINNINGS

Spring 2009

WE HAVE STARTED SLOWLY. I'm making seven or eight changes for every league match, looking at different options and combinations. Our championship team is fairly settled but we're looking at the players' contributions in a different way this year. We don't talk about starters and substitutes any more. We don't use words like "dropped" or "demoted". The key to our team ethic is the concept of game time. If a player comes on with 25 minutes left, that's his game. He has 25 minutes to empty himself. He knows he doesn't need to worry about pacing himself over a 70-minute game. He can go for broke.

The same applies for those who start. If they trust our panel, they can throw themselves into the game from the start, comfortable in the knowledge that someone else is there to pick up the slack. That was the great legacy of 2008. The panel is more flexible now. The trust within the group runs deep. Over the years I always wanted players to master a wide variety of skills: kicking and hand-passing off both sides, tackling, blocking. Good movement and awareness was always vital to play our system. The atmosphere we have promoted among the panel means every player is valued equally. Some might not be able to contribute as much across a game as someone like Brian Dooher, but they know they can deliver something vital. It's another strand of our core philosophy: respect uniqueness. Not everyone can deliver the same things on the field, but every contribution is priceless.

At the moment, we're not quite getting the return on our investment in terms of results, but I'm happy with our performances. Galway got away from Omagh with a win. We beat Westmeath with a goal in the last minute, then we lost to Donegal. Now people are worried about our next game against Derry. They're going well, but my instincts are telling me we can take them. I just need to try something different.

I call Peter Quinlivan on Monday. Peter has cut together video analysis pieces for me since I was with Errigal Ciarán in 2002. I've watched the Donegal match four times since Saturday night, and I can see the potential in this team. I usually get Peter to start my packages with some good Tyrone play, blend in some of our weaker moments and end the reel on a positive note. This time, I'm going to take this defeat and turn it into a complete positive.

I've found over 40 pieces of good play from our team. That's all I'm going to show them tomorrow night. Instead of running them into the ground, we're going to have a light training session. We're going to turn upside down every assumption they have about the upcoming week and our reaction to the Donegal match. I have already run the idea past Conor Gormley. By the time I finished our conversation his mood had already lifted. He reckoned he hadn't performed well. Having studied the video, I could highlight a handful of things Conor had done well. We're all going to leave that meeting room with a new outlook and a new positivity. Next Saturday night we will ambush Derry.

Result: Tyrone 0-14 Derry 0-11.

I HAVE FOUND a theme for the rest of the year. When I speak at business seminars, I always emphasise the need for people to hunt for good behaviour among their staff. If I'm preaching that mantra, why am I not living it?

Everything I say to the players this year from now on will be positive. Our video sessions will be based on positivity. The language I use when I talk about their form will be positive. If I want to highlight episodes in our play we need to improve on, I'll use similar errors committed by our opposition. We're constantly looking for new ideas to reinvent ourselves, to set this year apart from 2008. The hunt for good behaviour is a start.

I'm reading Anthony De Mello. His ideas are striking a chord with me again. He asks simple questions that require a rare kind of candour to answer. Do we live in a humdrum, routine way or do we embrace each day as a potential for growth? It's how I look at every day – not as a chore but as an opportunity. He talks about awareness a lot. You can only make changes if you're aware of that requirement to constantly pursue a better way. As players and managers we often overlook that need, especially when things are going well. Once you discover that awareness, it opens your mind to all sorts of methods, ideas and possibilities. That's what got me thinking about hunting for good behaviour this year.

I'm also reading Wayne Dyer. He talks about disarming yourself of your ego. It's reminding me how that core principle served us so well last year. Once you leave your ego behind, you discover the true source of life. People call it the source, the power of intention, the higher value. God. Subsuming your ego for the good of the collective is part of a journey to understand and explore your version of God. It also creates the sense of selflessness that can underpin a functioning, thriving team. To me, both journeys follow the same path. And it's a path I've walked before.

The Beginning

I WAS RAISED in the townland of Ballymcilroy near Ballygawley, right beside St Malachy's church, across the road from the graveyard. As children, we grew up witnessing funerals and all the rituals of grief. Strange, when you grow up beside a graveyard you never really have much fear of them.

I was born on 19 October 1954, the youngest of ten children, six brothers and two sisters. One girl, Veronica, died when she was young. I never knew her. My father was Peter. He worked as a labourer with the county council, tending to the roads around Tyrone. My mother's name was Mary and while my father went from place to place, she was always at home, doing everything for everybody.

She truly was an amazing woman, and her influence still has a profound impact on my life. She rarely left home. Even when it came to getting the weekly groceries, it was Daddy who went to the shops. I might have come home once or twice as a child to find she was away somewhere, but I can still remember that terrible, empty feeling when Mummy wasn't there.

But most days she was our anchor. Dinner always seemed to be cooking. Champ – potatoes and milk mashed with butter – warming in a big pot on an old range, a wee brown crust slowly forming on top, with bacon and sausages alongside. As children we'd run home to eat. As adults, if we were ever within reach of home, the house would be invaded. If she cooked enough food for four or five and six or seven people called, she would make it stretch. If anybody called, they got dinner or a cup of tea. She made soda bread till the cows came home. With seven boys there was never any fear of it not being eaten.

My parents were good, honest people with a deep connection to their faith. My father believed deeply in the prayer life. St Brigid's crosses were always the order of the day in our house.

When the Easter Holy Water was blessed, my father always wanted to get one of the first bottles so we could bless ourselves after midnight Mass on Holy Saturday night. Blessed candles from the Easter ceremonies were a major part of our lives as well. Mummy always prepared a May altar in honour of Our Lady. We said the Rosary daily as a family, all year round. When October devotions were being said in the chapel, the Hartes were always there.

Church life defined my parents to a huge degree, but it's not what I remember most vividly about them. The biggest thing about them both was that they reached out to everybody.

People would visit our house, simply to talk with Mummy. She always listened. Neighbours would come. People who lived on their own. Elderly people who perhaps didn't have anyone else to confide in would empty their souls to Mummy about what life was doing to them. People came so regularly she might hear the same story every week, but she would act like she'd never heard it before. She just sat at the table and listened.

My parents had a huge respect for everybody. Travellers would call to the door when I was a child, begging. Mummy would give them what she had: milk, tea, maybe some bread. Later, when they came calling with trinkets and religious ornaments, she'd buy a few bits and pieces from them. Years later, when she was confined to bed in the last months of her life in 1996, many of those people who had called in times past came to visit with her. She had cared for them when they were low. Now they tried to help her.

My father was also a Pioneer and a member of the local Pioneer council. When I reached 14 years of age, I didn't even think twice about joining. It was never a case of being compelled to do it by my father; it was simply an automatic choice. All my brothers and my two surviving sisters had joined before me. I followed them and that commitment has been a special part of my life ever since.

Football was the other great commitment sourced from home. Back when I was a child, Daddy looked after the Ballygawley jerseys. There was only one set for the entire club and they lived in an old army duffle bag that resided in our house. I'd often look out the back to see a row of green and gold striped jerseys fluttering in the breeze, the collars pulled out of shape from the different-sized necks being forced through them.

Peter was the first to take football seriously in our house. He went to Queen's University in Belfast to study civil engineering and played football for Tyrone in the sixties. He was a powerful footballer, terrifically aggressive. He loved a robust game and could hit shoulders all day. The Ballygawley pitch was in Dunmoyle, about four miles away on the other side of the parish, so we threw up a pair of goalposts on a patch of land Daddy used to graze a few animals. When the brothers travelled across for training, I would often pile in with them and spend the evening kicking about with a few boys on a piece of scrubland behind the goals.

Dunmoyle was basic then. The dressing-rooms were four concrete walls with a tin roof and a partition down the middle. Sometimes, though, they became a classroom for lessons in football.

Back in the sixties, Paddy Joe McClean was the man. He was a teacher and spent more time than was usual thinking about football. In an era when catch-and-kick and looking after your own wee zone of the field was the primary duty of every footballer, Paddy Joe talked tactics. He even brought a blackboard to draw diagrams and lay out systems of play. In 1963 Ballygawley reached a county semi-final against Omagh St Enda's. I was nine years of age with brothers on the team, stuck in the middle of everything.

One evening before that game, Paddy Joe had the boys in the dressing-room, blackboard out, chalk in hand. I can still see him drawing X's and O's to explain what he wanted. He talked about a scenario where the half-forward got the ball. Instead of hoofing it, Paddy Joe wanted precision delivery. The corner-forward would run out, leaving space for the full-forward to move across. That space was where Paddy wanted the ball played.

He talked to the boys about rotating the forward line to keep the opposition backs moving around. When a move broke down, he said, everybody within reach should revert to tackling the man with the ball.

Stuff was sticking in my mind. Peter Canavan's father, Sean, was another man with ideas. Attention to detail was his thing. Back then when football boots got wet, boys generally tended to leave them in the dressing-room. Nobody would look after them. Because the laces didn't have the wax covering they have now, they would rot after a while, making them dangerous to wear and prone to snapping at any time.

This would wind Sean up. Sometimes he would come into the dressing-room and see someone's rotted laces. He'd bend down and simply rip them out. "What good would they be to you if you play a match on Sunday?" he'd ask. "If you have to tie up your boots and they break, where are you?" It was a small thing, but it struck a chord. Preparation was everything.

As it turned out, Ballygawley lost that match against Omagh. Heavily. For me, though, that was only half the story. A few months later, in the depths of winter, Ballygawley met Omagh again in a local cup final. Same players, same assumption that Omagh would steamroll them. Instead, Ballygawley won.

Even then, that turnaround struck me. How could a team that had been stuffed a few months before come out and beat the same team that had crushed them? It was my first experience of complacency and how deep that virus can go. Maybe it showed me how endless football's possibilities were, too.

As children, Peter's achievements were the target for the rest of us. Martin was the second youngest and played for Tyrone under-21s with me. My other brothers, Barney, Paddy, Francie – father of current Tyrone player Davy – and Joe played club football with Ballygawley for years.

Back then, big was everything in football, and I wasn't big. But I had speed. Burning, searing speed.

I was hugely determined, too. I was a one-dimensional full-forward in one sense. There was only one thing on my mind: score. As I matured, I learned to lay ball off and slip other forwards through, but when I was young, it was all about scoring.

And I always got scores. At senior level with Ballygawley I could shoot the lights out: 1-5, 1-6, 0-8, 0-10, 3-3. But it took me time to build that confidence. As a child I flitted in and out of school teams. I didn't really shine with Ballygawley either. Tyrone didn't come looking for me as a minor in 1971, but they did in 1972. I couldn't figure it out, but I didn't dwell on it too much. I got stuck in, and had a place on the county team by the time the championship began.

It was a good time to be playing under-age for Tyrone. We had won the Ulster minor title in 1971 and won another in 1972. We played Meath in the All-Ireland semi-final that year, which gave me my first trip to Croke Park.

The week before the match, my brother Joe took me shopping. He brought me into a sports shop and pulled down a set of boots from the shelf. In those days, a decent pair of boots cost £6. But Joe wasn't having that. He handed me a pristine pair of black Adidas boots. The price tag said £12. It was a huge gesture that I never forgot.

So, I headed for Croke Park with the Predator boots of 1972 in my kitbag, cool as a breeze. Back then, playing in Croke Park didn't feel like a big deal to me. I liked playing football. Croke Park seemed like the best place to play it, so I was happy to do that. I remember the old dressing-rooms under the Cusack Stand were dead on, but they wouldn't exactly blow you away. They were just very ordinary. We beat Meath, I ended up scoring 1-3 and we headed back up the road again. Apart from Joe's boots, there was no fuss. No nothing.

The final was against Cork. The last time Tyrone had made an All-Ireland final was in 1948, but again we weren't bothered by history or hype. We knew little about Cork beyond a few names. Bob Wilmot was their star, a talented mountain of a man who looked closer to 25 than 17. Word had wafted north about Jimmy Barry-Murphy. We were aware of him too, but we weren't worried. We had Frank McGuigan.

Even then, Frank's talent was drawing plenty of attention. He could win ball in the middle of the field at his ease. His distribution was good. His speed was deceptive. He could fist balls farther than some boys could kick. He was superbly strong, yet when he leapt in the air to field a ball he could also float there like a feather. When you had McGuigan, you always had a chance.

This time, though, even Frank's genius wasn't enough. On the day, we were our own worst enemies. We let slip a soft goal before half-time that put us on the back foot for the rest of the game. Then Jimmy Barry-Murphy popped up for a goal. I managed to stick 1-1, but we couldn't turn it round. In the end, we lost by a goal. As if that wasn't bad enough, our tally of 2-11 set a new scoring record for the beaten All-Ireland minor finalists.

For the next three weeks I hobbled about, having injured my hip some time during the game. I consoled myself with the thought that I hadn't even imagined I'd get near a Tyrone minor panel that year. I hadn't underachieved in an All-Ireland minor final either. Croke Park and the big day hadn't bothered me at all. I really didn't think too much about any of the pitfalls and nightmare scenarios. It was a blessing I often wished for later in life when I got more preoccupied about the venue, the opposition and how good they were. Back in 1972 my mind was completely uncluttered, and I performed.

That autumn I went back to school in Omagh CBS and nailed my place on the McRory Cup team. They even made me captain. In December I got a call from Jody O'Neill, who was in charge of the Tyrone seniors. He wanted me down to train in Dungannon. The following Sunday I was on as a substitute against Down in the National League. Sean O'Neill was still there for Down. Three All-Ireland medals Sean O'Neill! Later to be Team of the Millennium Sean O'Neill! Class.

I had learned to hold my own as a minor, but senior football was a different scene again. It took me about five minutes to learn that lesson. Back in Ballygawley, Paddy Joe McClean had taught me a neat trick about dealing with full-backs. When the ball is dropping towards you, lean into the defender. Stick your arse into him, make him move backwards. That way he was slightly off-balance, and you were in a better position to get under the ball and catch it out in front of him. It used to work a charm at minor level. Why not now?

First high ball comes in. I start backing into the Down corner-back, bumping away. He counters my deft piece of chicanery with a stinging punch in the ear. He doesn't retreat an inch, collects the ball and clears it. Back to the drawing-board.

I stayed with the seniors till the following March when McRory Cup commitments and my A-Levels started taking precedence. We made the McRory Cup final in 1973 and lost, but I rolled along. Later that year, Martin and myself made the Tyrone under-21 team. Martin had an Ulster under-21 medal from 1972 already, and added another with me in 1973. Mayo stopped us in the All-Ireland semi-final, but Tyrone were accumulating titles and players.

Then it started going wrong. We met Antrim in the under-21 finals in 1974 and 1975. Lost both. Gerry Armstrong was starting out as a soccer player at the time, but travelled home during the summers to play for Antrim. He was a powerful footballer and Antrim had good teams, but we really should have done better. By 1975, Tyrone had a terrific base to build from: Ulster minor champions in 1971, 1972, 1973 and 1975. All-Ireland minor finalists in 1972. Ulster under-21 champions 1972 and 1973. There was enough talent in all those to win an All-Ireland under-21 title, even with Kerry starting to produce the great footballers that would dominate the seventies and eighties. But we never took the next step.

When Tyrone produced a similar run of under-age success from 1997 to 2001, those boys made no mistake. But we had nothing like their belief. We hoped we might win. There really wasn't any serious planning or preparation before matches. I'm not casting aspersions on those coaches in charge of us – that was the way things were everywhere back then. We didn't think about how success in one year could feed into the next. There was no sense of process or improvement.

Generally the best players always won matches, not the best team. Teamwork, developing a team ethos, building connections within the team weren't really given any attention. You were all in the same jersey and played for each other, but there was no calculated sense of team. If that collective bond didn't occur incidentally, you invariably lost. People didn't fully appreciate what you could do if you could develop that vibe of togetherness. It took years to nail that one.

Training was grim. The winters were spent running in pitch darkness up and down a field in Dungannon. The facilities weren't there to do much else. It's the sort of running that strikes me as a complete waste of time now. As a light, mobile corner-forward I didn't care for it back then either.

We might play a little backs and forwards, but there was nothing particularly strategic about anything. You were accustomed to this being the way it was. We came together, trained a bit. Went home. You were proud to be part of a county panel. You were just glad to be picked. You never thought, "How good is this? How good are we at what we're doing? Are we just going out in matches clinging to hope?"

That was precisely what was happening. People were hoping that some day we might be ahead at the end of an important match. But we had no concrete thoughts on how we might make that happen.

I returned to the senior panel in 1974 and stayed there for the bones of eight years. Won a couple of McKenna Cups. Lost an Ulster title in 1980. That was the real killer. Armagh beat us, 4-10 to 4-7. It was back in the era of the hand-passed goal, and there were more balls thrown to the net that day than anything else. By 1980, eight years had passed since my All-Ireland minor final experience. Enough time to realise what had slipped through our fingers that day. I was 25 now. I needed to get back to Croke Park. Even better, the Ulster champions were drawn against the Connacht champions in the All-Ireland semi-finals that year. That was always the easier road. If you were drawn against Munster or Leinster, you were a dead duck before you even started.

So, aside from losing an Ulster final, we had missed out on an All-Ireland semi-final and the best chance we'd ever have to reach a final. It was desperate. Just pathetic.

PEOPLE SAID I DID all right as a footballer, but I have always felt I underachieved. Psychologically, I could have been better but there was no one there to help me. Sometimes I backed off from challenges I should have been taking on. I didn't always deliver my best in the biggest games. I was too concerned with not being able to do things instead of focusing on what I could do. Years later I read a wonderful quote from John Wooden, the great American basketball coach. "Don't let what you cannot do interfere with what you can do," he said. I sometimes wish I'd heard that 30 years ago.

I needed someone to say: this is what you're good at. Concentrate on those strengths and you won't even notice your weaknesses. You can always work on those, but if you recognise your strengths, you can work from a positive base. Instead, I let my weaknesses dominate me.

When it came to Tyrone, I was a classic victim of the system. If things were going badly for us in a game, if the centre-half-back was being beaten up a stick, if midfield had fallen apart and the wing-backs had folded, who got taken off? The corner-forward. I went into games knowing that unless you got a serious few scores early on, you're not going to last. It felt sometimes like numbers 13 and 15 were merely an attachment to the team, not a key position.

I never had the mental capacity to cope with that. Instead of playing the game to our strengths, teams played to their size. Everybody kicked the ball into the big man. Then you had to win your own ball, a theory that annoys me even now. Why must any player win their own ball? Surely they should only be expected to avail of the advantage if the ball is delivered properly. There are times when players have to battle for a ball if it's kicked in under pressure, but that should be the exception to the rule. Use your strengths, not your size.

When I looked at what Tyrone were doing in comparison to more successful teams, it felt like we were on another planet. Winning wasn't something we even expected. Football was largely about defeat. I had lost an All-Ireland and a McRory final. When I went to St Joseph's College in 1974 – or The Ranch as we knew it – to train as a teacher, the defeats kept coming. We lost a colleges' semi-final to a Thomond College team speckled with class. One year they had Ogie Moran. Another year they had Pat Spillane and Brian Mullins. These guys were operating at another level, and we knew it.

You looked at them, and wondered. Sometimes I thought, "We're simply not good enough. End of story." But I could never fully convince myself of that.

Defeat in that All-Ireland minor final started to nag at me as I got older. I wanted to rewrite that history. I still reckoned the teams I played with could do better. I felt I could do better. I just hadn't figured out how.

I was willing to learn, though. From 1972 I became a fixture in Croke Park on All-Ireland final day. I've only missed one final since, in 1992 when I had to take a youth group from Ballygawley to Italy. Outside that, Dublin became an annual pilgrimage. I would travel with my brothers and head for our sister Mary's house out in Castleknock. Colm McAleer was an old friend from Omagh CBS and played with me on the 1972 minor team. His brother Gerard was a Christian Brother in Dublin and shared the same passion for football as I did. The car filled with Harte boys would arrive and Gerard would join us at Mary's. In later years we'd bring the children to Mary's place and let them loose on the big green in front of her house. When we came back after the match the shortening autumn evenings were illuminated by a game of football. You always felt summer ended that night. The football was over. Next year felt a world away.

Those All-Ireland final days were funny affairs. As Tyrone people it felt like we were visiting somebody else's domain. All-Ireland finals were for Kerry and Dublin. Cork, Meath, Galway and Down. Not us. When Tyrone finally reached one in 1986, we were nearly apologetic about it. Tyrone were in an All-Ireland final. What more could you wish for? We never thought, "We need to win this final." Maybe the players believed in themselves, but they were eight points up and in a strong position to win that game and still lost. We were all afflicted by the same condition.

Back in the seventies, Gerard would go out to Parnell Park and watch the Dubs train. He watched Kevin Heffernan and the way he developed his team. Gerard noted the savagery of the training, the sheer lengths these players were willing to extend themselves. They pursued excellence relentlessly. That was the key.

When it came to watching Dublin in Croke Park, we were students too, in the greatest classroom of all. Tony Hanahoe was the first centre-forward we ever saw who didn't play conventionally. He actually wandered about. Imagine. He was into the business of getting the centre-half-back out of the middle to create space. It was an unprecedented choice for the defender: come out here and mark me, or I'm going to get plenty of ball.

We watched Bobby Doyle drift out from corner-forward and involve himself in the play, giving hope to tormented corner-forwards all over the country. Kerry and Dublin had used a merciless training regime and superb levels of skill execution to play football at a higher pace than ever before. At the time it looked the greatest deal on earth. On reflection it's not as good as we thought at the time, but in the seventies Kerry/Dublin were the last word.

It gave me plenty to think about.

6

MOVING ON

I MOVED TO BELFAST in 1974 for college, leaving behind the quiet countryside of Ballymcilroy for a city that was turning into a war zone. I lived in digs off the Falls Road, up on the Whiterock Road. Maybe it was the naïve courage of youth, but we treated life in Belfast like life in Ballygawley. A crew of us would go to dances in the Starlight ballroom down in the city centre, get a black cab to the bottom of the Falls afterwards and stroll home. We never realised how potentially dangerous that was.

It was an era when black taxis also provided cover for murder gangs. Victims were being picked up in their own areas, murdered and dumped somewhere on the other side of the divide. When you heard about it the following day, the automatic reaction was to ask: what were the victims doing in that part of town?

I remember one classmate in first year was walking along the Andersonstown Road near Casement Park one night when a black cab pulled up alongside him. The back door swung open and he was dragged in. It was the Shankill Butchers. They slit his throat from his left ear to the corner of his jaw but as they were drawing the knife across his neck, the lights of an oncoming car distracted them. He managed to wriggle free and escape. When he returned to college, I'll never forget the necklace of stitches reaching from his throat to his ear.

Looking back now, it must have been the grace of God that saved us from trouble. Of the gang I hung out with, one of us always had a car to commute to and from college. At the time, a bunch of young men cruising around the Falls Road in a car was an object of sinister interest to the armed forces, but it never even crossed our minds as dangerous.

The rural perspective on the Troubles was slightly different. In Belfast the hostility between both sides of the community and towards the police and army was naked and bitter. You could see people physically preparing to riot and the aftermath. It was urban warfare.

Out in the countryside, things were more subtle. You never heard of things happening, but people had a sixth sense about strange cars moving through the area. People looked out for each other. You might hear of things being moved around. We were never fully aware of exactly what was going on, nor did we want to be.

It was a strange, difficult time. We were always open to checkpoints, being pulled out of the car, delayed and generally peppered with questions. Sometimes it was our own neighbours in UDR uniforms. Often you'd roll down the window to see a neighbour in uniform, asking your name and your destination. It seemed ridiculous at times: old Protestant neighbours asking questions they knew the answer to, but we kept trying to remember where they were coming from. Both sides were scared and suspicious. If we wanted to survive that time without incurring any scars from bitterness or resentment, we had to try and understand that.

Belfast was also about finding new friendships and strengthening old ones. Tony Donnelly had been around Omagh CBS when I was there. I could remember Tony wishing me and

Colm McAleer well before the All-Ireland minor final in 1972. He was a smoker. I didn't partake, but I knew the best spots for those who did. It was always cat-and-mouse stuff for those boys: out the lecture room hall at three, down behind the handball alley, through a field and down to the bus depot in town. When we finished school I got a college place in The Ranch. One summer day I met Tony in a dole queue in Ballygawley. He was at a loose end. "Why not go for the teaching?" I suggested. He did. For the next few years we were inseparable, forming a friendship that would last for life.

Sometimes I wonder what strange quirk threw us together. Tony likes a good drink. I don't. He's a great man for yarns and slagging. I'm a little lower key. Our personalities might have been different, but I guess our bloodlines were similar. He was one of seven brothers and one sister, Helena, and grew up in the countryside near Augher. His parents always reminded me of my own. To this day Marian and myself would visit Tony's mother Irene. His father, Pa, was a great football man, with stories that could last all night. He was the kind of man that went to Croke Park when there was only one car in the country, but Pa Donnelly was always the man who had it. I listen to Tony tell stories and crack jokes now and I often think of Pa; same temperament, same demeanour.

The Hunting Lodge on the Stewartstown Road was our place in Belfast. Tony would sip his pint, I'd sip something softer and the nights would pass with all sorts of chat. Then there was the common room in The Ranch. Being a pub man, Tony was pretty tasty at darts. I was okay, but I was good to have a go. If anyone was looking for us, the dartboard in the common room was always a good start.

We hung out with boys from all over the north. Plus, there was a good chunk from Omagh CBS there, too: Tony Marlowe, Barry Campbell, Gerard O'Neill, Sean Healy. It was a wee home from home populated by Gaelic men with the same passion for football as myself and Tony.

Among our lecturers was Jim McKeever, the wonderful former Derry footballer. It was often said of Jim that he was too nice to be a footballer, and there was no doubt he was a gentleman. His approach to teaching and talking football was illuminating. He was deliberate, methodical, meticulously explanatory in everything he did. I can still see him talking, moving his hands about in that expressive way. I don't know whether all nice guys make great footballers, but this one did.

Life was taking off in a different direction beyond The Ranch, too. One weekend I was at home in Ballygawley. It was a Sunday night, and my brother Francie was suited up and ready for a dance in Carrickmore. He was looking for company. He'd drive. All I had to do was sling on some decent threads, and we were gone. I didn't fancy the hassle, but he talked me round.

Later that night I was standing in the Patrician Hall in Carrickmore when I spotted someone. She was pretty. Nice smile. I half recognised her face, but I couldn't quite place her. I walked over to say hello. Her name was Marian. Would she like to dance?

She would.

When the song ended, we stayed talking. I knew her brother Conall. He had been in school with me in Omagh. Her surname was Donnelly. She only lived a few miles from my house, in the first house of the parish next door. I noticed that smile again. She was easy to talk with as well. In a Patrician Hall the only drinks available were minerals, but that suited me. Turns out she didn't drink either.

At the end of the night, I asked her if I could see her home. Well, I asked if I could see her home while Francie drove. We got back to her house and she invited me in. We drank tea and talked some more. She was in Belfast, working in the bank. Maybe we'd meet again?

Maybe we would.

Soon after, I met her on a night out in Belfast. That night I strolled back to her flat along with her friends. Little things were starting to accumulate. She lived on Fitzroy Avenue, barely a half mile from my digs on the Whiterock Road. Her family were country people like mine. She had just emerged from a long relationship and, like me, had to be cajoled into heading to Carrickmore that night. We had actually been confirmed on the same day, in the same chapel. She went to primary school in our parish, which meant she was part of my confirmation group that year. Many years later, Carmel Coyle, who was in school in Altamuskin with Marian and became a lifelong friend, produced an old black-and-white picture from the day. Sure enough, I'm in one row with Marian standing nearby.

We continued to see each other, falling slowly in love. She was the eldest in her family, but her parents were wonderfully warm towards me. I didn't drink and probably seemed pretty sensible. In our house you simply didn't go wild anyway. As the youngest in a big family, you certainly didn't. Maybe you dinged the odd wing mirror if you squeezed on the accelerator too much when driving around at home, but you were only damaging yourself, no one else. Marian's father was also big into sport. No harm having a Tyrone footballer about the place.

I first mentioned marriage in the summer of 1976. Marian reckoned we should wait a little while. I was still in college. She was working. Not long, just a little while.

That Christmas, we got engaged. We headed down into Belfast and bought an engagement ring. I see the pomp and procedure now when each of our children, Michaela, Mark and Michael, got engaged, between getting consent from fathers and arranging venues and moments. There were no big scenes in 1976.

If anything, we were pretty pragmatic. We decided to get married once I was finished in The Ranch. The date was 8 July

1978, followed by a honeymoon in Malta. We returned to a flat in Belfast but we didn't really want to stay there. We had already been saving diligently over the previous couple of years, so one evening we decided we had to buy a house.

The following morning I headed off, looking to buy a house, thinking like a man looking to buy a suit. Find one I like. Take a look. Try it for size. Pay.

I eventually found a place in Glengormley. It wasn't as straightforward as I imagined, but we got the required mortgage. Then the interest rates started spiralling. By the time they peaked at 15 per cent, our monthly mortgage repayments were £153. My monthly salary was £152. Marian was still working, though, and that's what kept us above water.

Then Marian became pregnant with Mark. He was born on 21 June 1979. Marian was back at work six weeks later. If we wanted to live, we had to work.

By then, I had spent almost five years in my first teaching job in Kircubbin, a small place perched out on the Ards Peninsula in Down. The post-primary school housed teenagers with social problems. There were children from broken homes who had been fostered out or had fallen the wrong side of the law. Others had been moved from different institutions, having grown too old to stay there. It was a difficult place to work in many ways, but it was a job. That was all that mattered.

In my first year I had been paid some disturbance money to move to Kircubbin, which helped. Once we settled in Glengormley, it turned out that a woman called Maura Hobbs from the area was also a primary school teacher in Kircubbin. She travelled with me, which helped with the petrol money. I took the children for extra activities after school four days a week, till five in the evening. Every penny counted.

Beyond supporting my new family, though, Kircubbin shaped my life – and my outlook – in so many ways. You couldn't enter that environment with the attitude of a conventional teacher. If you were thinking about subjects and getting through that workload, Kircubbin would have blown your mind.

You needed a different mindset. You needed to accept that there was more to these children than what they might or might not know. You needed to work out their background and family history. You had to find a way to see where they were coming from.

For that, I leaned back on an old lecturer from The Ranch. Willie McCarney had taken us for Youth and Community Studies back then. He had a very humane approach. Youth work is always informal. People don't have to respond to you; they don't have to attend your youth club. That means you must try and engage with them. Willie never judged people. He always saw them as they were.

I remember he once told a story about his son, Liam, who would go mad writing on the wall in one room at home. He would draw and scrawl and scribble, all sorts of stuff. I thought of how Mummy might react if the same thing happened at home. It just wouldn't.

But Willie felt that's how his son expressed himself. It's what he needed to do, and Willie was going to accept that and find some understanding for his behaviour. You're allowing somebody to be who they are.

It's a philosophy that came to mean more to me as life went on. Sometimes people might come to me and say, "Would you put that Owen Mulligan in his box? He's too flamboyant, too flashy. Would you just nail him? Tell him who's boss."

I have to battle with that myself. Owen is not like me but we click in other ways. I would be more structured, but as long as Owen plays good football and works within the context of what the team needs, I'll grin and bear it. The battle goes on within me all the time, though.

In Kircubbin, accommodating that individuality was one lesson you had to learn. My mother's empathy was also a deep influence on me in that time. She showed me that if someone needs something, try and reach out to them. Be aware of them. That's what I did in Kircubbin. Even though you could swing for those children at times, you constantly tried to identify with their difficulties and problems.

I tried to make a connection with them. Find some common ground. Talk cars or soccer. Then let them steer the conversation. Sport was a fantastic tool. I was handy at most sports, and I was fiercely competitive. They liked that. When we played football, a De La Salle Brother might take the other team. We really went out to win those games.

It was mad, but that's how we were. There was always slagging with the boys in those games and sometimes fellas might step over the line. You could lose your own temper too, though, and you'd have to realise you lost it too.

The boys were split into four houses, each one with "house parents". These were people from the community who had volunteered to act as surrogate parents to the residents of each house. That could mean dealing with 13 boys. People did their best in difficult circumstances.

You had different variations: one house might have a De La Salle Brother and a woman from the village who'd come in to cook and clean. Another had a retired army officer and his wife. Some houses were strictly run. Others had a more *laissez-faire* attitude. It must have been hard for some boys to figure what was going on when there were so many conflicting methods in one vicinity, especially when they needed stability most of all.

Then there was sometimes a perception among the house parents and staff that the teachers saw themselves above them. It was all in their minds. We just worked in a different way with the children. For a young teacher trying to learn, even the staff was multi-layered with old-school disciplinarians and more conciliatory types. It was one serious learning curve.

But I took a lot from it. I saw that life offers different opportunities to different people. My upbringing hadn't been extravagant, but it was privileged in one sense: I always had stability and support at home. Despite all the pressures and strains that were exerted on those boys, though, some of them were still coming out the other side.

Take Declan Gallagher. Declan was the son of a Kenyan doctor and a white nurse. He always had a wonderfully bright smile and a terrific outlook on life. When I see Barack Obama now, Declan Gallagher's bright optimism still flits through my head. Whenever I meet him he still calls me Mr Harte, even though there's barely nine years between us. He had come through a difficult start to his life, but has shown the courage to emerge as a rounded, kind, warm human being. It's a privilege to know him.

Some boys weren't so lucky, though. Geordie Burke was a lovely lad who couldn't read or write so well. One week we came into school to hear that Geordie had been killed in a motorcycle accident. He was barely 16. I often wondered about the kind of life he had been dealt. What could his take on life have been? Kircubbin gave us a brief glimpse into so many sad stories, but my mother had the same experience at home. I knew from the way she listened that my only hope was to be as upbeat as I could be for these children. Those years made me appreciate the life I had, and always helped me keep that balance in years to come.

BY 1982, WE WERE on the move home. Finally. Marian and myself had always seen ourselves back in the parish, but we certainly didn't think it would take five years to get there.

A new post had been created in St Ciarán's school: youth tutor. I would take PE for half the week and run a youth club for the rest of the time. It sounded ideal. We rented a house from my brother in Dungannon and got stuck in. At first, I was away a lot. The youth club demanded my time three nights a week, and football claimed me the rest of the time. Sometimes I wouldn't see Marian till 11 at night, but it's what we had to do.

At least my work in the evenings gave me more time with the children. I got to drop them to school, take them to the doctors, all the little jobs some fathers miss out on. Then I got a notion to go back to school. I took an Open University degree for three years. I hooked up with Tony Donnelly back in The Ranch for an Advanced Certificate in Youth and Community Studies and did a postgraduate certificate in Computer Studies in Portadown Tech.

Another year I took a Masters in Education and Contemporary Society. My thesis was on the GAA and sectarianism, and whether the perception within Unionist circles that the GAA was essentially the sporting wing of the IRA had any merit. My contention was that sport was the driving force behind the association, nothing else. I did questionnaires with young people across the north about why they played. History and politics never came into it. I interviewed a youth team in Crossmaglen. If these boys weren't politically motivated, I reckoned, who would be? It turned out they didn't even know who had founded the GAA. They didn't care either. They just wanted to play.

Meanwhile the youth club was taking off. Having a youth club essentially meant a gym was available during the week. That meant indoor football. There might have been a dartboard hanging somewhere, but no one was using it. Instead, you might have 40 boys all hanging around for the night waiting to play two matches at five minutes a side.

The matches were savage. We put benches on their ends to use as goals. You played against wall bars and all sorts. Sometimes these games went right out of control. I often went buck mad myself as the games started heating up. There would always be a few girls around looking to chat to boys. Occasionally they might wrangle enough time for a game of netball, but 40 boys waiting to kick ball usually won that argument.

In time a new wing was added to the school housing a social area and a sports hall. The Youth Club had to reinvent itself. One day I went rooting underneath the stage in the hall. It was a wilderness down there, but I had an idea we could shape it into something. I got a few lads to help clear it out. We built a staircase down into it and cleaned out the basement. We got a snooker table and a dartboard, plugged in a few stereos and tossed a few beanbags around. Now the children had a common room.

Ciarán McCrumlish was a teacher in school who was handy with technical stuff. We got our hands on a control desk and a few record players and broadcast Radio Roundabout for a half hour every week. Martin McAleer had a background in scouting and joined us as a part-time youth worker. He taught the children some basic camping skills and brought them up into Kilbroney Forest and around the local area camping out. It was different and fun, and brought the children together.

My working life in Ballygawley had settled nicely. Coming back from Belfast I was thinking about football in Ballygawley too. I was looking forward to getting home.

I had no idea what was in store for me.

7

THE SPLIT

BACK IN 1969, when I was 15 years old, Ballygawley St Kieran's GAA club decided to fill the empty autumn months with football. Four teams were created based on the four different church areas within the parish – Ballygawley, Dunmoyle, Garvaghy and Glencull. Each team would get three matches each over the course of a few weeks, players would get a rare chance to stretch their legs in October and the road to Christmas would be shortened a little. No harm? No bother?

Wrong.

The dusting and danging went on over at the pitch in Dunmoyle for three hectic weekends. Occasionally a supporter or team mentor might be dragged into the trouble. If the matches took place now, the referee would have an aching arm from issuing cards of every colour. I stood on the side-line as a 16th man for Glencull. I was happy enough to stay there.

At least the aggression was confined to the matches back then, though. Once the games were over, people went back to being neighbours and team-mates. All the same, the club officials took note and conveniently let the idea slide when 1970 came round.

But memories fade with time. When I returned home to Ballygawley in late 1982, people were talking parish leagues again. Whatever about the potential for trouble, the idea of more football late in the year interested me. A few more people came on board around the parish and the idea gathered some momentum. If there were any worries the league might end up triggering the same hassle it did in 1969, no one mentioned them.

In the context of Ballygawley St Kieran's, Dunmoyle was the hub of activity for the club. The pitch was there and provided the club with its focal point. Garvaghy had a tidy pick from its surrounding area, while Ballygawley could choose a team from those living in the village and anyone who attended the school there.

We were fairly well stocked with players at home in Glencull, even though we didn't always have a significant representation on the club team. Apart from a few of my brothers and myself, we had Canavans and McNelises, Gormleys and McAnenleys. Maybe we didn't have as many first-choice St Kieran's players as the other townlands, but we had a good mix. With a little work, we could do well in this league.

Years before the pitch in Dunmoyle was developed, St Kieran's had used a field in Glencull. It was called The Holm, a flat piece of ground with a river running alongside. It was a funny little pitch down in a hollow beside the primary school where the river jutted into the pitch, cutting out one corner of the field. It was never big enough for full 15-a-side games but to Glencull people, it was their football field. When the club shifted across the parish to Dunmoyle, something of the club's meaning around Glencull changed. It was never mentioned, but among the older people that sense of disconnection was there.

As well as playing, I took on the job of managing the team and embraced the challenge. It didn't matter to me what the other townlands were planning or their attitude towards the competition. We weren't entering for fun. We were entering to win.

So we started training. The chapel car park across the road from our home had a floodlight which allowed us do some skill work at night. A wee circuit that ringed the chapel and went back around our house was ideal for running. That was as scientific as things got, but it sounded light years ahead of what anyone else about the parish was doing, which was pretty much nothing.

It wasn't long before word drifted around the parish. Glencull were training. People were surprised anyone would train for something like this. Most teams reckoned they would just play and be damned with it. We believed in doing a little more than that. The better we prepared, we told each other, the better we would play. It was good fun too. Players who had drifted away from the club returned to help fill out our numbers. It was a nice bonding exercise for old neighbours and friends in a different setting. The few weeks together had energised us all. The first game, against Dunmoyle, promised to be interesting.

THAT SUNDAY STARTED with my mind on other things. Marian was in hospital, having given birth to our second son, Michael. I was in Dunmoyle on the sideline. I had a twinge in my knee after all the nights pounding about the chapel's tarmac car park. With two matches scheduled, there was a good crowd gathered. Glencull were set. The whistle blew, and we went at it.

We always knew these games would be aggressive. You wanted to win. These were your neighbours. The local rivalry was even more acute than normal. The only uncertainty was the scale of the aggression.

We expected people to put in hits. A good hit was almost as useful as a score. If you could nail somebody – not with a belt or a punch, but a good shoulder or a thump that would knock them sideways – now that was the ideal thing. It wasn't a day for dancing around opponents with the ball. You steamrolled through them.

As the game unfolded, I was getting edgy on the line. Glencull were a point behind. Dunmoyle were controlling the game. My knee wasn't right, but instinct was taking over. Glencull needed to produce something different here, so I put myself on.

After all the talk of training in Glencull combined with my jagged competitive edge, my arrival might have lit a fuse with a few people. Either way, it didn't end well.

I was soloing up the wing at one point when I met Brendan McCann from Dunmoyle. I tried to pop a pass over his head to a team-mate. Brendan read my intention. He got a hand to the ball and knocked it into the air. We both jumped to fist the ball forward, but Brendan's jaw got in the way. I can honestly say I didn't deliberately go out to punch him, but that's what happened.

Instead of accepting it was an honest mistake, Brendan translated it as a naked act of aggression. When he landed on the ground, he took a swing at me. I ducked. Such was the force behind his swing, Brendan went sprawling. As he fell to the ground I landed on top of his chest and held him down, reminding him how vulnerable he suddenly was, particularly considering he had just tried to take my head off.

The referee jumped in. All hell was threatening to break loose around us. As he approached the scene, I saw a St Kieran's club official intercept the referee with a crucial piece of advice: send them both off. Brendan and I left the field as the game lurched from one skirmish to another. There was a punch in the eye here, a bang on the nose there. At the end of the day, players left Dunmoyle with more cuts, bruises and bumps than they should have.

By the time I got to Marian and baby Michael in the hospital, she had already welcomed a few eyewitnesses from Dunmoyle, and didn't need much help from me to flesh out the finer details of the story. On Monday night, the club held a meeting specifically to address the problems that had arisen the previous day. Reading between the lines, I reckoned Glencull were being depicted as the main culprits. The punishments handed down seemed to confirm my suspicions. As well as being banned from playing in the last two games, I was also barred from the side-line as Glencull manager.

This caused practical problems. In Dunmoyle, the crowd gathered on the dressing-room side of the pitch. Standing among them while trying to manage the team wouldn't have been ideal. The other side of the pitch was bordered by soft, heathery ground, which was impossible to stand in. Missing the games as a player didn't bother me, but the decision to bar me from the line made it impossible to manage the team.

I asked to be allowed on the touchline. The club officials refused. Things were getting messy. The same night I was being court-martialled in Ballygawley, Brendan McCann was playing handball for St Kieran's in an official competition. Now, if I couldn't manage my team from the side-line in an internal club competition because of the events of Sunday, how was Brendan allowed represent the club in a handball game? The club wouldn't move on the issue. The Glencull side was starting to harden, too.

The team met back home in Glencull and formulated a letter outlining our complaints. If I wasn't allowed to manage the team, Glencull would withdraw from the parish league and from club activities in general until this issue was sorted out. St Kieran's response was withering: no big deal. Let's move on.

I kept the Glencull boys together for training as the league went on without us. When it was over, there was still no word from St Kieran's. We had a decision to make. As it turned out, it was quick and painless. We weren't going back. Glencull was our new club.

It was a massive moment for us all. My entire footballing life had been devoted to Ballygawley St Kieran's. I had sat in the dressing-rooms as a child watching my brothers get ready for championship matches. I had spent countless nights travelling home from Kircubbin and Belfast for training and matches, just keeping the connection. I had been club chairman when I was still in college. At a time when few Ballygawley players represented Tyrone, my brothers and myself had made it. The old club jerseys had hung on our washing-line for years. All that history seemed to be scrubbed out in an instant.

However, this could be a fresh start for Glencull, too. It felt like football was coming home again to the older generations that had seen The Holm fall by the wayside in favour of the pitch in Dunmoyle. We also felt we had a strong case to be affiliated as an official club. In 1979, Aughabrack had broken away from their parish club, Owen Roes. Tyrone County Board initially rejected their application but following a hearing, the Ulster Council recommended Aughabrack be affiliated. The Board duly obliged.

In Tyrone, multiple clubs in one parish was not the exception either. Clonoe housed four. Coalisland had three. Omagh had four. We applied for affiliation in 1983 with confidence. Even when our request was rejected, we didn't worry. We headed for the Ulster Council with plenty of hope, given Aughabrack's experience, and duly received their backing. We headed back to the county board with that endorsement, expecting a change of heart. Instead, the answer was no. No explanations. No excuses.

We were stunned. Communication with St Kieran's had ended. We were on our own but were fuelled by the need to prove we could produce a club to be proud of. At the same time, we never thought it would take eight years to find a way back.

In the meantime, we set to work. We kept the team together and got a set of jerseys: gold with a green band. We ran functions and bought an old prefab from the YMCA in Portadown to use as a clubhouse. When he was GAA President in the mid-eighties,

Mick Loftus travelled from Crossmolina to meet us and discuss our situation. We tidied up The Holm and played nine-a-side matches there between ourselves every Sunday.

We continued to press our case with the county board. That autumn we filled up the cars, designed placards and picketed the board's annual convention in Eglish. We encountered no opposition from any delegates as they arrived. How could they disagree with our stance? A lot of their clubs wouldn't exist had they been subjected to the same treatment as we were.

Even though we continued to exist beyond the margins, we did everything we could to operate as a viable GAA club. We ran Scór sessions. We used a space in a local joinery factory or cleared out Gormley's Engineering Works to run social events and fundraising functions.

In time we developed an annual nine-a-side tournament and invited teams from Tyrone and beyond to play. Finding teams was tricky at first. The county board would warn visiting teams that we were an illegal entity. If anything happened at the matches in The Holm, Glencull weren't covered by insurance. Most teams didn't listen. We organised a decent tournament, and they were happy to play the games.

In turn, we travelled anywhere we were welcome for matches: Fermanagh, south Derry, Armagh, anywhere in Tyrone. Before we played the senior games on a Sunday, we ran training sessions for the local children. I got a teacher in school to run Irish language classes in the prefab. One year we ran a raffle selling tickets at £10 each that raised over £40,000. I can still remember the dark nights traipsing through south Derry, selling fists of tickets. Every penny was priceless.

We mightn't have been officially affiliated, but because we had to prove ourselves capable of running a viable club, we probably started up more initiatives than most clubs around us. In fact, I know we did. Unlike other clubs we couldn't read our results on a Monday morning in the *Irish News*, but I carpet-bombed the local press with club notes. If a fly stirred over The Holm, it got reported.

All the while, any movements towards resolution fell apart. The parish priest tried and failed. My school principal, Eugene McSorley, had a quiet chat with me one day in school about the situation, but there was no easy solution.

In 1984, we applied for affiliation again. Another rejection. This time, I decided on drastic action. At that year's convention, a group of us marched into the hall and demanded to be allowed speak. Our request was denied.

"Well, we came here to tell a story," I said, "and if you'll not give me permission, I'll speak anyway."

I spoke for about 20 minutes and laid out our story. No one interrupted me. No one left. No one booed and I didn't get kicked out. Maybe it didn't help our chances of improving relationships with the board but we felt we had nothing to lose. They weren't going to let us in anyway.

For eight years we applied annually for affiliation. For eight years they kept us outside. Ballygawley reached a county final in 1989 and lost. If they'd had access to the Glencull players sitting at home that year, they probably would have won.

Those years brought other missed opportunities for all of us. Tyrone won an Ulster title in 1984 with my old minor team-mate Frank McGuigan scoring 11 flawless points. I was heading into my thirties by then, but my competitive streak hadn't aged. If I had still been playing club football, maybe I could have made it.

In 1986 Tyrone even made an All-Ireland final. They led Kerry by eight points in the second half but still lost the game. Paudge Quinn from Ballygawley scored a goal that day, but it didn't register with us. We felt he might as well have been from Dungannon, Moy, Aghayarn. Anywhere. Maybe I might have made those teams. I was 32 in 1986. That age wouldn't have been an impediment to performing at the highest level back then. But it was all irrelevant. Whether I liked it or not, that chapter of my life was closed.

Like any conflict, things could have been done differently but no one person doing things differently can solve anything. A variety of people have to force themselves out of their comfort zones and take a chance. If both sides had given a little ground at the time the problem might have been solved quickly, but we didn't.

Life in the parish continued in relative normality. Conversations could be dry, though. You talked about the weather, the traffic, mindless snippets of small talk that cover your lack of connection with someone. Football, though, was off-limits.

Generally, I didn't feel it impacted on my dealings with people in school or in the parish. I stayed friends with Brendan McCann, the player I initially tangled with at the match in Dunmoyle. Indeed the McCanns stayed firm family friends, and occasionally visited The Holm for our nine-a-side games. I didn't care where people came from, Ballygawley or Glencull. I treated everyone the same. Living in the north, you were always aware of having neighbours you didn't associate with much. There was almost as much suspicion between Glencull and Ballygawley at times.

Because I was at the centre of the original incident that caused the split I was quickly fingered as the ringleader, the one that needed rooting out. I might have been dogmatic and opinionated, but any suggestions I was leading people astray were wrong. One day someone put that to Sean Canavan, and I can still hear his reply. "Mickey Harte doesn't drink or smoke," he said. "If that's leading our young people astray, I'm happy with that."

The biggest problem for us was that we were seen as second-class citizens. We were viewed as having no rights. We weren't affiliated, therefore we were mavericks. We always felt our opponents never gave us any credibility. We were ordinary, decent people who happened to disagree with them on one issue. Anything we did was stained by that. They had the backing of the board and the moral standing as the official club. We were treated like a bunch of tearaways.

We felt we were still doing the right things, still living according to the ethos of the GAA. We were doing more than most affiliated clubs to live up to those standards, but never got the recognition. Ultimately, that's all we wanted. If somebody had publicly accepted that we were decent people who had followed a path we passionately believed in, rather than depicting us as pigheaded troublemakers, the whole problem might have been resolved sooner. But others thought differently, and the years dragged on.

THE FIRST CRACK of light came behind the post office in the townland of Seskilgreen where a small boy used the window of an old barn for target practice. The Canavan family had run the post office for years and fed footballers into Ballygawley and Glencull for just as long. Sean had been a powerful, stubborn player who stood back from nothing. His son Steven had grown into a classy player himself but the Glencull crisis stalled his progress with Tyrone and always left a question over how far his talent might have taken him. His younger brother Pascal was growing into a useful player, too.

Then there was Peter.

In time I'd watch him grow into a player in school but even as a boy, the greatest joys with Peter were always in the simplest things. Driving down the road in Glencull, you would see Peter heading for the shop, juggling a ball as he strolled along. Where most boys would kick a ball against a wall and catch it, Peter was constantly on the move, dinking and ducking, bobbing and weaving around imaginary opponents. In his mind's eye, he must have constantly been surrounded by defenders.

Before the ball would even land in his chest, Peter was already thinking a few steps ahead, twisting and turning, feinting to go one way before darting in the opposite direction. He didn't learn those moves years later. He grew up with them.

He was a decent player as a child, but back then there were even better ones. When Peter was 13, Leo Cuddy was the man. As an under-14 in school, Leo had the power and strength that allowed him to dominate the field at that age. He could run all day and had a kick like a mule off his left boot. Put a ball on the ground in front of him and Leo could kick it 55 yards.

It took Peter another couple of years to pass him out. When he finally did arrive, though, he was class. In two years he had found the strength and aggression he needed to make the space for his skills. He was fiery and sharp, like his father. When he got the ball in space, he was like no one you had ever seen before.

His emergence also posed a challenge for Glencull and Ballygawley. As a Glencull resident, Peter never played any official under-age football. When he reached minor level, Tyrone wanted him on board. Without a club, though, he was ineligible. At the beginning he was registered with Killyclogher hurling club to circumvent the rules. After that he made an All-Ireland minor semi-final in 1988 and continued to rip it up for the Tyrone Vocational Schools team. Killyclogher was a useful sticking plaster solution, but it wasn't enough. When Ballygawley lost that county final in 1989, Peter was among the boys left at home in Glencull. That removed any lingering doubts.

Peter Canavan needed a club. The parish had a new reason to come together.

Around the same time, a new curate arrived. In the course of his work, Fr Sean Hegarty had also spent time managing the Armagh footballers. Now he was landed into the middle of a

Cold War inspired by football. It wasn't hard to see how the bishop's mind was working.

For the bones of a year, Fr Hegarty went from one end of the parish to the other, knocking on doors and talking to people to find a solution, drinking coffee till late at night and smoking Benson & Hedges cigarettes down to the butt. He identified Barney Horisk as the most accessible person on the Ballygawley side. If he wanted anything to happen on the Glencull side, he figured out he needed to talk with me.

By then, though, both sides had started to develop an open mind about some form of reunification. Fr Sean carried messages between both sides, editing them as he saw fit. Sometimes the messages were perfectly truthful. Other times Fr Sean might be economical with the truth. At the back of our minds, we always knew what he was at. The key was to make both sides feel the other was ready to make a move. Eventually, both sides jumped together.

There were concessions. Glencull agreed to give up the idea of existing as an independent club. Ballygawley gave up their old name in favour of a new parish club: Errigal Ciarán. The Glencull contingent would also be allowed operate as Errigal Ciarán 2 in a lower grade for the first couple of years if they wished, until they felt comfortable enough to fully unite with the rest of the club.

There was still some resistance in Glencull. To me, the settlement felt like vindication. The idea of Errigal Ciarán 2 at least acknowledged we had shown the strength and substance to be regarded as an autonomous unit in our own right. That recognition was all we ever wanted. We didn't want to split the parish or the new club. In my mind, Glencull was never anti-Ballygawley. I always thought of the positivity being created around Glencull. I wasn't anti-anybody. I was pro-Glencull and what it stood for.

The legacy left by those eight years bears that out. Many people still feel the time spent in conflict was a terrible waste. I can only see the benefits. When Glencull broke away, it became a cause in that area. People who had drifted from the GAA returned to help fill out the numbers and support the idea behind the club. The socials and dinner dances, céilí nights and other classes and functions helped generate a community spirit that had been lost.

Ballygawley had a similar rebirth. When both sides came together, the interest in GAA across the parish was beyond anything the old club could muster in 1982. In 1990 I took the first Errigal under-16 team. I can still see Mickey "Harley" Mullin, an old clubman, showing me his wee notebook to record the scores, with "Errigal Ciarán" written on top of one page. It hit me in that moment. Errigal Ciarán was the future. It was my club. Everyone's club. After eight years' division, this was some change.

THE TIMING OF ERRIGAL'S creation seemed right in so many ways. In August 1990, myself and Marian took the children on holiday to Sligo. We were travelling back into Ballygawley with the children singing in the back of the car when I saw something on the road in the distance. I slowed down. It was a man. I stopped the car and went back. I recognised the thick glasses first. Then the bald head. It was my father.

I knelt down and spoke to him. To this day I often wonder why I didn't do the natural thing and whisper a prayer in his ear. His eyes were flickering but he wasn't responding. Beside him was a box of groceries. It seemed he was coming from the shops. Maybe he felt faint. When he did, he placed the groceries carefully on the ground first, and leaned against the ditch for a moment. The bottles in the box weren't even broken.

Then, he died.

I felt helpless. Marian took the car home and sent some people up to help. The doctor arrived and pronounced him dead. A few days later Daddy's coffin was carried from the chapel across the road from home draped in the Errigal Ciarán colours. After years spent caring for the Ballygawley jerseys, having reared a family of footballers, it was right he should see football returned to its rightful place in his own home before he died.

It wasn't an era when fathers and sons shared their feelings with each other, but I always admired Daddy. You watched him rather than talk to him. He possessed a wonderful serenity and a powerful faith that allowed him to accept whatever arrows life might fire in his direction. He did things straight down the line. No messing. While Mummy bequeathed a sense of compassion to me, Daddy taught me the need for best practice, for quality in everything you do in life. I have always tried to live those values as best I can.

ERRIGAL CIARÁN WERE a powerful force from the beginning. We had outstanding young players. Many of them were already playing minor football with Tyrone. For the first time in years, teams from the parish were entering competitions truly believing we could win. In 1990 we took Errigal under-16s to a county title, beating Donaghmore in the final. Two years previously, Donaghmore had won the All-Ireland Féile title as under-14s. That was a massive sign. I also took an under-12 team in 1990 that matured into a county title-winning team as under-21s. You could see the old barriers breaking down at training. Boys from Ballygawley would start slagging the Glencull players: "You're not playing by the river now boys." We took it well and the heat quickly evaporated from the entire scene. The talent was there in Errigal now. It just needed patience and nurture.

Three years after coming into existence, Errigal seniors beat Moortown to win our first Tyrone title since 1932. This was something else. When I played in the seventies and eighties, Ballygawley had been a decent side who did well in the league, but we weren't a championship side. The best I ever did with Ballygawley was a county semi-final that we lost to Carrickmore by a point. I was 36 when we won that county title, still playing reserve football, still on the bench for the Errigal seniors. I didn't play much of a role that year but I did all the training and cherish my medal.

We didn't have that negative mentality any more that had hung us so many times over the years. Now, we were a championship side. Plus we had a management team well versed in winning, with an enlightened approach to how teams should be prepared. Danny Ball had enjoyed tremendous success with the Tyrone under-21s in 1991 and 1992, winning two All-Ireland titles. Anthony Gallagher was there with him, and between them they honed the team superbly. There was no pointless running. The drills were cutting-edge. It felt new and vibrant. Peter Canavan was a genius and the rest of the team members were starting to grow as players. We were becoming a team of winners.

That success came so quickly helped wave away any lingering doubts among the locals about the idea of Errigal Ciarán, too. If it had taken time to convert that work into something tangible, it might have been a tougher battle. Some people still hold onto the past because they feel they need to; many others – including myself – have released themselves from those shackles a long time ago.

Winning that county title and our trip through the Ulster championship was another adventure that brought the whole parish together. When I look at the videos at home of the Ulster semi-final against Kilcar from Donegal and the final against Downpatrick, I see Peter with a mop of hair, men hanging out of him, going to ground and bouncing back up to turn the other way, gradually creating the space to open up the defence like the boy evading his imaginary defenders years ago outside the family post office.

Flags and bunting hung from telephone poles across the parish, linking up all the townlands. When we beat Lavey in the Ulster championship first round that year, they couldn't believe it. Lavey were All-Ireland champions back then. Who were we?

We took the Ulster title that December and rolled into an All-Ireland semi-final against Nemo Rangers. Even though Nemo travelled with all their tradition and status, we were now ambitious enough to start collecting regrets.

The first match was called off due to a waterlogged pitch. The second day ended level at the end of normal time, but for some reason extra-time was played. They beat us in the end, but the disappointment we felt reflected the journey we had already taken. They had six or seven Cork footballers carrying All-Ireland medals. That didn't faze us. When they wrecked Castlebar Mitchels in the All-Ireland final, that sickened us even more. A rare chance had been missed. It remains one title in my mind that's there to be chased.

The bigger picture still formed a beautiful landscape. Players had won All-Ireland Vocational Schools titles and Ulster minor medals and now county and Ulster medals with their clubs. They were winners. We were winners. A new era was beginning. Everything we knew before didn't seem quite so certain now. The future had become what we made it. We had players. We had hope.

And we had Peter.

8

MINOR LESSONS

AT LEAST FOOTBALL in school stayed cocooned away from all that trouble. From the day I returned to St Ciarán's in 1982, I threw myself into coaching. Robbie Hasson was a PE teacher from Dungannon who had taken football by the scruff of the neck when he arrived in Ballygawley. By the time I arrived, he was busy creating something special.

Willie McCarney's ideas about respecting people as individuals, and connecting with them as an avenue to reach your goals, was my coaching ethos in theory. Robbie's work was a practical application of all that. He always spoke about quality – in his teams, his players, his training methods. Our school teams always aspired to be the best, on and off the field. They concentrated on playing football. They were physical but never dirty. There was never any bad language in our dressing-rooms or out on the field. Our players never answered back to referees. There was no shouting and bawling on the field. Robbie Hasson was the key to all that.

Little things struck me about how Robbie got things done. Because the school buses left promptly after the final bell, any football training had to be done at lunchtime. That meant we had maybe 25 minutes for training. Everything was tailored to suit those constraints. We didn't do any physical work. Everything was done with the ball. This reinforced everything I believed in and showed me how these principles could work. We didn't need to be running boys around the field. Our time with them was to develop a group of footballers. A team.

We developed small ploys and broke up orthodox formations where we could. Like me, Robbie never believed in players having to fight like dogs to win their own ball when we could improve the quality of the delivery and create more space around them. Corner-backs generally stuck to their position back then, so we drew players out the field to upset the opposition's rhythm. When we had Peter Canavan in school, it was all about creating one-on-ones close to goal and withdrawing players to give Peter the space he needed.

The key, though, was always creating that sense of team. It wasn't about allowing anyone to soak up all the limelight or funnelling every ball through one or two players. We tried to teach players to take the right option, regardless of what player that might involve. That basic philosophy pervaded everything we ever did.

We won Ulster Vocational Schools titles all through the grades. The first under-14 team to win an Ulster title included Peter Canavan. When Peter was in his last year as an under-16 we had a team capable of winning an All-Ireland title, until Peter stepped on a nail at home the day before the first round of the Tyrone championship. We lost to St Patrick's Omagh by a point; they went on to win the All-Ireland. That one, and what that team could have been, still haunts me.

Aside from that, though, we enjoyed plenty of great days. In 2002 and 2003 we won two All-Ireland under-16 titles. We beat Rathmore Vocational School on the way to one of them. Fifteen years before that we would have been shaking in our boots if we'd met a team from Kerry. Victories like that were priceless in changing all that.

Then, one evening early in 1991, I received an invitation from Tyrone county board to manage the Tyrone minor team. Errigal Ciarán were in existence by then, but after eight years of boardroom skirmishes, I hadn't been expecting this.

It probably looked a strange appointment to anyone who had followed my various encounters with the board, but I was developing a decent record as a coach in Ballygawley. My brother Peter had been president of the Ulster Council. A few of us at home had also played for Tyrone, so they knew our stock and bloodlines. After being a chronic pain in their neck for eight years, they probably reckoned I wouldn't stand back from a challenge either. Maybe in the middle of all that conflict, they saw some value in that.

While appointing me might have seemed a gamble, asking Fr Sean Hegarty to step in alongside me made it an each-way bet. He accepted the role, but his parish work in Ballygawley kept him busy. As the preparations for the 1991 season began, the workload pretty much fell entirely on my shoulders. With Fr Sean stepping back, I rang Fr Gerard McAleer. Would he come on board? He agreed immediately.

There were three decades of thinking, watching and waiting in all of this. The memories of Croke Park, watching Kerry and the Dubs with Fr Gerard and Colm McAleer. Watching Tony Hanahoe drift and Bobby Doyle mock the traditional role of the sacrificial corner-forward. There were the beatings we took in The Ranch against those Thomond College teams speckled with stars like Spillane, Mullins and Ogie. We thought about what they did and how they must think. Why were they so good? Why are they ahead of everybody else? Is there something we can do about that?

We had to believe they were no different from anyone else as human beings, but what differentiated them from other footballers? It was their standards of preparation for sure, but ultimately their sense of complete self-belief had to make the difference. Until somebody decides they can also create that belief in themselves, and build a system that allowed the players to develop that mentality, we would spend the rest of our lives admiring these boys without ever truly competing with them.

It was all there in my head: Paddy Joe McClean's blackboard and the attention to detail of Sean Canavan and Jim McKeever, percolating around with my parents' compassion and honesty towards people; my brother Peter's toughness in the tackle; the mental frailties that held me back as a player, and the gnawing memory of 1972. The desire to win just once. I was driven to win that All-Ireland minor title. I wanted the Tom Markham Cup back home. This was my chance.

THE NIGHT I WAS RATIFIED as minor manager, Paul Doris of the Tyrone county board was among the first to congratulate me. "You've taken on the most difficult job in management," he said. I knew what he meant. Our time with these teams would be short. There were no back doors. We had one chance to stand or fall. If we wanted to succeed we needed to make things happen fast.

We started by working on the skills. I wanted people who were comfortable on the ball. Every session had to revolve around using the football. At least 95 per cent of the players' time at training would be spent with the ball, sometimes 100 per cent. I wanted my players to be comfortable on the ball on either side. I wanted them to be comfortable with each other. I wanted to fit them into a system of play that didn't define them but offered them a solid baseline from which to work – one with the flexibility to accommodate flair, to accommodate uniqueness.

Given all the time we had spent thinking and talking about good practice, myself and Fr Gerard weren't going to start cutting corners now. Fr Gerard had a nice phrase he borrowed from Michelangelo: "Trivialities make perfection. Perfection is no triviality." Every brushstroke from now was crucial.

The first test of our convictions came with our inaugural set of minor trials. As an exercise in democracy and diligence, I sent three slips of paper to each club in Tyrone, asking them to nominate three players to attend the trials. The response wasn't quite in keeping with the spirit of the arrangement. Instead of nominating three players, club officials photocopied the slips of paper and filled them out with nominees, regardless of their prospects.

I was left with 220 players to reduce down to a panel of 24. It caused untold problems. Apart from the logistical nightmare of organising trials over six weeks, carefully assembling teams on paper only to turn up and find half the players had stayed at home, the standard of play was severely compromised by the numbers.

We videotaped every trial and studied them. Sometimes we ran two trials a day. Once we put our panel together, myself and Fr Gerard started to put our system in place. We needed to create a new collective identity for these players. They needed to realise that playing for Tyrone was different from their club or school. It demanded a different standard of application and commitment. For that to happen, we tried to create the right mood.

We started with championship day. How you performed on championship day began with how you projected yourself. Back then, minor teams usually traipsed off the bus or out of cars into the ground dressed in their civilian clothes. That wouldn't be our style.

I indicated to all the boys that they should buy themselves a white shirt and a tie. That would be our uniform. It said that championship day is different. It's nothing to be scared of, but to be involved in such a day was a privilege in itself. It also helped create a connection between the players. It was a statement: we were going to set ourselves apart, on the field and off it.

It wasn't just about how you looked or played either, but how you carried yourself. We always encouraged the players to show the simple courtesies. If we were having a meal somewhere, showing common good manners was important. Back then, hotel and restaurant owners would often comment on the behaviour of the boys. To this day, I still find that Tyrone players are well received wherever we go. That's vindication enough.

We tried lots of things. We used music on the team bus to motivate the players. Michaela wound pieces of red and white wool together at home to create wristbands for each player. She laminated a set of cards numbered one to 24 that would be handed to the players as they hit the training pitch. The idea was to break up any cliques that might be there among players from the same schools or clubs. If we needed to break the group into groups of five, it allowed us to simply ask numbers one to five to join up, and so on.

We had just taken on a shop in Ballygawley, so we took the milk and biscuits for the boys after training from our own shelves. The garden shed was packed with footballs and cones and other training equipment.

Every night Michael, Michaela and Mark would come with me to training. Matthew would tag along in later years. Some nights back then Marian would be along as well to keep an eye on them all – the entire Harte family in the stand.

On match days the children would travel on the team bus with me. They saw players like Sean Teague grow into seniors in the early days. Then Brian Dooher and Gerald Cavlan, and the wave of boys that came in the late nineties. No one ever passed any remark on their presence around the scene. They loved being there and I loved having them around. Maybe the board knew. Once you got me, you got the rest as well.

The jerseys would also come home with me every evening after a match. On those nights, our house turned into a small

Chinese laundry. The jerseys and togs would first be soaked in the bath to remove any heavy stains. After, they were washed and ironed. Finally, the whole family could be found on our hands and knees in the living-room, carefully folding each jersey with the number facing out, piling the shorts into the right sizes and balling the socks together.

As we knelt there, folding jerseys and sorting shorts, the jersey became the focal point. It wasn't just a shirt that denoted 24 players as a squad. This jersey had its own history. To make the jerseys fit to wear, my wife and family had devoted their time to caring for them, as had countless people before us. If players tore off their jerseys after a game and tossed them in the corner, they weren't just disrespecting the white jersey, but all those people who cared for the fabric of the jersey. Receiving that jersey is a privilege. I wanted the players to feel that receiving and returning this jersey was more than it seemed. Maybe the players would reflect on their status more, and the responsibilities that came with it.

Before the next game, the jerseys were folded and left on a table in the dressing-room. Instead of simply grabbing them, each player was called forward to receive his jersey. Then, the players waited, and all put their jerseys on at the same time. After the game, they folded the jerseys again and placed them back on the table. That tradition started back then, and has never altered since.

Our first championship dawned. Because Dungannon Academy had progressed in the All-Ireland Colleges competition, we had to make some changes to the panel late on. It was a difficult situation. In the end we let seven players go to accommodate the talent available from Dungannon. I spoke to them all individually and sent them a letter. They needed to know they had done well. We respected the commitments they had made, but they knew this fate would befall some of them when they began. It was tough but necessary, and felt as hard as any decision I ever made in the years that followed.

Blending in a whole new set of players promised to be tricky. We tried to break up any cliques among the Dungannon boys and the players who had been there all winter. We also needed to make sure the new players adapted to our new approach. One night I was forced to call a Dungannon player to order over his behaviour in the dressing-room. I gave him a pretty severe dressing-down, told him that different standards prevailed here. It was probably a more public outburst than I might allow myself these days, but it got the message across.

Once we hit the field, though, the results of our work were promising. We met Derry in the first round. It was tight and tense and Derry missed some good chances to win the game in the last few minutes, but we got home by two points. We put Monaghan away early in the quarter-final and won by ten points in the end. The following day the *Irish News* described us as "well-drilled". That's the language I like.

We met Armagh next. They had always been blessed with good under-age structures and hard-working people involved to make the best of their resources. In 1991, Diarmaid Marsden and Des Mackin were their stars, and the match turned into a battle.

Sean Treacy was providing the core of our scoring tallies every day, but a nasty arm injury took him out early on. Meanwhile, Marsden was proving unmanageable. We were hanging on for long spells, but just when the game seemed gone from us, Colm Donnelly popped up with a point in the last few seconds to level the game. Draw. Still alive.

The replay was as edgy as the drawn game for different reasons. We held Armagh scoreless for over 20 minutes in the first half and got to half time with an 11-point lead. The Armagh keeper even saved a penalty, only for the referee to order it to be retaken. In fairness, the keeper saved the second penalty too.

With that reprieve, they launched a comeback. Diarmaid Marsden's last point brought Armagh within a point, but it was too late. We were in the final.

This was magic stuff. Donegal in Clones, and it looked good for a long time too. We got ahead early on, and still held the lead with five minutes left. A lad called Mark Boyle had been tormenting us in attack, but we were nearly home. Then, with a few minutes left, a Donegal player was snagged in the square. It didn't look a penalty, but Mark slotted the ball to the net. Donegal won by a point. I never forgot that referee.

We were gutted, but the county board were pleased with the work we had done on and off the field. We started the 1992 championship like a fireball and incinerated Derry in the first round with one of the best exhibitions of football I have ever seen from any Tyrone team. Eoin Gormley delivered a stunning performance and rasped a marvellous goal from 12 yards to set the tone. Martin Mulgrew and Brendan Mallon gave us a pair of strong men at midfield, and Derry never got a look-in. In the end, we strolled away by 10 points. Near perfection.

With Monaghan refusing to play our Ulster quarter-final after a dispute over the scheduling of the game due to exams, the semi-final brought us back against Armagh.

We could scent danger from the beginning. The press had cottoned onto our display against Derry. Having found a nice spot in the long grass, we were now raging favourites to win Ulster. Armagh would never be far off us. This promised to be tricky.

Armagh had the memory of the previous year to drive them on and a handful of new players to make the crucial difference. Paul McGrane was at midfield beside Barry O'Hagan and took our well-regarded pair apart. Marsden had another field day. They held us scoreless from play till just before half time. By then we were trailing by nine points. We managed to stabilise things in the second half, but not by much. The margin in the end was ten points. Armagh made the All-Ireland final that year. We didn't find much consolation in that for a long time to come.

By 1993, MYSELF and Fr Gerard were starting to get restless. We had spent two years with the minors and little to show for it. The board weren't applying any pressure, but we felt the heat on ourselves. Tyrone had enough players to be winning minor championships on a regular basis. The 1993 batch didn't promise much, but regardless of their individual qualities, we needed to make a stand.

Around the same time, I had started selling water filters as a side-line business, using the concept of network marketing as the basis for the operation. It was a simple idea. First you bought some product. If you signed up as an agent for the company, you could then invite others to join. If you got two or three other people also selling the product, you earned money from their sales. In turn, they could invite people to join and take a percentage of their sales.

Essentially, the more people you can bring in, the greater percentage return. It's a fair system. If you work hard, you do well. If you help the person you introduced into the scheme, you'll get a return from their work. If you introduce somebody and leave them to paddle their own canoe, though, they might do nothing. Helping them develop their business actually helps you.

It's not a bad way of doing business through a recession, either. The overheads are minimal. You don't need premises. You don't pay employees. The shipping costs are counted as part of the price. All you have is the financial outlay on the product.

The business was fine, but it was the lessons within network marketing that generated the greatest return for me.

George Zalucki has been among network marketing's greatest promoters. His ethos was simple: give a little of yourself to help people develop their own gifts and talents. Encourage them to do it. See them do well, and you will do well. You can't be selfish. If you're in it for purely personal gain, you'll go nowhere.

His message blew me away. It resonated with the same sense of respect for people that had been nurtured in me as a child. It also matched the ideas I was developing through preparing my teams. I started reading books by Zalucki and buying his motivational videos. Before this I had seen reading as a means to an end, not as an ongoing process of learning. Zalucki was leading me into a whole new world.

Zalucki never believed in limiting himself to anybody else's notion of what he could be. He suffered from polio as a child but battled through life to become a basketball player. He hadn't allowed defeat, rejection and crisis to prevent him dreaming and achieving. It worked in business. I was sure it could work in football.

I started noting players' reactions to our motivational approach – how they reacted to rejection and setbacks. Network marketing is also about your ability to take rejection and turn it into a result. You accept rejection as somebody's choice. They're free to make that choice, but it doesn't diminish your belief that you're right. Defeat doesn't mean the end, just a new beginning. It's about turning adversity around and defining it in a different way. It's something that makes you take a different view of where you want to get to. It makes you adjust. But it doesn't knock you.

The message was clear. As a minor management, we had to try harder to develop our teams. We had good individuals on the 1991 and 1992 teams. In 1993 we had a solid group of boys, but no stars. This was a new test, but with Zalucki's ideas pinned to the back of my subconscious mind, it energised me.

We started working with our new team. They worked savagely hard in training and on the field. There was a different feel to this group than the others. Colin Holmes was a stout centre-back. Gerald Cavlan looked a classy player in attack, and Brian Dooher was already becoming Brian Dooher. He came from Clann na nGael, a small club in north-west Tyrone where players of his calibre fell into their laps only every few generations. As a result they always sought him out on the field, so he carried the ball endlessly. Years later we'd start pruning those excesses from his game, got him thinking that his best work is done picking up loose ball, transferring quickly and getting it back off them farther up-field. Back then, though, we just let him loose.

He was totally honest. He never made a fuss about anything. He never stood on ceremony with anybody, or expected any plaudits for his work. With Dooher it was work, work, work.

He also took life outside football as seriously as his sport. One evening coming back on the bus from a challenge game in Mayo, I remember spotting Dooher with his chemistry books out, preparing for an A-level exam the following day. Travelling with a bunch of minors that just wanted to muck about on the way home didn't bother him. He was in the same cocoon of concentration he entered for matches.

Although the rest of Ulster wasn't taking much notice, we could see something stirring in these boys. We picked Raymie Gallagher as Fermanagh's key player in the first round, shut him down and eased to an 11-point win. Then came the sort of curveball we would spend the rest of our lives trying to deal with.

Arthur Mallon from Edendork had been added to our panel early that summer but picked up an injury before the Ulster semi-final against Donegal. While we prepared for the game, Arthur was left off the panel to recuperate. That weekend he was involved in a car crash, and died. If Arthur hadn't been injured, he would have been with the panel that weekend. He might have been at home that night preparing for the match. Instead, he was a victim of the road.

We grieved with his family and supported them as best we could. We didn't go through the steps that helped us process the deaths of Paul McGirr and Cormac McAnallen years later, but we needed the boys to accept how random this had been. It was reason to stop and mourn, not a reason to stop living. The game went ahead that weekend. We blew Donegal away.

After all the tests and tragedy, we had reached another final against Derry. This time would be different. These boys had reached this final against the head. They hadn't relied on the guidance of any stars, but made their own way. I dearly wanted them to win this one.

At a meeting before the match, one of the O'Kane brothers, Sean, crystallised what was on our minds. "Look at Mickey and Fr Gerard," he said. "They're at this three years and haven't got what they wanted. It's up to us to start delivering." I hoped they could, but not for us any more. For themselves.

We were ready. All the videos had been analysed. We knew what we needed to do. During the week Fr Gerard had a cassette tape made, recording Tina Turner's song "Simply the Best" five times in succession for the bus ride to Clones. I can still hear a few boys at the back of the bus, battering the seat in front of them with excitement as the song rang down the aisle. They embraced everything we tried that year. That day was their reward.

As watershed days went, it didn't lack for a touch of the biblical. The rain began an hour before the game and continued till half-time like a monsoon. The players slid and splashed through puddles. The pitch was almost unplayable, but Clones had a new terrace to celebrate. There was no way the game was going to be called off.

It was a day for character. Our captain, Brendan Sheehy, had returned from injury for his first championship game of the year and dived on a Derry shot to stop a certain goal just after half-time, like a soldier smothering a grenade. At the other end,

Gerald Cavlan was on fire. Dooher delivered a powerful performance. Derry got a goal late on to close the gap to a point, but we refused to yield. A Derry shot was cleared off the line. Another screamer was blocked by our keeper, Eamon Gallogly, onto the post and scrambled away. When the final whistle went, we were four ahead, 1-9 to 1-5. I looked for Fr Gerard. We had done it.

We headed for Croke Park to play Meath in the All-Ireland minor semi-final. Hindsight tells us exactly the sort of storm we were sailing towards. Meath started with Darren Fay, Trevor Giles, Ollie Murphy, Barry Callaghan and Hank Traynor. Three years later, these boys would be winning All-Ireland senior medals.

On the day, they used us for target practice. We tried what we could. Colin Holmes was named at corner-forward but swept across our defence. Didn't work. We switched him onto Ollie Murphy. Didn't knock a feather from Ollie. Gerald Cavlan had another big day but we looked nervy and unsure throughout the game. Too many bad passes. Too many fumbles. Meath were excellent, but we didn't help ourselves. The game ended 3-17 to 0-10. Meath won a good All-Ireland title and left us to deal with a new reality. Ulster was only a foothill. The steepest mountains lay beyond.

OVER THE FOLLOWING two years, our teams mixed with good and bad. In 1994, we led Armagh by four points in Omagh as the game entered the last ten minutes but they still grabbed a draw. The replay was a nightmare. We held Armagh scoreless for 25 minutes and had goal chances to kill the game dead in the last ten minutes. Instead Armagh landed a goal in the last minute, won by a point and went on to win an Ulster title. Sickener.

The following year we drew a Derry team blessed with the kind of strength Meath had in 1993. They hammered us by nine points. They went on to lose the All-Ireland final to Westmeath, but the sight of our conquerors striding out after they had left us behind was beginning to wear thin. The board were staying quiet, but for how much longer?

I reckoned the events of 1996 would surely prompt them into action. We played the first round against Fermanagh in Omagh, confident we could make some progress. Instead, we were left on the seat of our pants. Rory Gallagher caused us all sorts of problems, and despite the fact we were playing badly we were still ahead with a few minutes left. Then they scored a goal. A famous win for Fermanagh. A trip to the cliff edge for myself and Fr Gerard.

Fermanagh deserved their victory, but to the greater Tyrone public this was sacrilege. The seniors went on to pulp Fermanagh that afternoon. That was how Tyrone–Fermanagh worked. Not this.

It was truly the worst day of all. That was our black hole, where all the good work of the previous six seasons could have been sucked in. The public wanted us out. I seriously wondered whether we'd survive this one.

So we waited. And waited. But no call came. When we did meet, the board were happy to hear our case. We would begin a root-and-branch examination of our approach and seal up any cracks for 1997. One Ulster title in six seasons was a modest return, but we were producing players. Dooher and Cavlan starred for the seniors in 1996. Dungannon Academy had another good team making progress in the McRory Cup. Myself and Fr Gerard were still winded from the biggest sucker punch I have ever experienced. Getting our breath back seemed the greatest challenge the new season could pose.

We needed to get back on track. Instead, our journey took a dramatically different route.

EARLY DAYS: Posing for a school photograph in Glencull, aged 10.

MARRIED BLISS: With Marian on the biggest day of our lives, 8 July 1978. I didn't use the razor that day either!

A FAMILY AFFAIR: With all the family on our parents' 50th wedding anniversary, August 1988. From back (left to right), myself, Peter jnr, Martin, Paddy, Joe, Barney, Francie. In front (left to right), Mary, Daddy, Mummy, Bridie.

THE IN-LAWS: With Marian and her parents, Nan and Pat Donnelly.

RECOGNITION: Then GAA President Mick Loftus on a visit to the Glencull clubhouse in the mid-eighties. This was a huge moment for us all.

PAUL: Paul McGirr, back row, second from the right, with a team picked for the Munster team in the minor trials in late 1996. Back then, we would have no idea the impact Paul would have on our future.

LOOKING AHEAD: With Fr Gerard McAleer after the 1998 Ulster minor final. In pensive mood, thinking of bigger days.

A DREAM COMES TRUE: The Tom Markham Cup sitting on my kitchen table in 1998. Twenty-six years in the making.

HIGH WIRE ACTS: Members of the 2000 under-21 squad during a team-building day in the woods near Pomeroy before the All-Ireland final. We all went One Step Beyond together.

BEAUTIFUL MUSIC: Cormac McAnallen being helped over a wire to the dulcet tones of Kevin Hughes singing a Boyzone melody during a team building day with the under-21s before the 2000 All-Ireland final.

With school principal John Clayton, Martin McElkennon and captain Paul Marlowe after St Ciaran's Ballygawley won the Ulster U-16 vocational schools' title in 2003. The first All-Ireland title of the year was only weeks away. *(Photo © Kenny Curran)*

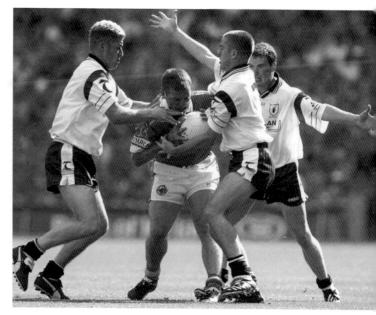

PERFECTION: Kevin Hughes, Philip Jordan and Gavin Devlin hound Kerry's Dara Ó Cinnéide during the 2003 All-Ireland semi-final. Some called it puke football. I reckoned it was the ultimate expression of team.

(Photo © David Maher/Sportsfile)

THE BLOCK: We had done everything to trump Armagh for 70 minutes, but winning the All-Ireland still came down a piece of heroism from Conor Gormley. Another example of our players taking One Step Beyond. *(Photo © Brendan Moran/Sportsfile)*

WINNING TEAM: Moments after winning the 2003 All-Ireland, I'm exactly where I want to be, with Matthew and Michaela. *(Photo © Kenny Curran)*

PRESIDENTIAL SEAL OF APPROVAL: It was a tremendous honour to meet Uachtarán Mary McAleese and her husband Martin in the aftermath of our 2003 win.

(Photo © Kenny Curran)

THE LAST HURRAH:
Cormac lifts the McKenna Cup
in 2004, his last act as Tyrone
captain. He died ten days later.

(Photo © Jim Dunne)

NOT ANOTHER ONE: Kevin Hughes, Owen Mulligan and Sean Cavanagh watch
Cormac's funeral cortege pass by. *(Photo © Ray McManus/Sportsfile)*

9

PAUL

28 September 1997

STANDING IN CROKE PARK. Everything about the scene was wrong. Laois had won the All-Ireland. I was with another beaten Tyrone minor team. A few days after the game, I met Josie Cassidy, a neighbour at home. She had heard me talking on the radio after the game. That defeat had been a terrible blow, but 1997 had become about so much more than football. Winning that minor title had been my obsession. Our collective obsession. But that summer had suggested that even defeat had to be accepted as a crucial part of the journey. Losing was a sickener, I had told the radio interviewer, but there was more to our lives that summer than football. "Maybe there's a reason for this, Josie," I said. "Maybe there's something better to come."

I might have said it. At the time, we didn't see where it might come from. How could we? I thought again about that Tom Markham Cup sitting at home on my kitchen table with its gleaming silver pot-belly and my reflection staring back at me. Winning that Cup had been my ambition for the previous 25 years. The last seven summers had given me a chance to finally settle that pang in my guts. But, after everything we had lived through, 1997 had left us with nothing.

I wanted to quit. I felt drained. I made my announcement at the team dinner that night. I had given everything I could. It felt like we had poured everything of ourselves into the first five years, then found even more to invest in 1997. We had dramatically shaken up our preparations. We had overcome unimaginable challenges. Young boys had forced themselves to become men. Great men. We had smashed moulds that Tyrone teams were usually happy to fit into. Michaela reckoned we were destined to win this All-Ireland. I had believed the script too. After everything we had all been through, it seemed the circle was about to be completed. Instead we had fallen victim to another twist.

After the game GAA President Joe McDonagh visited our dressing-room. It wasn't usual for the President to visit any dressing-room on All-Ireland final day, he said, but this was a day for breaking precedent. He told us of his admiration for the way we had carried ourselves through the worst summer of our lives. He used the word "dignity" to describe us. That meant a lot. He shook hands with every single player. It was a gesture that hinted at what men these players had become, but at that moment we were consumed by disappointment. Laois had played well and deserved to win. Nothing to do with fate or happy endings. It simply felt like an ending.

The following night we came home to a function in the Glenavon Hotel in Cookstown. I was sitting with Marian, soaking up my last few hours with the boys. Over comes Stephen O'Neill and Brian McGuigan. They're looking for me, but talking to Marian. "Please don't let him quit," they said. "Give it one more year. We'll win this All-Ireland."

After everything we had lived through that year, I couldn't dismiss them out of hand. But the words in my head were hard to shake: "This is history repeating itself. It's not in the script for you to win an All-Ireland. Face it. Move on."

That was the thing with 1997. We had tried everything. We had gained a huge amount of experience over the years and made an even bigger push in 1997. Then again, these boys had shown themselves not just to be special players, but a special team. And a lot of them were coming back again in 1998. I let the idea sink in. Could I go again?

◄○►

THE YEAR HAD BEGUN with a dart of acceleration. The horrors of 1996 had left me vulnerable as a manager. The board believed in what we were doing, but we needed to review our systems and improve them. Plus we now had some serious players coming through. Dungannon Academy had won the All-Ireland Colleges title, the Hogan Cup, early in 1997 with a good team. With that talent coming through and the lessons from the previous year, we needed to get everything right.

I started by trying to get Tony Donnelly to join myself and Fr Gerard, but Tony had a young family and couldn't sacrifice the time. Instead, I went for a colleague in St Ciarán's. Martin McElkennon had been showing some promise as a coach in school. I liked his attitude towards training teams. He was bringing some cutting-edge stuff to his sessions and the kind of personality guaranteed to bring some life to the scene. With Martin on board, I was certain we could bring the training to a new level.

Next, we had to make sure we found the right players. For years our system of trials had been an unwieldy, exhaustive round of phone calls, recommendations and lists bloated by hundreds of names. Sifting a panel from all that, you were guaranteed to overlook someone. We needed to create a more streamlined way of bringing players through.

I decided to split the county into four sections. I named them Ulster, Munster, Leinster and Connacht for fun and found four sponsors to buy some jerseys to match the provincial colours. Then, I found four mentors to put a team together from the players in each region.

From all that we generated some real games. Players were competing for themselves, but also for the good name of their area. We were uncovering talent, and boys with a streak of character too.

Training was spiky as the season began. Martin McElkennon was working out well as trainer and the vibes were good. Every night Stephen O'Neill would bound out in front of everybody else to grab that number one card from Michaela. If he was quick enough, Brian McGuigan would always try and nip in ahead, just to wind Stevie up.

Michaela was in charge of the milk and biscuits along with Sean Kelly, one of our drivers. To prevent the quickest players emptying the trough after training first, they carefully divided up the booty for the players. Even then, they knew how to keep a few happy: extra Milky Ways in Mark Harte's boots, a few Caramel bars in McGuigan's. Maybe a few Jaffa Cakes in Michaela's own pockets to keep the hunger away too.

Down were up first that year. Years of colleges football told us any under-age team from Down required careful handling. Plus, Dungannon's success meant we didn't have our full panel together until a week before the match. Down could cause us problems.

In the end we hit two goals in the last five minutes, including a stunning shot from 20 yards by Stephen Donnelly, and got home by five points, but it hadn't been without its difficulties. Once again Armagh stood in our way in the quarter-finals. In 1997 players like Steven McDonnell and Paddy McKeever were starting to mature into something special. Although Armagh always represented a huge hurdle for this team, we couldn't have imagined how this match would loom over us for the rest of our lives.

THE DAY BEGAN with the sun blistering the sky. It was the sixteenth anniversary of Fr Gerard's ordination, which put a little extra spring into his step. The boys were in good humour. We were starting to see some players make a special mark.

First, there was Cormac McAnallen. He was simply Cormac then, and always Cormac ever after. Everything about him was exemplary: his attitude, his enthusiasm, his willingness to take on a leadership role. He watched everything and learned from everything. He was totally focused on the simple but demanding task of being the very best he could possibly be.

Brian McGuigan was also something special. He came to us with a reputation from colleges' football, and lived up to everything we expected. He had guile. He had class. He offered something completely different from any forward we had. Plus, he was a unique person. The challenge with Brian was always communi-cation. You needed to know him to figure out the best way to understand and enjoy him, and get the best football out of him.

Being Frank's son might have burdened other players, but Brian never played that way. We saw him as an opportunity. He had the pedigree to be a great footballer, the ability and vision to make things happen. There was nothing difficult about having a McGuigan about the place. It was a privilege.

Then there was Paul McGirr. Number 12. I had known Paul when he was growing up in Ballygawley. He was always a jolly character, a boy with a neat line in quips and a quick wit. Paul had played his first few games of football with my son Mark too. His family moved to Dromore when he was around 13. With Mark also on the minor panel, they could renew old acquaintances.

Paul in particular got stuck into Armagh early on, kicked a good point and settled into the game. Then Richard Thornton took a ball in along the end-line towards the Armagh goal and fisted the ball across the square. Paul saw his chance. He dived at full stretch to reach the ball. The Armagh goalkeeper tried to smother the pass, but Paul made it. He flicked the ball to the net. The keeper's knees hit him beneath the ribcage. His liver was exposed because he was stretching so much to reach the ball, and ruptured on impact.

Our team doctor, Seamus Cassidy, went out to him. I followed. He was gasping for breath and hurting badly. It looked serious. Maybe a broken rib. Maybe a punctured lung.

He was treated for five minutes on the field. A stretcher arrived. I took one handle and helped carry him to the line. He was in a bad way. I remember seeing his eyes roll back in his head with pain, but rib injuries could do that to you. I'd see him later.

The game continued. Kevin Hughes kicked some great points. Stephen Donnelly kept pace with Steven McDonnell as the game settled into a free-taking battle. When it came to the crunch, though, our boys were learning how to survive in tight spots. We won by four points. Paul McGirr's four points. For a few hours anything seemed possible.

We headed over the road from Healy Park to Molly Sweeney's for a meal. I wondered about Paul. He might miss a few games between recovery and gaining full fitness again. After we finished I headed up to the hospital. A few lads had travelled up before us with Francie Goulding, one of our backroom team. They were coming out of the hospital. I met them at the door: Adrian Ball, Declan McCrossan and Stephen O'Neill.

"He's gone," they said.

"Who's gone?" I replied.

"Paul's dead."

The blood drained from my face. There was numbness. Disbelief. Total shock. I went up to the room. His parents,

Francis and Rita, were by his bedside. Paul was lying in the bed, still wearing his Tyrone kit. There was nothing to say. All you could offer was a presence. We stood there, trying to share the burden of grief that engulfed those in the room. Trying to silently let them know you feel for them.

This is when spirit comes into our lives. Words can't heal in these moments. All you can do is connect with your spirit and let those in most pain know you're going to do all you can in the weeks and months ahead to support and care for them.

I heard the full story later on. All the way to the hospital, Paul had kept asking his father one question: where had the ball gone? They had infused 20 pints of blood into Paul to keep him alive while a specialist from Belfast sped across the country, but the trauma raging within Paul's body was too much for him to bear. At around 6.30 p.m. the specialist was near the Ballygawley roundabout. At the same moment, Paul was suffering a cardiac arrest.

The sight of him lying on clean hospital sheets in his Tyrone strip, his grieving family at his side, is a sight that will live with me forever. A few days later he would be buried wearing the same strip.

I drove home. The next few hours were reduced to a muddled blur of thoughts and emotions. How many other sons went out to play that day and came home safe? Mark had lined out in the number 13 jersey, one ahead of Paul. What was in a number? A random moment in time?

Marian, Michaela and the boys were at home. Everybody had their own feelings of loss over what had happened, but for the children, the feelings were more acute. Myself and Marian felt we were too young to be dealing with something like this too. I could remember many young people dying in car accidents along the Ballygawley line over the years. The Somerville sisters, two neighbours of mine, were killed on that stretch. Their brother was in school with me. The date, 9 May 1965, is still etched in my mind. This sort of incident was hard for adults to deal with, but teenagers know it's a level of trauma they shouldn't have to face. That mental conflict was something we would have to deal with.

That night at home we watched *The Sunday Game*. Meath and Dublin had fought their usual battle in Croke Park. At the end Paul Bealin had missed a crucial penalty. The pundits talked about the disappointment Paul Bealin might feel tonight, but at least no one died. The programme ended with a shot of Paul McGirr running back out the field having scored a point. A smile was playing around the edges of his lips. He looked like a man filled with intent, ready to face up to the next ball, the next challenge. A few minutes later, all that exuberance and life was taken away from him, and from us.

Michaela kept scrapbooks for the minors that year. In that team photograph from Omagh all the players are staring at the camera, game faces attached. In the back row, though, Paul McGirr is looking away to his right. Maybe he's trying to spot his parents in the stand. Maybe he's looking at Armagh, rising himself for the challenge. The newspaper pulled out the image of Paul and used it as a headshot. There was a nobility and determination in his face that spoke of what his team-mates needed to be now. First, though, we had to mourn.

Those few days were tragic, but also a tribute. The long queue to his wake moved in complete silence. Micheál Ó Muircheartaigh was among the mourners. The image of him kneeling quietly at the coffin that evening saying a prayer stayed with us. At the funeral mass, Peter Canavan brought the Tyrone jersey to the altar as part of the offertory procession. The Tyrone minors were joined in the guard of honour by the Fermanagh Vocational Colleges team that Paul played with, players from his club, Dromore, and the Armagh team we had played the previous Sunday. Sadly, it wasn't the last time we would witness their proud dignity in these circumstances.

Our panel released a statement of condolence. Putting our grief into words seemed a futile exercise, but we needed to try. At the end, it said: "Our contact was limited yet our hearts are heavy." We will always carry that weight.

I GRIEVED FOR PAUL like everyone else. I felt the same sorrow and bewilderment. I also had a son on the panel who needed his father, and I felt a responsibility to those around me. We couldn't allow this tragedy to engulf not only the team, but the players as individuals. They needed guidance. They needed hope.

I found strength through my faith. When we were growing up at home, Mummy always left everything in the hands of God. She treated her life as God's instrument and accepted everything as being sent by Him. My father was a resilient man too. They both accepted the life they had without question. They were never angry with God, or felt that God had dealt them a bad hand. All they ever felt was acceptance.

Mummy had died the previous year. Her death had left a sad space in my life, but the strengths she blessed me with would play a special part now in helping me make sense of the loss of Paul. I knew this was never the way you wished things to be, but you had to accept it. The random nature of Paul's death might shake some people's beliefs. The strength I derived from my faith helped deepen my relationship with God and allowed me to begin to find a way to help the boys.

You had to find the positivity in everything. Sometimes that can be hard to see in these situations, but there is no other way. You must commit to doing as much good as you can despite what's going on. How can we help each other to cope with this? When you reach out to others, you don't get consumed by your own grief. That was one valuable lesson we all learned.

Myself and Fr Gerard had to use our life experience to process what was going on and lead the team in the best possible way. We needed to focus on the thing they liked to do: play football. We needed to get back to making them better players and, if we could, better people. It was the same philosophy I had adhered to from the beginning: you're not just looking at this piece of talent. You are looking at how being a good person can complement all those gifts. One could be enhanced by the other. In these circumstances, it all took on a whole new meaning.

Before we ever kicked a ball again, we brought all the boys together to talk. I leaned back on my training as a teacher and my work with youth groups in Ballygawley. Instead of holding a full meeting, we split the panel into small groups, creating the freedom for them to discuss things some players might have been too inhibited to say in a larger group. The smaller groups allowed them to get their feelings across and gave us the feedback we needed without making anyone uncomfortable.

Their feelings were what we expected: fear, anger, disbelief. There was a deep-seated worry that this could happen again; when Joe Campbell, a clubmate of Paul's, took a bang to the head in a game later that summer, he was terrified he was going to die too. The fear went that deep.

They needed reassurance. Dr Seamus Cassidy explained precisely what had happened to Paul and the unlikely chance of it ever happening again. Paul had died of a ruptured liver, the kind of injury usually only found in victims of major car accidents. For it to happen as a result of any other sort of contact, said Seamus, was a freak occurrence.

Dr Niall McCullough was a clinical psychologist and a neighbour of mine. As well as easing any medical concerns, we had to heal any mental cracks too. Niall joined us at a meeting in Cookstown and did a wonderful job for us. He reassured the boys that the emotions they were enduring were completely natural. He told them there were people they could talk to if they needed additional help, but that they could also safely lean on each other for support.

We reinforced everything Niall did for us. We tried to get the players looking to the future. None of us could live in fear, we told them. This was a terrible experience to endure at such a young age, but it wasn't par for the course. We had to try and start living again. We couldn't be afraid of what life might deal us. There was comfort and company in this group. No one should feel alone. We were in this together.

The entire experience was inexorably taking the group to another place. It felt like we had lost a family member. There was more to our relationship than football now. Working through our grief together consolidated our belief in each other. After Paul's death the results over the rest of the summer were a bonus, we told them. The important thing now was about how we carried ourselves. The year wouldn't become a crusade for Paul. We needed to honour his memory by doing the right thing. We needed to get back playing football. Where that took us was irrelevant. The important thing was that we just needed to be the best we could be.

Simply doing that provided the foundation for what these men became.

WE RETURNED TO FOOTBALL against Monaghan in the Ulster semi-final. We had retired Paul's jersey. The players seemed more comfortable in their own skin again. Bringing in Dr Niall, had provided the extra security blanket of professional help if they felt they needed it. They had been forced to mature a lot in a short space of time, but we could have no idea how that would impact on them.

I found out as we prepared in the dressing-room for that match. Without any prompting, team captain Declan McCrossan set the tone. The players would walk out in single file wearing their black armbands, he said. This was about dignity, and saying: "We remember." I looked around the dressing-room. This group was growing up fast. They were thinkers, capable of making the right decision at the right time. It was a trait that boded well for the years to come.

The mood was right. The balance between respecting the tragedy of the previous few weeks and moving forward had been perfectly struck by the players. Once the game started, the team was unstoppable. We hit 4-14 and won by ten points.

After the game we returned to the field with the Monaghan team and management, and lined up across the pitch for a minute's silence. It was impeccably observed. We were moving on, but Paul would never leave any of us.

We would never forget.

10

ON THE BRINK

A YEAR AFTER LOSING to Fermanagh in the first round, we had turned around and made an Ulster final, even though the season wasn't about justifying ourselves like that any more. Antrim made the final with a reputation for scoring goals, but we had momentum now. Serious momentum.

Apart from piecing a good team together, individuals were starting to blossom. Looking back, the list of players that started against Antrim is impressive: Ciaran Gourley, Brendan Donnelly, Cormac McAnallen, Declan McCrossan, Kevin Hughes, Mark Harte, Brian McGuigan. On the bench, Cormac McGinley was learning his trade, while Stephen O'Neill hadn't fully revealed his potential just yet.

We still had to fight, but these boys were leaving calling cards about their character in almost every game. Inside the first ten minutes against Antrim we were 2-2 to 0-1 down. By half-time, we were ahead. Declan McCrossan helped shore up our half-back line. Brian McGuigan roamed brilliantly from corner-forward. Mark accumulated 1-3 either side of half-time to get us a lead, and eventually finished up the game with 1-7. We won by six points. Declan McCrossan lifted the Cup and quietly remembered Paul in his speech as our motivation and our inspiration. Then he lifted the trophy again, and we roared.

It was a landmark victory for so many reasons. Crucially, it said so much about what this team was capable of. Given the journey we had made, it would have been easy for the players to yield. There would have been sympathy. No one would have said boo to them for losing. In a way, that made it an even harder game to win. It was to their credit they came through that. And it was continuing to say pleasing things about them as people.

We were chasing an All-Ireland minor title, but trying not to talk about it. Ideally, every coach should focus on performance, not outcome. In our case that attitude was being imposed on us. It didn't come from a good place, but it was still the perfect approach for our next opponents: Kerry.

For any Tyrone team, facing Kerry had always been the mountain that couldn't be scaled. This team had already shown they had a head for heights, though, and the ability to deal with any crisis. Beating Kerry now demanded we reject every conventional assumption about how these games usually went. We knew these boys had no fear anyway. That was a good start.

Noel and Tadhg Kennelly were the showstoppers for Kerry back then. Paul Galvin was there too. Galvin hopped one shot off the butt of the post, but we were well with them all game. In the second half, Mark ushered in a goal to level the game. That also gave Noel Kennelly his cue. He hit three points in a row and with five minutes left we were in trouble. I stood on the side-line in Croke Park. Helpless. Was our season going to end like this?

Since Paul's death, Fr Gerard and myself had kept his memory close to our hearts while being careful not to allow those emotions to overwhelm us all. In that moment, though, I allowed myself a moment's prayer and a small request. "Paul," I said, "if you're about there, give us something. If you have any sway, give us a shot."

Seconds later we hit a point. With injury time looming, Stephen O'Neill hit another. One down. Then Kevin Hughes took a ball, and slipped it to Mark. If Paul was looking down on his old friend, surely he'd see him right.

Mark was on the right-hand side, near the 13-metre line. The angle was tight, but Mark's left boot had been operating sweetly all day. He angled his shot over the bar. We were saved. The boys had refused to bow again.

The replay was originally fixed for the following Sunday week in Parnell Park before it was switched to Saturday. My antennae were up. Kerry wanted a Saturday match. Dublin County Board weighed in, looking to free Parnell Park up for club fixtures that Sunday. We wanted Sunday. We had made all our travel arrangements, put everything in place. Now this. Kerry were getting their way. We were left out in the cold. It was a small detail. On Saturday week, we could make it significant.

Everything seemed to be fitting into place otherwise. Then, the pendulum swung again. Six days after we drew with Kerry, Paul Hughes, Kevin's brother, was driving from coaching the Killeeshil under-16 team to watch a game in Eglish. A few hundred metres from Paudge Quinn's restaurant on the Ballygawley-Dungannon line, where we had gathered our boys after Paul's death to talk, he crashed, and died.

After everything we had already been through, it was another devastating blow. Myself and Fr Gerard sat down with Kevin that week. We told him the decision to play against Kerry was his. If he didn't, there wasn't a person in the world who would blame him for pulling back. But Kevin Hughes is made of special stuff. Mentally strong, even back then. His brother had loved Gaelic football. The match gave Kevin a focus, an escape from the grief around him. We still had a choice to make about how far we could push him, but Kevin Hughes made himself an option.

We decided to start him at midfield alongside Cormac McAnallen. His response was to deliver one of his greatest performances. Once again we traded punches with Kerry from the start. This time, though, both teams were hitting harder and were even more stubborn in their refusal not to take a step back.

Kerry led at half-time but by the end of normal time both teams had been level 11 times. Phenomenal. In the second half Kerry pulled three clear again, as they had in the drawn game. Again, we responded. Kevin Hughes was dominating the middle alongside Cormac. Mark would end the game with 0-11 from frees and one from play. This time Kerry were forced to scramble an equaliser in injury-time, and the game staggered on into extra time.

Men were out on their feet everywhere. I watched Cormac McAnallen being lifted and helped off the pitch with cramp. He lasted a minute on the side-line before Brian McGuigan went down with cramp. Cormac insisted on returning in his place. That was what they were prepared to give for that game. That was what they were prepared to give for something that was now so special to them. There was no rational explanation any more. It convinced me there was something extraordinary about them. Out of all the tragedy and uncontrollable drama the summer had inflicted on us, this team represented something to me about the mystery of life: there was something irrational, intangible and utterly brilliant about these boys.

Now they were about winning. Mark hit two late points in extra time. Kerry pulled one back. They won a 45. Seconds left. The ball lofted towards the square. Players rose to meet it. One player emerged with the ball. Kevin Hughes. Before he had time to clear it, the whistle went. We had won. 0-23 to 0-21.

This was a rare moment. Tyrone people in the stand cried that day. Beyond being a stirring win for these boys, this was a landmark for Tyrone football. To this day, many Tyrone people would say that victory was the most significant win in Tyrone's history. It was a statement of what was possible for us in championship football. That sentiment was beyond anything Tyrone people had ever imagined. It almost broke the impenetrable myth around Kerry that had been built by Tyrone people for decades and decades. At worst, it left a deep crack that Kerry couldn't repair.

I found the last few weeks into the All-Ireland final something close to a joy. This was it. We had survived all the tragedy and rebuilt. I thought this was destiny. Michaela was certain. We're going to win the All-Ireland. That Tom Markham Cup finally in my hands.

But just as much as I assumed we were destined to win, it was just as appropriate that we shouldn't. Laois were seeking their second successive title. We were rookies in an All-Ireland final, doing what we could to guard against nerves but still waiting to see how our players would react.

They looked jittery from the start. Although we talked for weeks about keeping things simple, the boys were overplaying the ball. Laois had a goal inside the first minute. By half-time we had drawn level, and kicked 0-10, but delivering the final pass was causing us problems.

Then a chink of light. Richard Thornton hit a goal soon after half-time to put us ahead. Laois's response, though, was clinical. They held us scoreless for 20 minutes while overturning our lead and putting enough daylight between us to get home. Gareth Maguire, our keeper, made some superb saves to keep us alive. Laois hit another goal, though, and when Gareth fumbled a ball and Laois scored a third, they were six ahead. The boys battled hard and reduced the gap to three points, but we were out of steam. I thought of 1972. Another All-Ireland minor final had slipped away. Gutted.

AT THE TIME it seemed like nothing could heal the disappointment. Looking back now, it was the best thing to ever happen to us. If we had won, there would have been a serious feeling of satisfaction, a sense that this had to happen. With the Tom Markham Cup finally won, I would probably have left football management entirely. I can still remember how distraught Michaela was that our script had been torn up, but behind all the disappointment I knew there were greater lessons, and a greater purpose at work.

Back in Cookstown the following night, I was sitting there with Marian. Beaten and broken. Worn out. We had deserved this. But here were Brian McGuigan and Stephen O'Neill, two teenagers, now telling me in their own way that we didn't. One year didn't define our time with them. These boys were already talking about 1998. Football went on. Our life with them could go on if we wanted.

Years later I read some lines written by Nick Pitino. The sentiments echoed back to 1997. "Success is not a lucky break," he wrote. "It is not a divine right. It is not an accident of birth. Success is a choice." It's what I already knew in 1997, but it took the boys to remind me.

When Fr Gerard and myself took on the minors in 1991, we made a decision to challenge the accepted norms of how to prepare a team. We made that choice. Not winning an All-Ireland title in 1997 didn't dilute the conviction that our methods would produce great players and people. It didn't invalidate everything we had done. Zalucki's ideas told me that.

We had turned players into teams. We had gotten agonisingly close to creating something truly special. I realised that 1997 wasn't an ending. The story would go on, with or without me. The boys wanted me back. The Tom Markham Cup was there to be played for next year if I wanted. That evening, Michaela scribbled out a list of aims for the coming six seasons on a napkin.

1. *WE WILL: Win the All-Ireland final in 1998 (minors)*
2. *WE WILL: Win the All-Ireland final in 2000 (U-21)*
3. *WE WILL: Win the All-Ireland final in 2003 (seniors)*

2&3 with special 1997 team

It seemed a massive task then, but she had faith. I drove home that night, thinking of Stevie and the boys. Thinking of Fr Gerard's compassion. Michaela's ambition. Thinking of Paul.

By the time I saw the lights of Ballygawley village, I wished the trials for 1998 could start the following morning.

11

SPIRIT OF '98

May 2009

We finished the league with three wins, three defeats and a draw. Even our scoring difference was only −1. We had broken even. We shuffled our team for every game, and having to guard against defeat in our last match against Mayo with relegation a possibility was no harm either. You don't want to be in those situations, but when you are, it's good to make the best of them.

Before we played Armagh in the championship, though, we needed to draw a line in the sand. Like a the end of 2007, we decided to talk to the players individually. The difference this time, though, was that there would be no whingeing. No complaining. This year is about positivity. We are using optimistic language and attacking the year as a series of challenges. We don't see hurdles and problems. This set of meetings was about what we could all improve on to take our performance to the level required to chase an All-Ireland. Nothing more. Nothing less.

Myself, Tony and Fergal met the players as a unit. It's good that they see us that way now. When we present our take on any upcoming game to them, the process is well established. Tony takes the tactical side. Fergal takes the feedback about the kind of approach we want to take when playing different oppositions, and tailors the training drills to suit. Our pre-match approach has also changed this year. Instead of loading the players with information on the morning of the game, we get much of the team talk out of the way on the Saturday night. By Sunday, they're getting a succinct version they can easily digest before the game. It seems to be working well.

The meetings were just as effective. Over the space of four sessions we interviewed all 35 players for 20 minutes. We even packed seven in on the morning of Niall Gormley's wedding. The energy was entirely positive. We weren't coming up with solutions, we were asking questions: what could we all do better?

Improvements could be made in the smallest things. If we have four crates that all carry eight drinks bottles, I don't want to see 22 bottles in them. I want to see 32. Carrying 22 bottles is a sign that not everybody is tuned in. It might sound stupid or simplistic, but it's not. It's practical.

How are players performing in training? Are they providing the required energy? Are we? Don't wait till the day of the game to show that energy. Let's see it now. Speak out. Drive things on. Nail your personal training schedules. Get to training early and do a little extra practice. We hand the players dietary sheets to monitor their food intake for a week before getting them analysed at Jordanstown to see where we can make improvements. Stick to them. Get the data right. Human nature always means we will push on and slacken back. Right now we need to create an atmosphere where we can progress from good practice to best practice.

Over the years I have learned the importance of telling players exactly what we thought of them. Even before our league game against Derry, I had taken Ryan Mellon aside for a chat. We had been struggling against Donegal in our previous match, and opted to shake things up by bringing Brian McGuigan on to add some creativity. We took Ryan off at midfield to facilitate that. I needed to explain our thinking to him. Just because you're taken off doesn't mean you have played poorly. In fact, when I watched the video back, it showed Ryan had played well. Ryan thanked me for explaining our reasoning to him. He hadn't been feeling good about it. I started him against Derry, and he performed well. We're constantly learning this lesson: don't just observe the football, observe the vibes.

The same sentiment carried through the meetings. Take Tommy McGuigan, for example. We could tell Tommy he had become a serious player in 2008. He has vision. He's excellent under pressure. He proved he could kick pressure frees in the championship against Down last year. He coped with setbacks like his performance against Mayo and responded with a classic performance against Dublin.

I told him he was creative. He was a mighty fielder of a ball. Every player that came into us got the same kind of message. We recognised every talent they brought to the table. Now, what could we all do to lift that again? When players tell us what they wish to improve, we can mentally note them. When we see them make those improvements, we can tell them. Provide them with another lift.

Stephen O'Neill was the same. He has struggled again with injuries, but his outlook is much more positive than over the previous few years. That was deeply impressive. We talked to Brian Dooher about his appetite to get back to full fitness. He was working savagely hard, but I didn't think he would have the legs to last a full game yet. I told him this. He said he respected that opinion but was keen to contest it. I told him I wanted his minutes on the field at the end of the match. For the Armagh game, he saw the sense in that, but his summer is never about cameo appearances.

Our communication with the players had clearly improved over the years. If we had problems getting our message across before, they seem behind us. Building a relationship with your players where they feel comfortable in your company is about the only comfort zone you want in a squad. I think we've managed that this year.

Before the Armagh match we headed to Carton House for a weekend away. Our routine never changes: we get settled on Friday night before two good training sessions on Saturday. That evening we have our meeting about the upcoming game, and focus on a few goals for the coming season.

The vibe is good. Our attitude towards Armagh this year is informed by our knowledge of them as tough opponents, but also the reality of their current plight. They have lost some major players since we met them last. This isn't the team of the McEntees, McGeeney and McConville any more. Paul McGrane, Francie Bellew and Paddy McKeever all went in one night alone this spring. If Armagh were coming to play us and we had lost 75 per cent of the team that had made such great breakthroughs, and they still had 85 per cent of theirs, we wouldn't give ourselves much chance. I expected Armagh to be more mobile than the old team, but they were inexperienced too. If we were serious about pushing on for an All-Ireland, this was a game we should be winning by a distance.

Before the game I showed the players some video from the end of our match last year against Down. We are shattered. Down are jubilant. That's our last experience of the Ulster championship. Do we want that again? The sun is beating down on Clones. The summer is here. The players are ready.

We pull away early on and look comfortable for much of the game. Armagh change tactics slightly and start pumping long ball towards Ronan Clarke. Conor Gormley has already coasted forward to crack a goal and put us eight points up. Now he is isolated close to our goal, trying to get a handle on Clarke. Ronan does a little damage and Conor picks up a pair of yellows. I'm not worried. We hang on to win by three.

Maybe we should have pushed on, but a comfortable win would mean we wouldn't be examining our consciences as we are now. That sense of mission is still there. That's good enough for June.

—◄○►—

THE SAME CONFIDENCE accompanied the minors into 1998. Driven by the disappointments and tragedies of 1997, the players tore into the season. We won the Ulster minor league without too much trouble and faced into the championship fuelled by a sense of mission. We weren't turning the year into a crusade, but our ambition and expectations were growing. Anything less than winning that All-Ireland title wouldn't be enough.

Our preparations had to match that scale of ambition, too. Before our first Ulster championship match against Down, I asked the players from the 1997 minor team, who were now over-age to take part in a training match with the current panel. I got a set of jerseys from Aghaloo GAA club. Their colours are red and black, the same as Down's. I wanted our players to start thinking about that jersey. As well as that, though, I wanted the 1997 panel to be in their minds too. I wanted Paul to be with them. With us all. We were starting a new journey, but we still needed our old friends around us.

As usual, though, we got nothing easy. Take the match against Down. After 15 minutes we were seven points behind and struggling. Our response was superb. Cormac McAnallen took over at midfield with Kevin Hughes. Stephen O'Neill nailed a pressure penalty. We had pulled level by half-time. Stevie seemed to have turned the game again with a goal at the end of a 50-metre run but we fell away badly. Down hit five unanswered points and went two ahead. The boys bit back again. We clipped the deficit to one, before Enda McGinley skimmed a shot over the crossbar to secure a replay.

The week in between was an interesting one. I could see the boys had taken the draw badly. Because of our recent history, the interest in our games was more intense than normal for a minor team. This match was going to draw a crowd. If we were serious about righting the disappointments of last year, this was the time to show the world what we were about.

Our performance showed the value of that week's learning. We were ruthless. While Down shuffled their team around, we simply worked hard on getting our team to lift their performance levels. Over 5,000 people turned up in Newry for the replay, and saw a statement of intent that rang out for the rest of the summer. We led by three at half-time and cruised home, 0-12 to 0-6. I strolled down the side-line at the end towards the dressing-rooms feeling more certain than ever before. This team wouldn't be beaten.

Around this time, I had started looking more closely at our style of play. Coaching minors didn't allow much time to develop systems and tactics. Once you had moulded a team together, you generally looked for the simplest playing methods to get the job done. We used plenty of long ball. We withdrew the corner-forward over the years to help around midfield and defence, but it was relatively crude stuff.

Now, though, we had a group of intelligent, quick-witted footballers. It was time to start challenging them, and myself.

Over the years Fr Gerard's philosophies always chimed with mine. Like me, he had trained as a teacher and applied many of the same principles to coaching teams as I did. We had both studied philosopher AN Whitehead in college and favoured the idea of process theory. The concept is based on the notion that, just as the universe is constantly changing, God is in the same state of flux. There is no end to learning or development. Translating that to a team means focusing your energies on creating an ethos, a framework that can accommodate the development of a real team. It echoes science philosopher Karl Popper's idea about little steps adding up to one giant leap, like a long-jumper. We never verbalised any of those ideas with the players – we barely discussed them between ourselves – but this was where our ideas had their root.

I went back to the simplest principles that governed my attitude towards football. We needed players to make the best of their own talents, then find ways to encourage them to improve themselves. If you were a skilful ball player, you needed to improve your work ethic off the ball. If you excelled as a workhorse, improve your score-taking and distribution with the ball. The team would defend from the front. Once we lost the ball, every player became a defender. When we broke out from defence, everyone became an attacker.

Controlling the percentages also meant working on our possession game. To make that work, the player in possession needed the oxygen of support. He needed options. We conjured drills to work on our angles of running. Instead of bursting straight out, we hit passes at a different angle and switched play. Players never ran in isolation. Other players chased them in support. Players up-field moved to make themselves available.

The keys to lock it all together, though, were a commitment to work, concentration, loyalty. That needed something extra from all the players, a kind of statement not every team could manage. We knew we had potential stars on this team, but that wasn't enough.

As the great Chicago Bulls and LA Lakers coach Phil Jackson once wrote, the goal is "to find a structure that would empower everybody on the team, not just the stars, allow the players to grow as individuals as they surrendered to the group effort". In

1998 we knew we had the boys that could make this system work.

On top of a good pile of players from 1997, we could now add Packie McConnell, Gavin Devlin, Mickey McGee, Owen Mulligan, Ryan Mellon and Enda McGinley. Stephen O'Neill was stepping up too. Gavin Devlin was becoming a truly great defender. He was the lynchpin of our new system. He was our sweeper. He didn't mark anyone, and his vision and ability allowed him to sweep effectively across the back-line, adding an extra layer of security. Even he took time to adjust to the idea of forsaking his marking duties for another role. Now that Horse was cantering around the defence adding extra cover, everyone had to work extra hard to cover the spare man.

Our drills were simple but effective. Knowing that one fumble could change a game, holding onto the ball was everything. One night I asked Michaela to pick one player and count how many times he touched the ball in a single session. The total came to 259 touches over an hour's training. Add that up over the course of a career.

We started with simple drills where two players would fling a ball at each other's face. They might get down on their knees and throw the ball at each other or to the left or right. Sometimes they would bounce the ball at their partner. It was all part of sharpening their concentration, their skills, their awareness.

We spent time working on their tackling. We taught the players to tackle with their near hand when running alongside an opponent, allowing them to flick the ball away once the player in possession decided to solo, punch or kick the ball. We taught them to dispossess an opponent from behind. On Saturdays, we worked on tactics. Everything centred around the collective effort. We sometimes split the teams into groups to explain their roles. When the ball was launched into our full-back line, for example, the message to our half-backs was simple: leave your man behind, get back and crowd the space around the ball. Hustle to get the ball back, then break at speed.

As Fr Gerard used to say, "There isn't a Berlin Wall across the field." Players were dismantling that concept, brick by brick. Some players took time to adapt to an approach that demanded more from each player, physically and in terms of their skill levels and adaptability. Our wing-backs Ciaran Meenagh and Philip Jordan began to appreciate the value of tracking back when the play had gone behind them. Their role wasn't entirely confined to marking their opponents any more. Stephen O'Neill also developed an incredible work rate as the years went on.

We chalked up diagrams to illustrate our points on the back of dressing-room doors. Some of those faded diagrams can still be seen around Tyrone, like primitive cave drawings. People were already saying that the 1997 minor team was perhaps the best team ever to represent Tyrone. We knew that meant nothing. Like any other year, that talent had to be underpinned by hard work.

After we beat Down, Armagh posed their usual challenge in the Ulster quarter-final. This time, though, our boys weren't about to get drawn into a battle. Seven minutes gone, 0-4 to 0-0. Fifteen minutes, 1-6 to 0-1. Half-time, 2-9 to 0-3. Full-time, 2-15 to 0-9. It was dominant and brilliant and uplifting and devastating all at once.

Same story against Derry in the semi-final. A five-point win was as tidy as the scoreline suggested. Now we were back in a final.

Our minds also needed to be open to the threat Antrim might pose in the Ulster final, especially after the trouble they had caused in the first quarter of the 1997 final. This time, the boys were acutely tuned in. By half-time they were already 2-6 to 0-1 ahead. Cormac was dominating centrefield, and finished up with

1-3. Owen Mulligan was causing them problems and Aidan Lynch hit a cracking goal from distance that seemed to drain the heart from Antrim.

Gavin Devlin was wearing a corner-back's shirt and sweeping around the defence to good effect. Although Antrim pulled two goals back in the second half, we were never in trouble. Another Ulster title, but we were about far more than that now.

The Saturday before we played the All-Ireland semi-final, we took the boys away for another team-building morning. That afternoon, though, we returned to more tragedy.

We were at the school in Ballygawley for some football work. Jimmy McCann and Marty McAleer also set up some other activities for the players, target golf and archery. As the afternoon went on, we heard there had been a bomb in Omagh. I tried to make a call from the school office but the phone lines were down.

A shiver went through me. I knew Marian was heading to Omagh to buy a school uniform for Mattie. I tried to ring home. No joy. I pointed the car for home and raced through the winding roads towards Glencull. As I turned up the driveway into our house, I saw Mattie playing football. Everyone was safe.

Back at the school, we had sent everyone home to check on their families. Thankfully, none of the players were directly affected, but like people in every community across the county that summer, they grieved for others.

We played Leitrim in the All-Ireland minor semi-final soon after. By then, our momentum was nearly unstoppable, and we delivered a supreme performance. We could absorb 21 wides on the day and still win by 11 points. Cormac McAnallen was again our anchor. We had eight different scorers. Total dominance. Leitrim simply met a great team that day. Against those odds they stood no chance.

The build-up to this final felt different. Losing in 1997 had come as a shock to our collective system. We still had that memory, but we also had the confidence of a dominant campaign to heal any wounds. We also had Paul McGirr's spirit around us all summer, helping and driving us on. Before the All-Ireland final I got a set of tops printed for the players. It depicted two interlocking triangles. Inside one was the number 97 in black. In the other was the number 98 in red. One year was joined to the other. One year had led us into darkness. Another was bringing us towards the light, with Paul to guide us.

The players weren't fazed by facing these tests and processing these intense emotions. Their extraordinary commitment to open up their minds has always been among their greatest strengths. I have always deemed an open mind as one of the finest qualities anyone can have. If you have that, you will always believe anything possible.

There was no need to provide the boys with any carrots or incentives for the final. Ten years before many of these Tyrone players would face up to the task of stopping Kerry's surge for three-in-a-row in 2008, they addressed the same challenge against Laois. Beano McDonald was looking to make history with a third medal. Opinion was split about the outcome, but not inside our group. We just felt we were stronger. Over the course of six matches we had scored 9-75, an average of 17 points a game. Our average winning margin was almost eight points. These players wouldn't accept two final defeats. You never had that worry with them. The summer had engendered a terrific belief in our own ability, and was helping us make sense of the previous year. Our performances in 1998 were why we had been stopped short in 1997. We were told to wait a while. We needed to mature and appreciate what winning was about.

It was the same for me. For 26 years I had dreamed about winning the Tom Markham Cup. Paul's death was the catalyst to change my outlook on so much. It wasn't about the Cups any more, but the players. Before and after every training session, and before we sent them out to play matches, the boys always gathered in a tight circle, arms around each other. The energy inside the circle is special. We feed off it, and have been nourished by that energy ever since. Their skills were exceptional, but that spirit and energy was what already set them apart. These boys were special.

Still, the burning desire to win that Cup hadn't been doused either. The final was tight for spells, but like 2008, when the breaks came, we grabbed them. We had two goals inside the first 15 minutes, one from Owen Mulligan, the other from Enda McGinley. In 1997 we had been forced to chase Laois all day after conceding a goal.

Now we could be the hare.

As half-time loomed we were six ahead, but Laois were still threatening. A ball floated across our square and palmed towards the net. It looked a certain goal. Instead, Packie McConnell reacted like a viper, snapping his hand out to push the ball away with a fantastic reaction save. One step beyond.

Our response? A point.

By half-time we were seven ahead. With ten minutes left we were ten points up. Laois pulled back a few points, just as we did in 1997, but we were safe. It finished 2-11 to 0-11. Tyrone's first All-Ireland minor title in 25 years. Everyone knew this went much deeper.

When it was over, I hugged Mattie and Michaela. Of all the victories I have ever known, that was probably the best. It was special. I had lost the 1972 final as a player and watched several of my team-mates from 1972 win the All-Ireland with Tyrone in 1973. I finally felt I had achieved. Tom Markham would finally sit on my kitchen table.

Cormac lifted the trophy and proclaimed that, after a year spent grieving and battling and hoping, striving to find a crack of light in the clouds, Tyrone could at last enjoy a high point. For a moment, you wondered what else you could do in life.

As we left the field, the Laois team formed a guard of honour for us. Fr Gerard shed a tear. I smiled. Their grace in defeat reflected the realisation for us all about the journey we had made. Paul was still with us. Now we had an All-Ireland for him.

The dressing-room was an emotional place. Kevin Skelton, a local referee who had lost his wife to the Omagh bomb, came and visited us. He hugged every player, and thanked us for bringing a little joy back into the life of the county.

That night we celebrated. Cormac asked Michaela if she could laminate him a special number eight that he could keep as a memento of the year. Kevin Hughes fashioned a hat from a white napkin to start a tradition of wearing crazy, ridiculous hats to mark our greatest victories. I've seen him produce sombreros, oversized chefs' hats, all sorts of stuff. A Tyrone win isn't complete without a Hub Hughes hat. Having been deprived of his historic third All-Ireland minor medal, Beano McDonald still called to our banquet and hung out with our boys for a while. It was a marvellous night.

The job was done. For a while I considered leaving it all behind. My ambition had been satisfied but the bond with the players was too tight to break now. I would move on from the minors.

But not from these boys.

12

BATTLES AND BREAKTHROUGHS

"Heart speaks to Heart" –

the motto of Cardinal John Henry Newman

June 2009

Over the last few months, I have been thinking again about my time in Kircubbin and in Belfast as a student. As I watch my own children grow into adults, I have begun to realise how fundamental the experiences you have during that period can be to forming the values and beliefs you apply in your life. For me, college offered the framework for everything that followed in football and beyond. Every summer I search my books and my memories for new ways to address the challenges ahead. This time I'm being drawn back to my college life. Back then, Willie McCarney offered the inspiration. I wanted to reconnect with his ideals, the concepts he believed to be the foundation for good teaching and the kind of good practice that applied to anything you did. It was time to get back in touch with him.

One day I rang him for a wee chat. A few days later a long email popped up on my computer. It was from Willie. What he wrote impacted on me like nothing I had ever read before. He reminded me of a book by the nineteenth-century Catholic intellectual, Cardinal John Henry Newman. It is called *The Idea of a University*. It is the university's duty, wrote Newman, to provide a "culture of education". A good culture, he said, is one that allows people to uncover their true potential as human beings.

How you create that culture depends on your approach to your role as an educator. The approach Willie supported was rooted in the holistic philosophies of the great Greek thinkers, Plato and Aristotle. It echoed the teachings of St Augustine, who spoke of "*gaudium de veritate*", the joy of searching for, discovering and communicating truth in every field of knowledge. When the joy disappears from that search, no true learning can take place.

Willie suggested that educators needed to take account of the "lived realities" of their students. They needed to know where they were coming from. It all fed into Newman's concept of a university as a centre of excellence. To do that, you need to listen to your students, to understand their perspectives on life, then shape your approach to teaching them using that knowledge. Thirty years after leaving Willie and college behind, I realised that the lessons I had learned from him had shaped my entire coaching career.

When I took teams, I had never seen them as units requiring organisation, simple tactics and a straightforward approach to winning. I saw panels as living, changing organisms. Some players would become regulars. Others would challenge them. Some would need reassurance. Others would need the room and the right framework to give full breadth to their natural talents. It was my job to build that framework. Since I joined Robbie Hasson in Ballygawley I had been quietly refining those ideals. Because of Willie I uncovered the foundation blocks this year again. Redoubling my own efforts to understand the mindsets of my own players would help deepen relationships within the entire panel. The closer we could get, the better we could be.

—◁○▷—

IN 1999 WE STARTED our first year as an under-21 management team. It promised to be tricky, though. The natural progression to under-21 meant our core group would be sourced from the 1996 minor team that fell to Fermanagh. So we took a chance and promoted eight of the 1998 minor team to play Derry in the first round. On the morning of the game we attended Fr Gerard's mother's funeral. We wouldn't have been anywhere else that morning; it was just unfortunate we had a match to play that day, too. Either way, Derry were clinical and polished us off without too much bother. The boys weren't ready just yet, but it was worth a punt.

We picked up the pieces later in the year. The team looked different. More powerful, more experienced. Nine of our players had already been drafted into the senior panel in 2000. Cormac McAnallen was being hailed as the solution to Tyrone's apparent problem around midfield. Stephen O'Neill was already looking like a star. Success for these under-21s wasn't considered a bonus now, but an obligation. There was plenty of slack for us in 1999. Things were different in 2000.

We were comfortable with that kind of expectation. After we slipped past Down in the first round in 2000, we met Monaghan, the defending champions. They brought us to Ballybay, where the pitch is located at the end of a long, forbidding lane. It felt like heading into Afghanistan for a match. I sensed an ambush.

Monaghan's reception was suitably warm. Seamus McEnaney was in charge of Monaghan that day. He was down the line, manically driving his players on, setting the tone. Our boys thrived in that mood. Cormac McAnallen barged through to crack a goal in the second half that sent us seven points clear. Ciaran Meenagh was sent off early on for a phantom punch that never happened and Ryan Mellon had reverted from attack to right-half-back, where he excelled in his new role. It looked an odd move on paper, but there were no questions afterwards from Ryan or anyone else. It was the first example of a player subsuming his own ego for the good of the team. Those kind of cornerstones would support the success that would follow over the next decade.

Monaghan tried to muster a comeback, but we were in control and escaped Ballybay without a scratch. Back in the dressing-room, the players celebrated like we had won a title. They were delirious. I can still see Conor Gormley lifting the table off the ground, rattling the legs off the floor with delight. They weren't simply chasing cups. Like me, they were now on a journey to discover the best they could be. Right at that moment, just like our first minor match against Down in 1998, I knew we wouldn't be beaten that year.

Our system of play and our ethos was starting to help grow great teams. The Ulster final against Donegal that year was another annihilation. Owen Mulligan and Kevin Hughes provided the scores to underpin a 14-point win. In defence, Gavin Devlin was developing into one of those players you dream about. He was a passionate man. If he had pace he would have been the best defender I have ever seen. His ability to read the game was unrivalled. His control on the ball was sublime. For a defender, he had the feet of a dancer.

And he could talk. Off the field he was the centre of the banter. On the field, he could guide a defence through the game with his insights and vision. In time the increasing speed of the game would catch up with him, but his store of All-Ireland medals is a worthy tribute to a great player.

By the time we met Galway in the All-Ireland semi-final, I was becoming convinced of certain things about this team. That afternoon before the game, I pulled Cormac McAnallen aside.

He had already lifted the 1998 All-Ireland minor title as captain. I was certain he would do the same as an under-21 in 2000. I was also certain there was more in him. "You're going to lift three Cups," I told him. "You've lifted the minor, you will lift the under-21 and you'll lift the senior." You could tell he was quietly thinking something similar.

That day, the team didn't flinch when faced with adversity. Galway led at half-time after a poor performance by our standards. We needed to lift everything. The players responded. They outscored Galway 1-7 to 0-1 in the second half. Joe Bergin buried a fist in Cormac's midriff and got himself sent off. We didn't get distracted. We kept going, kept pounding. We won by seven points. Another All-Ireland final and nothing to fear.

We met Limerick in the final. Plenty of Tyrone people might have snorted at the notion of dealing with Limerick. We knew different. We had watched them win the Munster final and seen plenty to think about. They were a big, strong team. John Galvin was a powerful presence around the middle. Stephen Lucey and Brian Begley helped form a strong spine through the centre of the team. Throw in Jason Stokes and Conor Fitzgerald, and they were useful.

I was also conscious that this generation had lost their All-Ireland minor final in 1997. Three years had turned them into stronger players, but I wanted to make this final feel different. I had heard of a company called One Step Beyond, run by Hugh Campbell and Des Jennings. One Step Beyond specialised in outdoor activities designed to build up trust and team spirit. I knew we had a group of exceptionally determined footballers. Binding them together a little more could only help.

I had used camping and abseiling and canoe trips with the youth clubs back in Ballygawley to give the local young people a sense of togetherness and improve their sense of self-worth. This was taking that concept to a new level.

One Saturday morning we all headed to a forest in Pomeroy. High wires criss-crossed the sky between the trees over our heads. There were poles that ascended 40 feet into the air with a little plate on top. Bells were suspended in mid-air. Crazy, fantastic stuff.

One activity involved climbing that pole, strapped in a safety harness. Once you reached the top of the pole, you had to hit a target which would set off the bell. The plate atop the pole was maybe two feet in diameter. To reach the target you needed to jump from the plate. The harness pretty much guaranteed your safety, but it still required courage to take the leap. Any comfort zones were left behind on top of that pole. You could see where they got the name One Step Beyond.

Some boys were more comfortable with the heights than others. I can still see big Packie McConnell, teetering on the pole and listening to the rest encouraging him. They wanted him to step farther than he thought he could. They were the ones who could help him reach his target.

There was a high-wire exercise where two wires started very close together before widening out as they went along. Two people went up and linked arms with each other. It was easy at first, but the farther out you went, the more you needed to work together at maintaining your balance – another way of promoting the value of working as a team to escape a tricky spot.

One exercise involved getting one player over a wire without touching it. Another catch was that the two groups on either side of the wire could communicate only through the medium of Boyzone melodies. I don't think any of us will forget the sound of Kevin Hughes beckoning Cormac over the wire to the tune of "Father and Son": "It's now time, for you to come over . . ." Classic.

It was abstract and unusual, but it all helped reinforce an underlying mood around the team. Guys were working for each other. They were sticking together. They went on trust walks through the woods, where one person was blindfolded and reliant on the other to guide him through safely. We played a few games of volleyball. High fives all round when one team won a point. There was a game where a rope was stretched out at a certain height. The challenge was to get over it, which involved climbing on people's backs and shoulders. People lifted their team-mates over that rope and got them over the other side.

There was a terrific vibe among the group that day. We probably didn't think too deeply about the value of those activities at the time, but these were the little elements that were making us more than a team.

Because the opposition was Limerick, people might have assumed the final was ours to win. When we got to Mullingar that day, though, the scale of the challenge steepened. The town was rinsed in green and white. The Tyrone support was outnumbered by ten to one. Look around, I thought to myself. This felt like another ambush. Ballybay all over again.

The mood was good before the game, though. It was the first year we had asked the players to submit a song for inclusion on a cassette tape to play on the team bus. Michaela did the taping, and was still doing the job when we upgraded to CDs in years to come. As we gave out the jerseys, Horse Devlin couldn't contain himself any longer. As every number was handed out and the players waited to put their jerseys on, he got more hyped up. By the time we reached number 15, he was banging and battering tables and benches. Any more numbers, and there might have been killings.

We needed all that fervour to match Limerick early on. Until Richard Thornton hammered a ball to the net midway through the first half, Limerick were clipping at our heels. The goal gave us the breathing space we needed. Brian Begley cracked a shot off the crossbar early in the second half. Two minutes later

Richard had the ball in the net again, and the game was over. Brian McGuigan pulled the strings. Mark Harte kicked five points and competed brilliantly against Brian Geary. We had another All-Ireland. Cormac had his hands on the second trophy of the trinity. As you think, so you shall be. We tucked our medals away, and moved on.

THE BUSINESS OF MINDING the players was on my mind. Nine seniors was a big chunk of players from our panel and communication between Art McRory and Eugene McKenna at senior level and ourselves was minimal. The day we played Donegal in the Ulster under-21 final in 2000, some of our players were recruited to play the McKenna Cup final immediately afterwards. I wasn't happy with that. At that stage people were trying to get out of even playing in the McKenna Cup, yet here we were dogging talented players who had just won an Ulster title.

We had to be more careful with these men. They needed to be phased into the senior set-up, not flung in too early and burned out. The senior management's attitude was that they had access to all the players regardless of any grades. Every other competition was secondary to senior. Having seen the calibre of player coming through, I couldn't agree with them. Even now, I always allow any under-21s on my senior panel to play in their grade without interference from us.

Ironically, the foot-and-mouth crisis saved us from a similar problem in 2001. When a case was discovered in Ardboe, Tyrone were in trouble. The 30-day exclusion policy meant no matches for a month. Instead of leaving it there, though, the GAA tried to go further.

We had reached the Ulster final against Fermanagh but the match was called off that morning. I took Marian and the family to Lisburn instead for a day's shopping. As we drove along, the news came on the radio. Tyrone were being forced to step aside. Michaela was in the back seat in tears. I was stunned, but I couldn't accept that. "That'll not happen," I said.

Some parts of Fermanagh were closer to the outbreak than other parts of Tyrone. Why confine this to a county? I couldn't take this. I knew the quality in our team. We weren't just being asked to give up an Ulster final, but an All-Ireland. Fermanagh manager Dominic Corrigan suggested that if we stepped aside and allowed them into the All-Ireland semi-final we could play Fermanagh later in the year for the Ulster title. What was the point of that? Ulster titles weren't the height of our ambitions. We were about All-Irelands.

The seniors had already thrown in the towel and walked away from a National League semi-final without even looking for a deferral. They just accepted it. I couldn't understand that. Because the seniors took that attitude, maybe the board didn't think the under-21s being removed was a big issue. Why worry about them? If nobody else was, I felt I had to.

I revisited the mentality that had steeled me during the years with Glencull, and went to war. I spoke to any newspaper that would hear me out. I appeared on television to fight our case. I went on RTÉ radio one Sunday afternoon with Con Murphy, and laid out the reasons for retaining our position in the championship.

The GAA was an all-Ireland organisation, I said. If something bad happens to one of us, surely we should all take the hit rather than riding off smugly into the sunset. Adrian Logan also gave me a crucial 90 seconds on UTV news that helped solidify the campaign. If the same issue had arisen in another province, I'd like to think we would have stood with the affected county and tried to accommodate them.

The under-21 championships had often been delayed during the summer in the past and finished in the autumn. Holding off until later in the year wasn't going to send the GAA into meltdown.

Something I said struck a chord somewhere. Cork County Board secretary Frank Murphy might trigger all sorts of reactions among GAA people, but I will always owe him a debt of gratitude. Cork stated that if they beat Limerick in the Munster final, they would happily delay their All-Ireland semi-final against the Ulster champions until the crisis had passed. Fermanagh were now painted into a corner. Unless they wanted to look like they were shamelessly taking advantage of the situation, they would have to face us.

The day of the Munster final, Marian, myself, Michaela, Matthew and their cousin Peter were on our way to Kilmallock to see the match. I got a call between Newtownbutler and Cavan. It was Philip Lanigan from the *Ireland on Sunday* newspaper. "Mickey," he said, "you're back in. The semi-final is on September 9." I gave a composed response, very matter-of-fact, like I had never imagined the outcome any other way. When I got off the phone, the whole car erupted. Suddenly the seven-hour journey down felt a lot shorter.

The Ulster final was put back to midsummer. When we met Fermanagh, there wasn't much said in the dressing-room beforehand. We didn't need any motivation to eat them alive. After that, everything stopped until September. The senior squad members won an Ulster title. Stephen O'Neill picked up an All Star. Cormac was now a significant figure in the senior team. When they came back, though, none of them had any airs or graces about them. Perhaps they felt more like strangers in the senior set-up. Now, they were home again.

After availing of their kindness in the springtime, our All-Ireland semi-final opponents that September turned out to be Cork. We couldn't allow ourselves to express our gratitude. Instead, we played full-press football. We hustled and harried them all day and held them scoreless for the first half. We hit 0-10 and strolled home. The final against Mayo brought its own edge, too. Earlier in the year Mayo had beaten us in the Hastings Cup, a warm-up competition before the under-21 championship began. It was our only defeat all year. These boys didn't do defeats.

I could see the players were feeling the pinch. It was an extraordinary reaction to a defeat in a modest competition. Soak the hurt up, I told them. These players never lacked belief, but they weren't complacent either. It was a rare balance at their age. The defeat to Mayo was an unacceptable slight on their reputations. An All-Ireland final was the place to correct those mistakes.

The final in Sligo turned into a battle. Trevor Mortimer was Mayo's key player but we saw Philip Jordan as the right man for the job. Cormac and Kevin Hughes were immense again at midfield. The hits and the intensity were savage that day. It was an invitation to stand up and be counted. No Tyrone man stood back. Owen Mulligan continued his marvellous year. Stephen O'Neill kept the scoreboard ticking, while Philip Jordan had Trevor Mortimer reined in. Four points didn't seem a big lead at half-time, having played with a strong breeze, and Mayo pushed us hard. But we hung on again.

After the game, Mayo manager Kevin McStay expressed his congratulations and his gratitude. Word had reached us in the weeks before the game that his mother had recently passed away. We had all signed a condolence card and made sure he received it. Of all the teams in the country, we knew what that support from the wider GAA family meant.

As a victory, beating Mayo was massively significant. Winning those two All-Ireland under-21 titles were the foundation for everything that followed. We had challenged ourselves to achieve and we did. We had faced challenges throughout those two years and responded. When we were forced to fight for the right even to play, we had prevailed.

Our boys were moving onto the senior grade while I stayed on with the under-21 team. I knew it wouldn't happen immediately, but I needed to be part of their lives again. For them, their potential as footballers wasn't solely confined to their ability now. They had shown the capacity to face down all sorts of obstacles. There was nothing hopeful about what might transpire in the following few years.

In my eyes and theirs, everything that would follow was inevitable.

AT THE START of 2002, I looked to home for a new challenge. I was carrying on with the Tyrone under-21s and also added Errigal Ciarán senior and reserve teams to my roster. The Errigal teams were a different kind of challenge. After our initial successes in 1993, their progress had stalled slightly. While almost every player on the Errigal senior team had played with Tyrone at some level, they had never translated that talent into trophies. They carried the same sort of class as the Tyrone minors – albeit at a different level – but they lacked the same ruthless belief in themselves.

The word for the year with Errigal would be "steel". We wouldn't yield to anyone. With the right attitude and preparation, defeat wouldn't be countenanced. We sharpened up their training methods, which tested me, too. There were nights early that year when 60 players could be slogging around the pitch in Dunmoyle, all training with the ball. Working those sessions out and accommodating so many players required a massive amount of advance planning.

Steel. Steel. Steel. We worked our way through the Tyrone championship and made the final against Killyclogher. The theme was more of the same. We needed to be braced for a mini-war. We needed to be in their faces. Get our retaliation in first. Hit them hard and fair. Put them on the ground and see how they react. Hustle and harry. Work like dogs. Errigal had always been accused of having nice players with a caramel-soft centre. We needed to show them different.

Around the same time, the Tyrone under-21s were outstripping all our expectations as well. Only Enda McGinley and Owen Mulligan remained from the 2000–01 generation. Meeting Down, the 1999 All-Ireland minor champions, didn't promise much either. Sean Cavanagh had arrived on the scene and John Devine was in goals, but we wondered if that was enough.

As it turned out, the team ethic carried them further than any of us imagined. We won an Ulster title that year against the head. While the titles we had won the previous few years meant a lot, this meant just as much in a different way. It reminded me of winning the Ulster minor title in 1993. That team was the very embodiment of what we defined as "team". They were the first group to win a provincial title with us. They had what I call the hidden ingredient. Sometimes you look at a team that isn't dominated by stars and wonder why they work so well together. It's because that hidden ingredient is in the mix. It's their realisation that their individual difference makes the winning difference.

What made both teams work was that commitment to the team ethos, to our system. It was much more refined now than in 1993, and players were sold on the idea. Dublin beat us in the All-Ireland semi-final with a team dotted by players that still form the core of their senior team. We weren't too worried. We had already gotten so much from this team.

Back home, Errigal faced down Killyclogher. Peter Canavan hit 1-3 and the team withstood the burden of favouritism and anything Killyclogher could throw at us.

Now we turned to Ulster, and Crossmaglen.

OVER THE YEARS, some matches have stood out as defining moments in my coaching life: the draw against the Kerry minors in 1997, winning the under-21 All-Ireland titles, beating Kerry in 2003, the 2005 All-Ireland final. This was another.

Although most of Errigal Ciarán had played with Tyrone at some level, drawing Crossmaglen in the first round of the Ulster championship challenged the players to lift themselves to another level. Because of Crossmaglen's supreme reputation, they started as favourites. That suited us fine. Our players were acutely aware of what we could do. Crossmaglen were a major challenge, but not insurmountable.

The first game in Omagh, though, was a struggle. Peter Canavan was forced off injured after 20 minutes. We fell eight points behind with 20 minutes left. The players dug deep, and as the game entered injury time we were just a point behind. Errigal needed a little boost. I checked how Peter was. There was nothing in the rules that said we couldn't bring on a player we had already withdrawn as a new substitute. Peter went back in and immediately set up a point for Eoin Gormley. Level, thanks to a useful play. We were heading back to Crossmaglen.

The first half of the replay taught me another lesson that has never lost its relevance over the years. We were nine points down and in trouble, but watching John Devine beat away a shot just before half-time and our defence work furiously to prevent another goal told me the value of never letting go. One more goal and we were gone, but these players weren't ready to lose. We held Crossmaglen to a point in the second half and escaped extra time with a draw.

After the game, Crossmaglen's manager Oliver Short said something that reflected a mode of thought I was trying to turn on its head. "You can only do a certain amount anyway," he said. "We are a big physical team, we play to those strengths. They are not, they play to their strengths. It doesn't take brain surgery to work out what's going to happen again."

That wasn't how I was thinking. Replays are always about bringing difference. They are a challenge to your capacity as a coach to learn. Can you divine more than the opposition? Are you thinking your team might win, or can you discover trends that make you sure you can win? Replays aren't about lucky breaks. It's about showing you're not operating on a wing and a prayer, but that your team is developing from week to week. The Crossmaglen experience offered a classic example of that.

After two games Crossmaglen reckoned they knew what to expect from us. In attack, Eoin Gormley was physically powerful and a wonderfully talented footballer who had played for Tyrone and international rules with Ireland. Peter Canavan was still causing them terrific trouble. I knew they would focus on tying both players up. I needed to give them something else to think about.

Around that time, I heard about a piece of software called Focus which allowed us to analyse our match videos in a more efficient way. It allowed us to tag each individual's contribution to the game and passages of play, and develop new ways of analysing our game plan. The concept worked then. It still works with Tyrone now.

I reckoned the solution to dealing with Crossmaglen was speed. Eoin Gormley had a hamstring injury, but Crossmaglen would expect us to chance him on Francie Bellew. Francie was preparing himself for a physical battle. I decided to alter the state of play.

With Eoin's hamstring injury putting him out, I turned to Dara Tierney and Rory McCann. They were young, light and quick, and relatively unknown. Peter Canavan could play off that pair in the full-forward line. The other key player was Mark Harte. He was playing very well at centre-forward. His passing was clinical and his free-taking was excellent. Crossmaglen overlooked his importance to us, and he spent the day hitting perfect ball in front of Dara and Rory. They ran the legs off the Crossmaglen defence. We won by a goal.

The lessons I took from those three games would deliver an even greater return over the years to come. In seven championship seasons, Tyrone have lost just two replays – against Armagh in 2005 and Down in 2008. There hasn't been one draw we haven't learned from and improved as a result.

Beating Crossmaglen might have been a massive moment for Errigal, but it could have been the end of us, too. What saved us was the scale of the next challenge: Ballinderry. Crossmaglen might have had tradition, but Ballinderry were the defending All-Ireland champions. They probably assumed we were out on our feet after three epic matches. Instead I used different language with my own players.

On current form, playing Ballinderry meant we were actually moving up a gear. I told our players to imagine what Ballinderry were thinking. They couldn't possibly fathom how high our confidence was after beating Crossmaglen. When they thought about us, fatigue must be the first word in their mind. We knew different. We won by six points.

Retaining that attitude for the Ulster final against Enniskillen was harder, but we did enough to win. The perfect year had a perfect ending. In 2002 I had collected an Ulster under-21 title with Tyrone. Errigal Ciarán had brought home a county senior title, a reserve league title, a county senior league title and an Ulster club title. We had beaten Crossmaglen and taken down the All-Ireland club champions. The club had won 12 straight matches. At the end of the year, I could look back and find just one defeat in all competitions – a reserve match against Ardboe. We lost by only a point.

One point. It still sickens me.

I WAS GROWING MORE CONFIDENT as a manager. My methods were different, but they were working. I was finding out new angles to coaching and becoming more engrossed in the psychology of preparing a team. I was more conscious of my delivery now. I didn't rant and rave. Every time I spoke to the players, I wanted to deliver something of substance. I wanted to provide real information and present it in a way they could latch onto and use.

I looked at the paths taken by my old under-21 team. A lot of them were with the Tyrone seniors. Their summer ended with a crippling defeat to Sligo in Croke Park. I hadn't really thought about managing the seniors before, but the last few years had opened my mind up to different things. My record was strong. I wasn't going to canvas openly for the senior job at any stage, but something inside told me my chance might come a few years down the road. When that opportunity came, I'd be ready.

And I knew I could work with those boys.

13

SENIOR SERVICE

AFTER TYRONE'S DEFEAT to Sligo in the 2002 qualifiers, morale in the county was at a low ebb. Initially Art McRory and Eugene McKenna had been reappointed as a joint managerial team for 2003, but when Art stepped back a few weeks later, it opened up the situation again. There seemed to be an understanding that, when Art left, Eugene would automatically take on the job. That couldn't be the case. They had been elected as a joint managerial package. If Eugene wanted the job, he could declare his interest, but a process still had to be undertaken.

When the post became available, I immediately put my name forward. Brian McIver and former Derry player Peter Doherty were also in the running, as well as Eugene. All of us were called for an interview with the county board. I put a simple CV together, outlining my success with the under-age teams and Errigal. I set out the backroom team I would assemble. Initially I included Tony Donnelly alongside myself and Fr Gerard in the management team. That caused a potential problem for Tony at home. Eugene McKenna was also from Augher. People were already sore that Eugene had to reapply for the job. Seeing another Augher man on my proposed management team could cause all sorts of bad feeling.

I didn't see it that way. I had been friends with Tony for over 30 years. Like the issue with Glencull and Ballygawley, I wasn't anti-Eugene or anti-Augher. I was pro-Tony. Tony accepted the offer to come on board at first, but once he sensed the disharmony growing, he stepped away again. It was desperately disappointing, but I could understand his feelings. I knew I could still catch a few words with him at the wire or down the tunnel on match day. But I would miss him.

At the interview, one member of the board asked a simple question about my aims and ambitions. My answer was equally simple. An All-Ireland, based on a total belief in the players, the people around me and my own convictions. Everything I had delivered before was based on that principle. I knew I could do it again with these players.

Then things got messy. A few days before an announcement was made, news was leaked that Eugene McKenna hadn't got the job. That wasn't good practice. When it emerged that I was to be appointed senior manager, I somehow got dragged into the whole confusion. I had nothing to do with the leak. It wasn't my fault. All I did was apply for a job that was open and available. I set out my case and was appointed. I didn't hold any animosity towards Eugene McKenna. My usual critics reared up. It didn't bother me. After eight years living through an equally uncomfortable arrangement at home with Glencull, this was perfectly manageable. You get used to the sting of the arrows. Another few wouldn't damage me.

I knew one thing for sure. Even though some sections of the Tyrone media and public weren't overjoyed at my appointment, I would have the support of the players. Most of the squad were now graduates of my under-age teams. Peter Canavan was my clubmate. I had coached all the players on the panel at some stage apart from Chris Lawn and Ryan McMenamin. The vibe would be good. Our prospects were much brighter than 2002 suggested.

A new stage of our journey had begun.

I WAS ALWAYS CERTAIN about the heights that could be reached with the young players. When you combined their confidence with players like Chris Lawn, Peter Canavan and Brian Dooher, it already felt like a beautiful mix.

Now, we had to make it work.

The biggest task of all was to bond this vast spectrum of age groups and personalities. This panel had lived through a whole era of Tyrone football, enduring good times and bad. Some players were scarred by their time with Tyrone. Others were energised. Players like Cormac McAnallen had already won everything in football apart from an All-Ireland senior medal. Others like Peter Canavan had spent their lives chasing the one medal they truly needed. They needed to believe: in themselves, in each other. In the system.

To me it all came back to what the former LA Lakers' coach Pat Riley calls "The Innocent Climb". Being innocent means understanding that each player has his space, then setting it aside for the good of the team. Creating that innocence is a process that takes time and patience. When a gifted team dedicates itself to unselfish trust and combines instinct with boldness and effort, wrote Riley, it is ready to climb.

This all echoed my view that each player is unique, that all my efforts as a coach to extract the best from any team had to be governed by that need to communicate and relate to the player. In order to get the best from him, the player had to understand what I wanted.

If he did, and bought into it, that would naturally lead to Riley's state of innocence. He would buy into this selfless system of play. He would sacrifice his own preferences and habits for the good of the team. All these players had seen these methods at work before, but we were operating in a different landscape now.

Back home, they loved all the excitement. Michaela was on top of the world. Matthew was just as excited. Apart from having their brother Mark in the panel, their daddy was drawing all sorts of strange looks and attention. When we went to matches, they couldn't believe how many people would recognise me. I found it strange myself, but they'd be falling around the car on the way home laughing. We might be walking along towards the ground when they would spot someone nudge someone else with an elbow, point in our direction and watch them turn around, trying to get a good look at me. Matthew used to call it "neck strain". I had been coaching Tyrone for years, they chuckled. Why the big deal now?

That was the biggest change from other years: attention. Suddenly every utterance was observed and analysed. I never found that a problem, though. Living as a member of Glencull GAA club made you just as cautious about your language and tone. In general I saw our dealings with the media as a useful learning tool for the players. It came back to the decision-making process. I like to see the players thinking about what they have to say. If they think about that, they can think their way through a match as well. Do that, and the player will always feel more comfortable in his own skin and when wearing his jersey.

Looking at the team, it wasn't really a case of tearing the structure down and starting again. There were areas where we could improve, but the personnel were already there to make those improvements. In the past I always felt Tyrone were more inclined to trust bigger men, even when their most important player was usually the smallest man on the field – Peter

Canavan. Still, bigger always seemed to have a better chance with Tyrone. I didn't believe that creed when I played myself, and I wasn't going to convert now.

The team had also developed an overtly defensive mindset. We needed to address that. We would find ourselves branded with a similar tag before the year was out, but that criticism always seemed badly misdirected to me. Our teams were attack-oriented. Our players' first instinct when they got the ball was always to attack. I worked on creating players who could perform in any corner of the pitch. We didn't want any mental blocks about positions or size. When I was with Errigal, the watchword in 2002 was "steel".

With Tyrone in 2003, it was "quality".

Since 1998 we had really got deep into the development of a recognisable style of play. This was where Pat Riley's innocent climb steepened. Because Gavin Devlin was employed in that sweeper role, everyone else needed to compensate for his absence from his traditional marking duties. Every player had to work a little harder. If they didn't, the whole system would fall. It required that unselfish trust.

Connected to that is the need to recognise the opposition's strengths, and attack them. Your players must recognise that performance isn't always governed by what you do on the ball, but also what you do when you don't have it. When you lose the ball, every player is responsible in some way for regaining possession. If you need somebody – like Gavin – to withdraw and abdicate responsibility for their direct opponent, there has to be a shared workload, particularly in the middle third of the field. That was how this system evolved. Defenders could be attackers. Attackers could be defenders. When we attack, we move as a cohesive unit. When we defend, we apply the same principles.

Another cornerstone is preventing goals. Teams might get a big points score, but goals really nail you. They had drained us in the 1997 All-Ireland minor final. We have taken our cue from that game ever since. Most goals in Gaelic football come down the central channel. If we could clog that area with extra bodies, then we would. That approach again required a massive commitment from players to work back and tackle. Between 2003 and the end of this season we played 45 championship games. We conceded two goals or more in just five of those. Those returns were crucial.

We built on those basic cornerstones. Working on support play is a natural follow-on. When you attack and defend as a unit you need people breaking the line, taking passes. You work on your angles of running. You work on switch plays. You change the point of attack. It's work that we can do through drills and through simple ball-handling exercises. Showing the players how these drills can be translated into useful knowledge on match day is important, too. No player, from corner-back to corner-forward, can afford to allow those skills to decline in this system. While it rewards hard work, it also requires a high level of skill to execute it properly. When it works, it can be devastating.

Everything about our training sessions has always been geared towards that. We train as close to a match length as possible – 70 minutes. We move from drill to drill quickly and efficiently. Everything is done at high intensity. Match speed. In 2003 we installed a few things that players needed to get used to. We would train one night a week before upping it to two nights when the clocks went forward later in the spring. The other nights, they would work on their own. It returned me to the days with Robbie Hasson in Ballygawley, when all we had time for with our teams was 25 minutes at lunchtime. It was about quality then.

It was about quality now.

Paddy Tally came in as coach, which refreshed that side of things. He had been teaching in St Ciarán's when I took on the Tyrone job, and I got talking to him about training. I knew he was doing some work in The Ranch. I also knew I wouldn't have much time to train the team. He had some good ideas and he was working at the cutting edge at college in Belfast. He knew I was fanatical about keeping ball skills as central to all our drills and he had an excellent handle on the work/rest balance I wanted to sell to the players. The players took to him well. A few more critics clambered aboard, wondering aloud about the wisdom of appointing a 29-year-old rookie as team trainer. To me, he felt like the right man.

With more time on my hands, I could tend the details. I continued to work with Peter Quinlivan on video analysis and carefully wound more statistics into our game analysis. Binding the team together was crucially important, too. All the players were aware of my belief in the sanctity of the jersey and the ritual of donning them as a unit. They knew about the team CDs, about the importance of the team circle and the various elements I liked to build into our preparations during a season. They had also been together as a group for a year or two. The likes of Cormac and Stephen O'Neill had already been successful seniors. Others were still making their way. Players knew each other, but the panel wasn't a whole unit yet.

We had to work on that. When we held team meetings, I was careful that the groups contained a good mix of young and old. I wanted to hear voices on the training field. I encouraged players to communicate. I asked for comments on our training and our form from different players. I was always conscious of giving the older players a platform. They might have assumed I had a natural warmth towards the younger ones. They had to understand that I didn't carry any baggage into that dressing-room.

And players did talk. Cormac transcended every age group. Peter Canavan and Chris Lawn were heroes to these boys. Brian Dooher and Colin Holmes always voiced their opinion. Kevin

Hughes rarely spoke, but when he did it carried a lot of weight and made a lot of sense.

Gavin Devlin was always class. He was constantly bouncing with exuberance. He crackled with talk and banter. When training got quiet, Gavin's voice would fill the vacuum. His was the constant voice through those early sessions, but the important thing was, he backed up all that confidence and good humour and opinion with football. For the older players, seeing this young buck deliver on so many levels must have been a huge source of encouragement.

I also wanted to connect with Peter Canavan. I had known Peter since he was a boy kicking ball against the post office wall at home, doing his best Micheál O'Hehir impression as a child on the videos of Glencull matches which we recorded at The Holm; I played with him in 1993 and coached him in 2002 with the club. But this was different.

I started to see how outstanding he truly was. His skill levels were always obvious, but there was an unquenchable fire inside him. He had grit that many people didn't appreciate. Second best meant nothing. Like me, he was a bad loser. If you like losing, I have always reckoned you'll get plenty of it. I could see that outlook in Peter, too.

When dealing with Peter, I had to be aware of a few things. I had a bunch of young players who were familiar with my ways. Peter wasn't coming from the same place as these guys. I knew he would appreciate the quality of our training sessions and our practices. At the same time, though, I had to give him the right place in the mix. We needed his leadership. I didn't want him becoming isolated from a young band of players. He had taught Owen Mulligan in school. He was a hero to all of them. We could feed off his experience if the environment was right.

I would bounce ideas off him. I talked to him about what was going on at training and observe what he was doing. I would always ask for his input at team meetings. If a training session was starting to lag, I'd ask Peter to say a few words and give the whole mood a dart of energy. At our first team meeting he made a statement that has endured through our history as a team. "I don't want to be a great captain," he said. "I want to be a captain of a great team." I felt a shiver of excitement race through me. I knew we were on the same track.

Chris Lawn was also fantastic at that. One evening Chris and Peter both talked about winning their under-21 All-Irelands in 1991 and 1992, and the pain they felt having failed to make the next move. It was a tremendously valuable contribution to make in front of a group of players who hadn't known anything but winning. It also showed I wasn't a dictator. I wanted and appreciated every player's view. I knew I didn't have all the answers. We were learning from each other.

Other things changed. We dispensed with challenge matches. I could never see the point of them anyway. If both teams are experimenting, how can we make a value judgement from a match like that? At least if I see a player doing well against Philip Jordan or Stephen O'Neill in an internal trial, I know they can play.

We also wanted to install a culture of winning. Early on in my time with Tyrone, I said I wanted to win every match we played. It was a catchphrase that stayed with us, but it was more than an idle sound bite. We needed to make a statement every time we went out. Our ambition and our mixed record in the recent past demanded it. There had been a huge sense of disappointment in Tyrone in 2002. We had won the league title but watching Armagh win the All-Ireland was hard. Reflecting on the strong position the team had been in against Sligo before being overhauled posed even bigger questions.

There seemed to be a psychological chink in the team. They were vulnerable. That had to be eradicated. There would be no more excuses. The quality of our preparations would form the basis for that attitude. At one meeting during the year, we asked the players to rate out of ten our chances of winning an All-Ireland. The average rating was six. It didn't worry me at the time but it suggested we needed to keep building on confidence. Winning was an obvious way to do that.

The best way to do that was to create a winning mentality. After years of treating the competition like an outcast, we embraced the McKenna Cup and pursued it. Ironically, we over-experimented in the final against Monaghan, played poorly and lost by two points, but it served our purposes. Without challenge games, we needed good matches in January. The McKenna Cup fed off our enthusiasm. We got a stir going about it then, and it's never looked back since.

People were still ready to have a pop from the start, though. We lost two of our first three league games – to Dublin and Roscommon. Both slipped through our hands by a point. A few weeks later we beat Donegal, but delivered an appalling performance in the first half. That day I cut into the team in a manner I can't imagine doing now. I told them to forget about diets and stats and ice baths and videos. This was about showing some pride in the jersey. As I walked out for the second half, someone shouted from the crowd. "Harte! That was the worst Tyrone performance in 20 years!"

"You know what," I replied, "you are probably right."

It was early in the year to be looking for carcasses, but the vultures were circling. It didn't surprise me. Sometimes the critics make a lot of noise, but it doesn't mean a lot of people are in the chorus. I have always known some people don't want me as Tyrone manager for their own reasons. I've seen the newspaper articles and heard the barbs from the stands. That's fine. Maybe people would have preferred a former player with a higher profile than mine. Maybe there's a single-mindedness about me that can rub people up the wrong way too. I won't always say what pleases everybody, but I'll say what I think is right. That approach can sometimes aggravate people. If that's the case, so be it. It's not going to deter me.

Fr Vincent Travers wrote a book, *In Touch with God*, where he compared criticism to accepting a gift. If the receiver declines the gift, where does it go? It stays with the giver. It's the same with criticism. I'm not responsible for how these people feel. I don't need to accept the way they feel. I'm only responsible for how I feel. I can only work on that.

I always believed I could make things happen for Tyrone with the players we have. We have dealt with so many setbacks anyway, a few critics aren't going to register too strongly on my Richter scale.

In time, we started to get things right. We played Kerry in the league and beat them by two points in a good game. We clogged up the middle, limited the goal chances and turned over mountains of possession. We could have been out of sight by half-time but a goal from Peter Canavan was the cushion we could lean against for the rest of the game.

Little things stood out that day. Brian Dooher worked back to block out a Colm Cooper shot inside our full-back line. As some of our players argued with the referee and Kerry took a quick free, Cormac McAnallen hared back into defence in time to make an interception, win a free and clear the danger. Darragh Ó Sé won plenty of high ball at centre-field but Cormac and Sean Cavanagh shared 0-3 between them in reply, and we still won. That fractured one theory: that if Darragh wins ball, the opposition invariably loses. Useful morsels to nourish us as the year went on.

We reached the league final against Laois and won it, though after the disappointment of 2002, having won the league title, it wasn't a huge cause for celebration, even if it suitably reflected our winning mantra. Of greater concern was losing Gavin Devlin.

The cameras caught him treading on Colm Parkinson. We knew he was in trouble, even though it wasn't the most vicious thing in the world. He received a three-month suspension, which seemed harsh. He was gutted, but he remained a central part of the scene all summer. As soon as the suspension was over, I wouldn't have any hesitation in returning him to centre-back.

With Gavin gone, we prepared for the Ulster championship and almost got caught cold by Derry. It was a massive day for me, and reflected the fine lines between success and failure. For the last few games of the league, I had been worried about Ryan McMenamin's form. He had been carrying an injury and was struggling to deliver his best. When it came to the Derry game, I didn't pick him.

At the time I didn't realise the gravity of that decision. I was simply picking the best team for the given day. I never considered how Ryan's absence would be perceived. I didn't have Ryan before as a minor. Was this going to be seen as a classic example of favouritism towards the others?

Ryan took the decision well but also consulted Peter Canavan about it. Peter's advice was well-observed: hang in there, fight your way back. Ryan came on that day against Derry and was instrumental in saving the game for us. By the time the replay came round, his form had recovered. He never looked back.

From the beginning of the year I had wanted to incorporate more patterns of play to suit the players we had, systems with the capacity to bend and adapt when necessary. Derry provided the perfect test for that aspiration.

To beat Derry, we simply tried to continue what had worked in the league. We kept Peter Canavan and Owen Mulligan close to goal and planned to feed them ball.

Derry had our number that day, though. They strung up a defensive barrier in front of the two boys and forced us to play around it. Our naïvety almost lost us the game. Like

Crossmaglen, though, we learned lessons from the draw. Next time, we put Kevin Hughes at full-forward, pulled Peter out the field and ran at Derry along the flanks to draw them out. We knew we had the finishers if we could create the space. It worked, and we eased home comfortably. It was a good sign. We could be flexible when we needed to be.

Now, with the thrill of beating Derry percolating around the county, we needed to refocus. One night at training, Chris Lawn had a few things on his mind. Beating Derry always means so much in Tyrone, he felt the need to guard against any sense of a job being done. We stood in our circle, and Chris spoke.

He asked the boys if they had All-Ireland senior medals. He reminded them that Tyrone was surrounded by counties that did: Armagh, Derry, Donegal, Down. We had no right to assume anything about ourselves. He recalled the team being six points up against Sligo the previous year. He remembered the sloppy passes and mistakes that crept in. At half-time the body language could be translated into "We'll be all right". He could even recall seeing a few players joking about where they were heading that night. Forty minutes later, he said, Tyrone were beaten.

In January 2003, himself and Peter Canavan went on the All Star trip feeling like second-class citizens without their All-Ireland medal. We could put nothing before this prize, he said. Wives, girlfriends, job, family. Everything had to be put behind us. We had four months to fulfil our potential. Four months. The circle broke up.

The edge never left us again.

WE EASED THROUGH ANTRIM to make the Ulster final. It was an exciting time. Marian and myself were married 25 years that July. The children were loving our adventures that summer. Mark was doing well with Tyrone. Then, the Friday week before the final, I received a sad phone call. Sean Canavan had died.

It was a terrible blow to us all. He was a character in the parish, a man who ensured that any trip to the post office was accompanied by a lengthy discourse on the state of football. Sean had provided me with such staunch support during the Glencull era and he loved his boys, but he never mollycoddled them.

While the rest of the country gloried in Peter's ability, Sean always challenged him. He didn't tell him what everyone else was saying, but what he felt Peter needed to hear. He loved skilful football. Even though he came from a different generation, he appreciated the new approach I was bringing to my teams. He was as straight as any pass Peter ever made.

At the removal in Sean's house I stood at the bottom of the stairs with Peter, talking about his dad and how he adored the game. I told Peter how proud his father had always been of him. "I know," he replied. "but he might've missed the best."

We both knew. This was the year. It was achingly sad that Sean Canavan wouldn't be there to witness it.

DOWN WERE WAITING in the Ulster final. Having gotten our shock against Derry and worked our way past Antrim, we felt we should have enough to win. Maybe that was the problem. We were doing okay, but we weren't pushing ourselves hard enough. Watching the game from the line, I felt we could win this whenever we decided we wanted to. When Gregory McCartan got sent off before half-time, we eased ourselves even deeper into the comfort zone.

Then Benny Coulter scored a goal. We were busy trying to free up Brian McGuigan as the extra man. Down weren't allowing us to indulge that luxury. Ten minutes into the second half they had hit three goals. Coulter tapped over another point and we were nine points behind.

I stood on the side-line, bracing myself for the worst. This was where we needed to attack that innocent climb. We needed to make that effort. We needed to be bold with our convictions and our belief. Old Tyrone teams had died sorry deaths in matches like these. I always felt these boys were different. They had to prove it again now.

The comeback started with Peter. When a Sean Cavanagh shot was tipped onto the crossbar by Mickey McVeigh, Peter was there to grab the rebound. The defenders leapt on him.

Penalty.

Peter's penalty-taking record in the Ulster championship was mixed, but his team needed him. He stepped up, and slotted the ball home. Six in it.

The team was revitalised. Down were in full retreat. With five minutes left, we had drawn level. The game was wide open. Then Down seemed to snap it shut again. It was infuriatingly simple. Long free from Liam Doyle into the square, up went Dan Gordon with his fist. Ball lands in the net.

It was a sickener, but the team refused to wilt. Owen Mulligan broke a tackle to hit a point. Ciaran Gourley intercepted a pass and pushed forward for another. Brian Dooher found Peter with a pass. He drew a foul and converted it. Players stood up again and took responsibility. Another crucial foothill scaled on the innocent climb.

It was hard to figure at the time, but I knew it was better we didn't win that day. We needed that chastening. The players could see it. We had gone to the edge and dragged ourselves back. Now, we needed to learn from it.

14

ATTACKING THE SUMMIT

June 2009

WE HAD A LOT to think about after Armagh. Everyone was happy with the result, and the players were mature enough to realise the benefit of Armagh's comeback for us rather than strolling away with an easy win. At that stage, though, none of us could have imagined that brief 15-minute skirmish would represent our hardest battle on the way to an Ulster final.

Derry had talked all year about championship. Championship was everything. Damien Cassidy had used so many players during the league and still got to a league final. That was a message. He was preparing the team to cope with missing players if required. Now they were meeting us without Enda Muldoon and Fergal Doherty at midfield and a handful of other influential players. By Damien's gospel, though, Derry were ready for this.

We looked at the situation differently. We knew the missing players were crucial to them. With those players out of the equation, we should be winning this game. Damien was on a part of the road to building a championship team we had passed through many years ago. Derry had much to learn yet.

That said, Tyrone don't take chances against Derry. I took the video of their game against Monaghan and ripped it apart for clues. In the end, I boiled their approach down to three key players: Barry McGoldrick and Sean Leo McGoldrick on their half-back line, and Gerard O'Kane who nominally lined out at corner-back. Most of their attacks were launched by these three players. Barry McGoldrick was Derry's spare man all the time, and a lot of ball went through him. Sean Leo also channelled a lot of ball to O'Kane. Watching the Monaghan game, I noticed that Gerard broke every one of his tackles. The first man never stopped him. Allowing that to happen wasn't a good idea.

After that, Derry's entire attacking ploy still revolved around feeding the two Bradleys – Eoin and Paddy. Monaghan tried to play a sweeper in front of them, but he didn't seem too sure what his job was. We felt our corner-back, PJ Quinn, had the pace to handle Eoin and had done a good job on him in the league match. We weren't going to focus all our efforts on two Bradleys; we were going to focus on Paddy, and Paddy's space.

Justin McMahon was physical enough to give Paddy plenty of it one-on-one, and with Conor Gormley covering the space in front of Paddy, life promised to be difficult for him. Joe McMahon came back from wing-forward to take up Conor's position at centre-back as an extra bolt on the door. When it came to kick-outs, we reckoned Derry would try to exploit our use of extra men in defence by playing their kick-outs short. We practised endlessly combating those in our in-house games and ended up giving them no free options. We also worked out a way to contest with them under the long kick-outs. Conor would slot back to centre-back, Joe would push into centre-field, while Tommy McGuigan would pick up the spare man left by Joe.

In the weeks between the Armagh and Derry matches, we focused entirely on Derry for one session, assessed our own performance against Armagh in another and worked on some pointers from our in-house games. We tape every one of those, too, and use clips from them just as much as any competitive match. We need the players to see it's not just for show. It all matters.

Peter Quinlivan's video analysis has now evolved to a point where we can project tactical line-ups onto a screen and shift icons denoting the players using a mouse to the areas of the field we want them to be. It's a long way from the days of diagrams and arrows blotching up the paper. We had so much stuff in our locker to cover a variety of those scenarios. On the day, we didn't need most of them.

Brian Dooher had been close to returning for the Derry game, but was a victim of his own manic commitment. After the Armagh match, he trained Monday and Tuesday evening, had a session with physiotherapist Louis O'Connor on Wednesday, trained again Thursday and played a club match at the weekend, where he had to come off.

I understand where Brian is coming from. His confidence on the field comes from knowing that no player has worked harder than him. That's his safety net. I still needed to pull him up this time, though. He needed to train smart. Too much work had prevented him from starting the Derry game, not bad luck. He was visibly frustrated at the news, but it was a point he needed to take on board.

Even our approach to the game took us away from the traditional blood and thunder of Tyrone–Derry games. People thought we would focus on 2006, when Derry held us scoreless to half-time and beat us well on the day. I had a different take on things.

I have been reading a book by Eckhart Tolle called *The Power of Now*. Its core message is the importance of now. The past is an illusion. Time itself can be seen as an illusion that exists only to help us make sense of the world around us. It's challenging stuff. It really forces you to try and break out of your traditional way of thinking.

Tolle also focuses on the importance of controlling the ego. If you can detach your mind from your ego, you can achieve a better sense of awareness. You can look at your reaction to things. Is it ego-driven or truth-driven? Do you have to put yourself down to rise yourself up? Do I have to make Derry and Damien Cassidy an enemy to find a reason to win this game? Do we need to revisit 2006?

I don't care how anyone else is doing, I tell the players. This year is about us. Why are we judging them? I respect Derry and Damien. Look at the quality of our work. Our team. We are the only people we can judge. Tony might throw in a low ball about Derry now and then, but that's fine too. The overall attitude is positive.

On the day, we dominate and win by eight points. Derry can barely lay a glove on us.

People are hearing me talk about developing our play and looking hard to spot the changes. It's more subtle than that. We're not talking about tearing up our script, just refining it. We want to be about variety. It comes back to developing the thinking player. We want to play our support game when appropriate and kick the ball long when appropriate. Improving our long kicking is a key element to training at the moment. We're decent as a support play team, but we want to mix it up more.

Tackling is another serious issue. Perfecting the near-hand tackle has been a blessing to us over the years, but we can move that on a stage too. The first stage of any tackle is to dispossess. Now, we can talk to the players about completion. Knocking the ball away isn't good enough any more. We don't want to see them flick it away from themselves, but towards them. If they do, they can regather possession, and set us on our way.

Our video work is about working on the players' minds. Why should they carry the ball, for example, in certain situations? Why kick the ball in others? You carry the ball to attract attention. Knowing the right time to release it is key, but you also need someone to release it to. We find examples of intelligent play, and silly play. We highlight the differences. We embed good practice into the players' minds until it starts to become second nature. It's layering on the knowledge and confidence to do the right thing in a pressure situation at the right time. We won't fall back to old habits. We are forming new ones. Our tactical framework is always there, but the players need to be flexible within that. That journey probably picked up pace in the middle of 2003.

––◦––

I HAD RESISTED the ridiculous notion all that year that Tyrone were too small to win an All-Ireland. I still believed that, but after conceding four goals against Down, I could see we needed to do something in defence.

Chris Lawn was an excellent full-back, but Dan Gordon was causing too many problems for him. Having conceded four goals, John Devine had to pay a price as well. Packie McConnell had a size and presence we needed back there. As for a full-back, I knew where to go.

A few nights later, I sidled up to Cormac McAnallen in training and asked how he felt about playing full-back. We needed his physical strength back there, and no one could adapt to such an imposing task as quickly as he could. He loved attacking the ball and was always hugely determined and aggressive when he got it. He was up for the challenge from the start. In the back of my mind, I knew where Cormac would go with this. He would embrace this challenge. He had only days to figure Dan Gordon out. He spoke to Chris Lawn and soaked up every drop of information he could. I knew he would pore over videos, figure out what made Gordon tick. If Down thought their performance in the draw would be enough to win the replay, they hadn't factored in the attitude epitomised by the likes of Cormac.

The following Sunday, Cormac's approach set the tone. The rest of the team followed. We blitzed Down early on, got five points ahead and continued to pull away after that. We hit 0-23 and won by 15 points. When he received the Cup, Peter recalled the day he watched Frank McGuigan kick 0-11 for Tyrone in the 1984 Ulster final with his father and how he wished his father had witnessed another wonderful game the previous week. At such an emotional moment, it was a wonderfully dignified way to remember his father.

> *"Be more concerned with your character than with your reputation,*
> *Because your character is what you really are,*
> *While your reputation is merely what others think you are."*
>
> JOHN WOODEN

OUR NEXT STEP was an exercise in ruthlessness. The last time Tyrone had played a championship match in Croke Park, Sligo had beaten them. Peter Canavan had ended that game believing his last chance to win an All-Ireland was gone. Tyrone had lived up to its stereotype as a county that produced classy under-age footballers who knew how to turn a step in the league, but lacked the gravel in their guts for the championship. I never believed that. The only way to convince the rest of the country, though, was in Croke Park.

Fermanagh were waiting in the All-Ireland quarter-final. I knew we were the better team but we could leave nothing to chance. A week before we played Fermanagh, we held a meeting.

By now the players were splitting themselves into suitably designed mini-groups, unconsciously mixing younger players with the more experienced ones themselves. There was no need for us to supervise their make-up any more. The players were comfortable with each other.

I resurrected the Sligo game, showed the players some footage. The message was simple and withering: this is what can happen if we don't approach this right. This is the standard people expect Tyrone to be at. We're going to be better than that.

I drove it home and rose the bitterness inside them. A lot of the players who had lost to Sligo were still in that room. Remember how much in control we were before we lost the game? This time the team were not allowed to take their foot off the pedal. You get into the lead, and you tramp on. Bottom line. Nothing else is satisfactory.

The night before the game I showed them cuttings from the day's papers. Every single piece mentioned our defeat to Sligo. This was how the world truly saw us. Among the questions raised were to mark their belief in winning an All-Ireland. Now the rating had climbed to ten. Fermanagh were going to suffer for the sins of 2002.

By half-time we were 1-11 to 0-2 ahead. I always approach half-time with the mentality that the game is still scoreless. Even though we were well in front, it applied even more that day. No disrespect to Fermanagh, but we were there to bury them. Take it up, take it up and take it again. No holding back. There were no other safe way to win this game, either on the scoreboard or psychologically. In the end it was 1-21 to 0-5. A massacre. Our ghosts were exorcised.

A day later we watched Kerry ease past Roscommon in their quarter-final. We knew all year we would have to beat them to win an All-Ireland. Think of 2003 and I think again of Riley's rules of innocence: trust, instinct, boldness, effort.

The steepest part of the climb lay in front of us. This team was ready to attack the summit.

A FEW WEEKS BEFORE we played Kerry, there was a line in the *Irish News* that got me thinking. Apparently, Tyrone had never beaten Leinster or Munster opposition on the way to an All-Ireland final. Never beaten a Munster side? That anomaly had me hooked. This wasn't just about winning a semi-final or making an All-Ireland final. Tyrone had done all that before. This match promised to be a landmark in every way. I have never been afraid to promote those ideas with the players either. Those are the little incentives that offer players a fresh edge. Some teams cower in the face of history. I raised my teams to embrace and challenge it. That was what facing Kerry was all about.

How did Kerry see us? I was pretty sure they viewed us as did the rest of the country: a group of whippersnappers who did rightly in the league. They're in an All-Ireland semi-final but Tyrone can't have the confidence to beat us. Kerry probably felt their traditional superiority would be enough to win the game anyway. If I was wearing a Kerry jersey, that's how I would have been thinking. I felt that already gave us a useful advantage before the battle began.

We were meeting Kerry at the perfect time, too. The belief factor within our team was so high now. The overriding attitude among the majority of the panel was simple: we're here to win things. Even if they doubted that optimism, the older players could see this view was palpable. The younger players didn't consider any sense of inferiority. They were capable of delivering any day, anywhere. I remember falling into conversation with Stephen O'Neill back around that time about the possibilities within that group of players. Some time in the next few years, I said, we'll win that All-Ireland. "In the next few years?" he replied. "Why wait?"

There was no sense of awe any more among the Tyrone players about Kerry. There was just the simple conviction that we would win this match. This wasn't 1986, when winning an All-Ireland semi-final and getting a big day in Kerry's company was enough. We were journeying to an All-Ireland title. That was the bottom line. Maybe that sounds smug and arrogant, but it's also the truth. There was no fear of Kerry in 2003. Respect, but no fear.

Part of our approach has always been shaping our own tactics to attack the opposition's strengths. In 2003 we played some magnificent football of our own. Dealing with Kerry, though, was slightly different. I looked at them more closely than any other team that year. We couldn't be consumed by their strengths and we couldn't let it dictate everything we did, but it was a factor. And there was a way to stop them.

This was where Peter Quinlivan's video tagging system came into its own. When I looked at how Kerry beat Roscommon, a few trends emerged. Mike Frank Russell and Colm Cooper were their key men in attack. Although named as corner-forwards, they did their most devastating work in the central areas in front of goal. They made their runs from the corner, towards the D, 25 metres from goal. When they landed in that zone, Kerry hit them with well-placed diagonal balls.

Their style indirectly matched our defensive system. If we lodged somebody in the area around the D for the entire game, Cooper or Russell would never be allowed a free shot. In fact, every time they got the ball, they'd be faced by at least two men.

Plus, we finally had the right man for the job. After three months kicking his heels, Gavin Devlin's suspension had expired. He had accomplished this job for us as a minor on numerous occasions. This approach might take Kerry by surprise, but it was second nature to Horse. He was straight back in.

We needed to stop Darragh Ó Sé, too. Kevin Hughes would be a key component there, as was the need to free Gerald Cavlan up to receive kick-outs from John Devine. We wanted people disrupting Darragh's charges towards Kerry kick-outs, stopping him winning clean ball. Once the ball hit the floor, I was sure our work rate on the ground should do the rest.

We headed to the Citywest Hotel a week before the game. We talked about Cooper and Darragh. What Kerry might be thinking, where our heads needed to be. We talked about what the public would expect. That wonderful 1997 All-Ireland minor semi-final would inevitably come up during the week. Our league game had been a decent match. People would speculate on the joy of watching Séamus Moynihan take on Peter Canavan. We had hit more than 0-20 in our previous two matches. Kerry had riddled Roscommon. That public expected a festival of football.

We didn't.

Everything about our game needed to be tighter and harder than anything we had produced all year. We would try and score big, but we couldn't allow Kerry the same liberty. I thought back to Errigal Ciarán's county final against Killyclogher in 2002. That was a day for steel, for Errigal to front up and demolish some assumptions about themselves. This Tyrone team wasn't built to play negatively, but we had to raise a type of fury we hadn't touched before.

To catch Kerry, we needed to hit them with sheer pressure. Blast them with heat. Work rate. We knew deep inside that if we worked as hard as we could, Kerry wouldn't be ready for that. If we hit that mark, Kerry might be taken by surprise for long enough that we could escape into a lead. By the time they knew what was happening, it might even be too late. It was high-stakes stuff, but I reckoned it was worth the gamble.

The mood that weekend was perfectly pitched. I had designed a new logo for the team: a "0" with a number 3 on either side. 2003 was about committing to split the game into

30-second batches of concentration. Every game was broken down into those bite-sized, easily digestible pieces. That was more crucial than ever when facing Kerry.

We had new gear and another new symbol for the rest of the summer: a "T" within a circle. The circle represented everything about us. It was where we could bare ourselves, where nothing but honesty was acceptable. The circle unified us and kept us together. Within that circle was a profound trust we had worked for years to create. The circle was our greatest strength on weeks like this. Our haven and our arsenal.

We also had our new song. I had fallen into conversation with Adrian Logan a few weeks before about the national anthem. He recalled how he travelled to matches with his brother, and the pride and exuberance they put into singing the anthem before every match. It felt like a tonic, a shot of adrenalin before the match began. It got me thinking. How unusual would it be for a bunch of bucks from the north, with minimal grasp of the Irish language, to end up in Croke Park singing *Amhrán na bhFiann* with perfect musical and linguistic accuracy?

The players clicked with the idea straight away. A week before we met Kerry, we stood in a room in Citywest, singing *Amhrán na bhFiann* with a ferocity and pleasure that lifted all our hearts. In a week we would stand together in Croke Park again and sing our anthem without missing a word. Breaking down the stereotypes had started before the whistle was even blown.

We all knew what needed to be done that day. There could be no room for error or respite. We couldn't take a step back. To beat Kerry we needed to put them down on the seat of their pants from the start. They needed to know this day wasn't going to transpire like all the rest. We were still fighting old assumptions about ourselves. Tyrone didn't have the stomach for the biggest days. That myth still needed to be shattered for good. To do that, every player had to take responsibility for his own battle. It was George Zalucki's definition of commitment made flesh: doing what you said you would do long after the mood in which you said it has left you.

Talk was over. Time for action.

WE MADE THAT DAY our own. We grabbed it from Kerry's grasp and never allowed them near it. Our energy and drive was infectious. We ripped into Kerry from the start. When they had the ball, we chased them incessantly. Players funnelled back after the player in possession and choked the space around the Kerry forwards. When we had the ball, we burst from defence, moving the ball crisply and at speed. Gerald Cavlan was winning kick-outs. Kevin Hughes was tormenting Darragh. In attack, we were ruthless in front of goal.

The one problem was Peter. He went over on his ankle inside the first 15 minutes. A chill ran through me for a moment. Then I started to think.

If Stephen O'Neill had been playing with any other county that year, teams would have shaped their attack around him, but in 2003 the right opportunity never quite came his way. He now offered us a potent alternative from the bench. After bracing himself to deal with Peter, Séamus Moynihan now had to face an entirely different package. Stevie was left-footed. He was physically bigger than Peter. And, what other county could replace one All Star with another?

It was another challenge to the rest of the team. Were they going to lean on Peter forever? If this was a day when every Tyrone player had already committed to stand up and deliver a performance beyond their normal capabilities, this made that challenge even more acute. There were no hiding places now.

The team's response was typical. They never lifted their foot off the accelerator. Every time a Kerry player took possession, he was cornered. The enthusiasm for work was infectious. When players saw other players scavenging for ball and hustling Kerry players all over the field, they followed suit. You couldn't just stand back and watch. Everyone wanted to be part of this. When they saw this approach was working, the players became even more ferocious.

When your opponent doesn't expect it, the results can be devastating. As I hoped, Kerry were now doubting every assumption they had made about this game. The one scene that was deemed to epitomise the game was the sight of Darragh Ó Sé in possession, hounded into distraction by a pack of Tyrone players. In the end, Darragh just hacked the ball away. It was the action of a tormented man. It screamed: just get me out of here. The loose ball was picked up by Brian Dooher, who in turn was dragged down. It was such a contrast to the disciplined, aggressive tackling executed by our players just a few seconds before. This instance captured the contrast, and ultimately told me who was going to win. I don't think you'll ever see a scene like it again.

By half-time we had hit 0-9, and led by seven. Perfection. The mood in the dressing-room was electric. Now, though, we had to finish the job. Before the match, I reckoned if we could pull off our ambush, we should have compiled a sufficient lead to pick off our scores and keep Kerry at arm's length. What we couldn't do, though, was slacken off.

I reminded the players of the 1986 All-Ireland final. Tyrone held a similar lead over Kerry then with less time remaining and lost the game. That wouldn't happen again. Before they left, Peter asked one question of them. "It's not often I've asked anyone for anything," he said, "but do this for me. I want back in an All-Ireland final."

For the rest of the game, we kept it tight and attacked the lead when we could. We effectively drew the second half and won 0-13 to 0-6. At the end of the match, I went to Páidí Ó Sé and shook hands. He was disappointed, but gracious. "I hope we can achieve as much as you did," I said.

It was a few hours before the full scale of public reaction to our performance became clear. We had delivered something no one was expecting. It didn't sit well with some people. Pat Spillane had already labelled our performance as "puke football". Sean Walsh, the Kerry County Board chairman, was talking about introducing the mark and changing the rules of the game to prevent the sort of mass tackling we had engaged in. Crazy stuff.

None of it bothered us. I saw the first half as one of the best 35 minutes of football we ever played. It contained everything you could ever wish from your team. I'm not interested in foul counts. I'm into sheer energy, work rate and determination. That was all there. If the foul count is high, the referees are there to deal with those.

Instead, we were being branded with all sorts of tags: puke football, blanket defence. We were disappointed with that and confused by the definitions. Was there anything wrong with blanket defence? To me, blanket defence means everybody defends when you don't have the ball. That's what football's about. Who has the right to abdicate their responsibility to win the ball back? Nobody.

As far as puke football goes, there was nothing unseemly about what we were doing. I thought it was refreshing to see a group of people embracing the challenge of doing a job collectively. No one relied on anyone else. They worked for each other. People missed the point. It wasn't a defensive approach. We scored 0-9 in the first 35 minutes for a start. We were trying to counteract Kerry's strengths to some degree, but we weren't hell-bent on winning the game 0-5 to 0-4 either. When we had the ball we were determined to score as much as we could. Indeed, 0-13 would have got us close to winning a few All-

Irelands over the previous few years. It was actually enough for Kerry to beat Mayo in 1997 and Dublin to beat Tyrone in 1995.

I was looking at everything through different lenses. People around Tyrone were jubilant to be in an All-Ireland final. To me, it was worth a moment's satisfaction. The job was done, but the beauty of the journey is there's always more to do. I thought back to that line from the *Irish News*. Tyrone had never beaten a Munster team on the way to a final. That was a first.

There was one milestone left to go.

15

HEAVEN

"Life is constantly testing us for our level of commitment, and life's greatest rewards are reserved for those who demonstrate a never-ending commitment to act until they achieve. This level of resolve can move mountains, but it must be constant and consistent. It is still the common denominator separating those who live their dreams from those who live in regret."

ANTHONY ROBBINS

AS THE WEEKS DRAINED down to the All-Ireland final, people already had the script written and the rights sold. Peter Canavan had lived with the tag as the greatest player never to win an All-Ireland. He had lived too long with that line. For years he had been such a crucial presence for Tyrone. He was the go-to guy.

Now, for the first time in his career, he had much more help. This would finally be his day.

The respect between him and the younger players was immense. They didn't deal in second places. They played to win, just like him. Getting Armagh in the final upped all that a little more. We needed to strike the right balance. This wasn't a final we could lose, but it rebelled against every fibre of our collective system to put result above performance. If we failed to deliver against Armagh, the result would take care of itself.

That's where confidence comes in. If you're certain about the performance you can deliver, then why worry about the result? Like so much of our work with this generation, creating that confidence takes years. By 2003 we were talking about when we would win an All-Ireland, not if. The likes of Peter, Brian Dooher and Chris Lawn now realised there was a dynamic here that could finally deliver their All-Ireland. That mix was everything.

I was lucky to be in a situation where I could elevate everything about our preparations to a new level. Winning an All-Ireland isn't just about playing the game and getting your tactics right. It's about mental tactics too. That's the real thrill in this whole business for me. The skill and ability the players have to perform on the pitch is one thing. The amount that can be done off the field to help them perform even better is incalculable.

That was the realm we were in now. We needed to think about how our players ticked, how a word here and there could change their mood and get them thinking in a different way.

Around this time Terence Donnelly, who was involved with Club Tyrone, mentioned Bart McEnroe to me. He had invited Bart to talk with the salespeople in his car dealerships. Terence had found him beneficial in terms of focusing his staff on the nature of their jobs. He got them thinking about how they sold cars, their methods, their language, their tone and style. If I thought it might be worth meeting him, Terence offered to set something up.

It sounded interesting. When we met, I wasn't disappointed. Bart's style was in-your-face. Aggressive. He asked hard, straight questions. If you were tentative or easily ruffled in any way, Bart wasn't the right person to talk with. If you were defensive and felt deep down that you already knew all the answers, he wouldn't be for you. He drilled deep, looking for answers. You had to be ready for that noise.

He asked me about my approach to the All-Ireland. What was I doing with the team? What was I thinking of changing as the game got closer? How could I make things different? He asked about tactics and dealing with players. How would I deal with Steven McDonnell, for example. Although I had already settled these issues in my head, verbalising them opened everything up to scrutiny again.

Sometimes when you think your way through a problem, you can conjure a solution that seems to fit in your mind. When you don't share that verbally, though, you risk not challenging your own thinking. Do my ideas make sense when I communicate them to someone else? I was thinking my way through these problems again, honing and refining my response. Then Bart might pick more holes in my ideas. The questions would begin again. It was intense, but it challenged me. I was glad it did.

It got me thinking about my approach with the players. Was I communicating effectively with them? Did they know where I was coming from? Did they understand what we wanted them to deliver?

Bart brought me into the realm of "ownable behaviour". Instead of imposing your ideas on his performance, you allow the player the space to define what a good performance means to him. It gets him thinking about what he needs to do to reach those levels, and reveals how he sees himself rather than relying on other people's perceptions of him.

Gerald Cavlan was a classic example of this idea at work. Gerald had been in and out of the team during the year. He had missed a few training sessions and taken his time getting back from injury. When I looked at Gerald, I saw a player with the potential to be among the best forwards we had ever seen. At times, though, I forgot my own best lessons.

I wanted him to play with the guile of Gerald Cavlan and work with the ferocity of Brian Dooher. I needed to respect the uniqueness within his game. If I did that, he might begin to develop the other sides to his game that this team needed.

That's where "ownable behaviour" came in. As part of our build-up to that final, I visited with every player. When I met Gerald I asked him about his perception of how I saw him. "Poor tackler," he replied. It amazed me. That wasn't the message I wanted Gerald to carry with him. I needed to understand more about where he was coming from and allow that to shape how I dealt with him. He needed to give us more in some ways too, but the change needed to start with me.

We kept prodding at the players' mindsets all the way to the final. One evening Peter Canavan, Chris Lawn and Paddy Tally recalled the mood after losing the 1995 All-Ireland final to Dublin. They remembered the darkness of the dressing-room that evening, the vast differences a margin as slim as one point can make. Back then, those boys thought they'd be back again. Instead they had endured eight thankless years. We might have felt a certainty about our destiny as a team, but as George Zalucki said, the mind can create all kinds of trap-doors. Peter Canavan said it in the dressing-room in 1995: making an All-Ireland final didn't make it a good year. It was all or nothing.

ARMAGH WERE STRANGE but suitable opponents to meet. In some ways, you wanted the novelty of meeting a team from down south in the All-Ireland final. In other ways, though, Armagh represented the kind of challenge this team thrived on. They were defending champions. They had beaten Tyrone in the 2002 Ulster championship. If we lost, Tyrone were staring a 2-0 defeat ratio in the face. Despite the stakes being so high, our players seemed perfectly relaxed throughout the build-up.

When we attended the *Irish News* GAA Awards, we received the best endorsement yet that our approach was right. We sat at our tables along with our wives and girlfriends, and enjoyed our night. The Armagh team arrived late and alone. They sat by themselves, ate their meal, endured the formalities and disappeared out the door. They seemed uptight. We were loose and relaxed. That's how I wanted it. Respect. But no fear.

Although plenty of the players knew each other outside football, there was never any great warmth between the teams. There wasn't real animosity either, but there was a distance.

Although people lazily labelled both of us with the same "Ulster football" brand, I always thought we were very different from Armagh. I thought there was more versatility to our team. Our players were there to work as a collective. They had the adaptability to change as the game demanded. Armagh were more rigid in their tactics and approach. Try and impose our style on that Armagh squad, and I don't think it would have worked.

Making that flexibility count on the day was another thing. After years of battling with them as minors, we knew how tenacious Armagh were long before they became fashionable. We also knew where we could hurt them. Armagh's strength was the cornerstone that supported everything else. If you allowed them get round you when in possession, they would smother you. They loved turning the ball over. It was like a tonic to them.

Paul McGrane was a crucial player at midfield. Their attacking system pretty much revolved around Ronan Clarke and Steven McDonnell, and sending high diagonal balls into them. Oisin McConville was sweeping about too, collecting any loose ball. It was all highly effective, but it was also predictable. We had already overcome an almost identical system with Errigal Ciarán against Crossmaglen in 2002. When there's that much predictability about a team, you should be able to put something in place to stop them.

We already had our sweeper system in place to deal with Clarke and McDonnell. We needed to pressure their kickers. John McEntee was a good ball-winner and a key launching pad for delivering ball to Clarke and McDonnell, but he was never going to carry the ball at speed. We were always going to have the chance to catch and pressurise him. If he did release the ball unhindered, though, we were in trouble.

Our trump card was pace. We needed to spread the game out and move the ball quickly. We couldn't afford to run into cul-de-sacs. We couldn't launch ball in from distance and give the Armagh defenders a 50/50 chance at winning the break. If we could develop one-on-ones by running at their defence and offloading the ball at speed, we could draw fouls and create scoring opportunities. Gerald Cavlan was a crucial presence there. We needed him to stay available as a spare man to pick up passes if players ran into trouble. With his kicking ability, he could pick off points outside the defensive blockade.

The greatest emblem of our support play all year had been our eight-man midfield. Aside from Cormac McAnallen and Kevin Hughes, our half-back and forward lines committed themselves at every breakdown to get the ball back. Add in Enda McGinley coming out from corner-forward and it was a formidable challenge to any team. If teams tried to crowd us out, no problem. That suited us.

Finally, we promised ourselves to attack the final ten minutes. Over the years Armagh's ability to pick off teams as the game neared the end added immensely to their aura. Instead of wilting, though, we would match them. It was a massive psychological challenge. But if we could pull it off, it could send the kind of statement that wins All-Irelands.

With all that in place, our only problem was injury. Ciaran Gourley picked up a bad shoulder injury. In the end, he made the team only by the grace of God and the good work of Marie

McElhinney, a chiropractor from Derry, and the work of our own medical team. Brian McGuigan was exhibiting flu-type symptoms, but that was sometimes the way Brian's system reacted to big games. We had seen this kind of reaction when he was a minor, too. He might not carry as much energy as usual into the final, but he could cope.

A bigger problem was Peter's ankle. We knew from the beginning he was facing a race against time to make the final. If he was fit for anything, that would be a bonus. Because it was a final he could probably get patched up, but how long would he last?

A week before the match, I met Peter in his parents' house. The bottom line was simple. I didn't want the team announced without his name on it. I could imagine the sharp intake of breath among the supporters at the news, and the spring it could give Armagh's step.

I also knew there wasn't 70 minutes in him. Ideally, I wanted him at both ends of the match. We had done a version of it before with Errigal Ciarán against Crossmaglen, so the idea of starting him and re-introducing him wasn't a complete mystery. It still required consideration, though.

Peter wasn't sceptical, but it hadn't really occurred to him that it could be done in an All-Ireland final. Apart from the psychological reasons to start him, I also felt the opening half would be a nervy time. There promised to be plenty of shadow-boxing and frees. We could do with someone with Peter's confidence and authority to kick those early frees over.

In the end, he agreed to go with it. If he got to half time, he would take an extended break then and return for the closing quarter. I was pleased we had talked it out. It confirmed the importance of making players completely aware of the rationale behind your decisions. It allowed them the chance to buy into them and contribute in some way to refining them.

It was also a brave decision for Peter to make. It's not easy returning to a game of that pace and intensity carrying an injury. For most players that would have represented a heavy psychological burden. Not Peter. He might have been surrounded by a special group of players now, but he still had a magnetism and strength of character no one else in that panel had.

We continued to tend the smallest details. The weekend of the All-Ireland hurling final, we headed to Donegal. That afternoon we watched the final together, but not as punters. I told the players to watch the build-up. See how long it lasts? Watch the warm-ups. Listen to the noise and see the colour. It all helped the players adjust to what was ahead of them.

The weekend before the match we headed to Killiney Castle for a dry-run of the weekend to come. We timed everything to replicate what we would do the following Saturday. We stopped for our food in Monaghan. We arrived in Killiney and the players went to the same rooms they would use the following weekend. Some people still feel this kind of preparation isn't necessary, but if you want to do the job in the best possible way, it's not just necessary, it's essential.

I would even prefer if the players were billeted along the same corridors and in the same rooms every time they visited. You want a situation where they can walk to their rooms in their sleep. You shouldn't even have to think about it, which frees your mind to focus your thoughts elsewhere.

The day before the final passed peacefully by. We played a show-reel for the players, highlighting their best plays of the year. We re-emphasised the different elements of our game-play that we needed to get right the following day. On the morning of the match we gathered one final time. I had heard so much about Armagh's physical size compared to Tyrone's, I decided to test the theory. I worked out both teams' average weight and height.

It turned out Armagh were seven ounces heavier and three-quarters of an inch taller.

This was something we could use. I got a piece of paper and measured it to three-quarters of an inch. I borrowed seven ounces of coffee granules from the kitchen and passed them around the room. "Would that bully you?" I asked them. "Would that knock you out of the way?"

The players were amazed. Why should we be pushed around by these boys? Where is the physicality in this? It gave them a tangible way of saying: I won't be knocked down. This man isn't stronger than me. This team isn't stronger than us.

I returned to the importance of the last ten minutes. The public perception insisted that if Armagh were still in the game with ten minutes left, they would walk all over us. We were saying no. We were looking to the last ten minutes. We would be the dominant team. It was a simple state of mind. As you think, so shall you be.

We were ready.

FOR ALL THE HYPE that accompanied this final, we knew that winning would come down to simple things. No rabbits were going to be pulled from a hat. We knew Armagh. We knew what we had to deal with. We were going into the game with our eyes open. We had prepared as well as we possibly could. Sometimes people look at me on the biggest days in Croke Park and wonder why I seem so detached. It's a sign of contentment, I suppose. I know we can't do any more. I also know that any sign of panic from me if things stray off course transmits the wrong message to the players.

Inside, though, I rarely find my emotions churning over. That day in 2003, none of us felt even a tingle of nerves. We didn't even see defeat as a threat. There was no fear. No worry that we might choke. Michaela had written it all down in 1997. The mix in that team was special. We were blessed to have it for that day.

In the end, it turned out as we expected. Using Peter from the start worked like a dream. The referee was giving a lot of frees and Peter was slotting them over. He nailed five points that day. In a tight game, each one was crucial.

Gerald Cavlan picked up a point outside the blockade. The boys were watching Paul Hearty's kick-outs and deciphering the coded messages about where he would flight the next one. By half time we were 0-8 to 0-4 ahead. Time to give Peter a break.

I told the players to forget the score. It's nil-all. Start again. Then, Peter ratcheted up the intensity before the players headed back out.

"We've been knocking on heaven's door for 35 minutes, boys, and she's opening. Now keep knocking, and inside will be heaven."

"We'll not be fuckin' knocking," replied Brian Dooher. "Start kicking it, boys! We'll go through her!"

The second half turned into a pitched battle. Too many fouls. No room. We squandered goal chances all day that would have made life much easier for us. We were ahead by the end and hanging on, but the boys remembered our focus on the last ten minutes. We weren't fading. We were rising to the occasion.

Diarmuid Marsden was unfortunate to get sent off for Armagh, but we kept going. Kept fighting, kept attacking. With six minutes left, I looked for Peter. Was he ready? He said he was. The crowd erupted as he hit the field again. With a three-point gap to bridge and time slipping away, it gave Armagh something else they didn't need to think about.

As the final few moments drew in, we were ahead by three points. One last chance for Armagh. Cormac and Sean Cavanagh go for the one ball. It breaks off them. Armagh get it to Steven McDonnell in front of goal. The world pauses for a second.

In that moment between victory and defeat, someone needs to come forward and decide it. McDonnell shoots. From nowhere, Conor Gormley dives on his foot, deflecting the ball away. It was miraculous. It said everything about our mindset that day: there was no such thing as a lost cause.

Soon after, we finally heard the whistle. The noise engulfed everything, but in that precious moment, I had something else on my mind. Michaela. We had made an agreement that if we won, I had to see her first. Brian Carthy came looking for a radio interview. I didn't want to talk to anybody. I didn't even enjoy the moment till I found her.

I finally saw Michaela, battling to get through the security cordon. It was a special moment. We had talked about it so much, anticipated what this moment would be like. A wave of satisfaction was breaking over me. She was near delirious.

Matthew was there too, with that bright, beaming grin. We gathered in a spot near the tunnel in front of the Hogan Stand and watched Peter collect the Cup. This felt right to me. This was how I wanted to cherish the greatest moment in my sporting life. The whole family had been an integral part of everything from the very beginning in 1991. It had become their way of life as much as mine. They were part of what this entire group was about. It was so special.

I eventually walked the steps of the Hogan Stand and put my hands on the Sam Maguire. I lifted it over my head. It almost felt that this moment was what we were born for. There was no sense of "what have we just done?" We were simply fulfilling the wishes of these young men. Fulfilling the promises we had made to ourselves through our hard work, our belief, our trust, through the wish-list on Michaela's napkin, through the painful times we had spent together. This was for Paul McGirr and all the boys. We hadn't achieved an impossible dream. We did what we expected to do. Now we could savour it.

PEOPLE REACT DIFFERENTLY to winning. Some enjoy it and set it aside. Others let it consume them the way others allow defeat tear them apart. My feelings have always been the same. The greatest satisfaction comes in the hours after the game. I spend time with Marian and the children. We have some family relations about the place and share the evening with them. While plenty of others will have a few drinks and take off into the stratosphere, I know I'll not be going anywhere. I soak up the atmosphere and all the good vibes. The reward for a long year.

The following day we brought the Sam Maguire Cup through packed streets in Aughnacloy, Ballygawley and on to Omagh. Such a sight. Although my mind was already moving on, the following couple of weeks demanded I stay in the moment. I spent 14 nights solid on the road with the Cup, visiting every club with a connection to the panel and plenty more besides. We had a bus that ferried us all about. On the first night the bus was full of players and backroom staff. By the final night, I think I counted five.

It was exhausting. You were repeating the same words everywhere you went, desperately trying to inject the same exuberance into them every time. I had taken a few weeks out of school before the final. Now, with all this travelling and commitments, I wasn't sure if I could get back to school. The work was tiring, but this was an important way to add value to this victory. We needed to get the Cup out there among the people. Schoolchildren needed these experiences and memories to drive them along as footballers. A couple of people in Club Tyrone got together and allowed me to take more time out of school to concentrate solely on promotional work with the Cup. In the end, I never went back.

Around the same time, we also decided to leave the shop we had kept going in Ballygawley. One late night that autumn coming back from a function somewhere, the same thought struck myself and Marian. Usually we would have to swing by the village to sort the tills and get the orders ready for the morning. Now we didn't. I diverted into Ballygawley and drove past the old shop, just to prove the point. We looked at each other and smiled. Life was free and easy. We drove home, just the Sam Maguire Cup and each other.

Because of our victory, I was being invited to all sorts of functions: conferences, club dinner dances, school prize-givings. I felt it was a privilege to be asked, so I felt I needed to reflect seriously on what message I wanted to impart when I spoke. I didn't want to impose my ideas on them, but I wanted to leave them with a set of thoughts they might be able to draw from in time. If they found them useful, fine. If not, they could leave them behind.

When I spoke to GAA audiences, I focused on the club. Why were they part of a club? What were they giving to the club? What is the value in being a club member? I talked about the value of the GAA club as part of the wider community. It gave people and places a sense of their own identity. I spoke in schools about the discipline a sportsperson requires to succeed and the benefits of carrying that into your ordinary life. If you do that, then you're doing more than nourishing your chosen sport.

It was all about our efforts as a team to live a life of value, within football and beyond. People could pour those ideas into their own mould and make what they wanted of it. That's how I believe any kind of wisdom or knowledge can reach different places.

The moments I cherished the most, though, were the private ones. Jim Rafferty was a solicitor in Dungannon, a wonderful Tyrone fan and a great friend of mine for many years. He had suffered from cancer for some time, but I think Tyrone's run kept him alive that year.

One day I called to the house with Sam. Jim was thrilled. He looked at the big Cup, with its fat, silver belly and thick handles.

"There's something I always wanted to do," he said, "and that's drink from that Cup." He had a bottle of water nearby, unscrewed the cap, poured some water in, and sipped from the Cup. It was a profound moment for me. That Cup has visited thousands of sick people through the years and helped them in so many ways. That day, we could give Jim something he had always wanted to do. He died that October.

The Tuesday night after the final, I finally got home, holding the Cup for safekeeping. I put it down in the hallway and looked at it. The rest of the family gradually joined me, sitting on the floor, staring at Sam. We looked around at each other, smiling. Is this really happening?

Sam bunked in our bedroom that night. The following morning we woke up with the morning half-light peeping through the curtains. Everything blurry and undefined. Then, the glint of silver. The outline of the Cup sitting in the corner of the room.

A dream mingling with reality.

16

CORMAC

CORMAC MCANALLEN RETURNED to a team floating on air at the start of 2004 but still with their feet close enough to the ground. Some of them might have partied hard that winter, but they were sensible enough to do the right thing, to project the right mood. There was still enough experience there in Peter Canavan, Brian Dooher and Chris Lawn to remind them how fleeting success might be unless we worked even harder to maintain our progress. The entire country was waiting to take a shot at us, but the team was young and ambitious. There was more to come from them.

We first had to sow the seeds of awareness in the group, then cultivate them. Things had worked for us in 2003, but I knew we needed to be different in 2004. If we could generate that awareness in the players, change would come.

I saw Cormac as a vehicle to drive that change. Peter had been captain and achieved what everyone wanted for him – to lift the Sam Maguire Cup. Now his career was nearing its end and we needed to prepare for that. We could start by developing new leaders. Cormac had always been an excellent captain for me. Maybe it seemed like I was stepping over a few people, but I didn't care. He was the man.

The only other person I considered for the captaincy was Brian Dooher, but Brian was already giving everything he had. I reckoned being captain could lift Cormac's game to new heights. Plus my promise to him before the 2000 All-Ireland under-21 semi-final was ringing in my mind. He would lift them all: minor, under-21 and Sam. I knew another All-Ireland was coming. I wanted his hands on that Cup. Like Stephen O'Neill says, why wait?

Before we convened for our first meeting of the year, I took Cormac aside to tell him the news. He was thrilled. Peter was also happy with the change. As it was, he was already planning to reduce his involvement through the year. Cormac would have all his support. So we split into our groups and formulated our aims for the coming season. Settling on two-in-a-row didn't require much time. Then, I announced the change in captaincy. Cormac rose to speak for the first time. The words were simple, and special. "I've got an All-Ireland medal at 23," he said. "I don't want to look back saying, did I only get one?"

The group was silent. It was an incredible statement of intent. These weren't the empty, idle words of a man saying what he thought captains should say. Cormac meant it. He was living that ambition. It was an invitation to greatness.

He drove us on. We swept through the early rounds of the league. We reached the McKenna Cup final and travelled to Ballybofey to take on Donegal. Over 12,000 people turned up, breaking the record for a McKenna Cup final. Before the game, Cormac led us out through a guard of honour formed by the Donegal players. The crowd came for a show. They witnessed something special.

We ripped through Donegal like a hurricane, leaving them in tatters. Brian McGuigan cracked a stunning goal, Mark Harte and Gerald Cavlan split 11 points between them. We led by 11 points at half-time and strolled home by 18 points. It finished

1-22 to 0-7. It was one of those games I have enshrined in my memory. It was a day when we simply clicked. Cormac collected his first trophy as senior captain. I watched and smiled, imagining bigger days that summer and into September. This was only the beginning for him.

Ten days later, it was suddenly over.

THE PHONE CALL CAME at 5.30 in the morning. Marian answered. Paudge Quinn, the local undertaker, was on the line. I knew from Marian that something serious had happened. When I heard it was a player, I thought one of them had been involved in an accident. When Paudge said that it was Cormac, that he had died at home, I couldn't believe it.

Of all the faces and names that flicked through my head in those terrible moments, Cormac was never in there. He lived life sensibly and well. He looked after himself meticulously. He was a fitness fanatic. He always did the right thing when it came to tending his body. To hear he had died in such simple, random circumstances, another young casualty from sudden cardiac death. There was no way to describe it. It was a total shock.

I rang Fr Gerard. More bad news, I said. He asked what was wrong. It's Cormac, I said. "He'll never get to lift the Sam Maguire." Saying his name suddenly made everything real. I broke down and cried.

I let the rest of the house sleep till nearer the morning. Then I started waking the children up. I went to Mark first. He couldn't believe it. "Not again," he said. Michaela was in pieces. Later on I told Matthew. He was devastated too. I contacted Michael in college in Belfast. He made for home immediately. We all felt numb.

Then the phone started ringing. Word had filtered out to the media. They all wanted a few words from me about Cormac. I obliged, but it all felt so hard. These were strangers calling at a time of profound grief. Over the next few days it felt like I was handed the responsibility of conveying the gravity of this tragedy to the general GAA public from a Tyrone perspective. I needed to be extremely sensitive to the family's needs too. I was in at the deep end, trying to keep my head above water. Every word had to be weighed and uttered with the utmost care.

Through all these trials, though, I felt God with me, providing guidance and help. Just like Paul McGirr's death seven years before, I didn't feel any detachment from God despite such an apparently senseless tragedy. It brought me closer to Him. There was no way I could have found the words and the will to continue through those days without that Spirit to guide me. People needed leadership. They needed strength. Hope. You had to reflect on how shocking this tragedy was for Cormac's family, but also immediately remember a wonderful life. That took us away from the darkness towards a new dawn.

Getting to that new place took time, though. The first night Cormac was waked at his home in Brantry, I walked down the laneway from the road to their house. Everything was silent and peaceful. I entered the house and saw him laid out in the coffin; such a powerful, vibrant presence in life now lying still.

The rest of the evening and the following few days blurred into each other. I can see our boys sitting in the house during the wake, their chairs lined up along the walls of the kitchen. I can see Dara Ó Cinnéide, Séamus Moynihan and Darragh Ó Sé sitting opposite them supping tea with Peter Canavan. Pat McEnaney, the referee, had collected them off a flight in Dublin airport and driven directly to Eglish. Sean Boylan was in the living-room, listening to Cormac's brother Donal tell the story of how he had found him in his bed in the middle of the night, struggling for air.

The Armagh team arrived in Eglish for the funeral and lined up to form a guard of honour with our team, his old friends from Queen's University and the Eglish club. It represented a huge mark of respect and was always something we appreciated as a group. This wasn't a piecemeal thing; this was dedication Armagh-style. They recognised the important things as footballers and as people. We will always be grateful for what they did that day.

Later that day we laid him down into the ground. Micheál Ó Muircheartaigh recited a poem by the grave. At the end, he hugged Cormac's father, Brendan. This experience left us feeling unlike any other tragedy we had encountered as a group. Paul McGirr's death had bound us together and propelled us to the heights we had reached as footballers, but this was different. Paul's death had brought us together as friends. This transformed us into a family. We had spent so much time together with Cormac over the previous seven years. There was a sense of connection between us all. We knew we would have to support each other and do what we could to help each other through.

It was going to take different kinds of leadership. We were lucky to have Fr Gerard with us again to offer a spiritual dimension and to draw on the many tragedies he had helped people process through the years. He brought stability and wisdom. He carried that sense of dignity he always has. These were things that could help us.

Beyond our own family, Cormac's death had a remarkable effect on the entire country in the space of those few days. This was the GAA as a living entity. The local community around Eglish tightened around the family. They ran buses to the top of McAnallens' laneway, ferrying thousands of people to the house over the space of a couple of days. Stewards marshalled the roads. People provided tea and sandwiches after the funeral. The GAA club opened up their facilities for use.

People made long journeys to be with the family and make that brief connection. It felt like Cormac's death had reminded people about the important things in life. By the age of 23, he had won everything Gaelic football could offer him. He had excelled as a student and found a happy job in St Catherine's College as a teacher. He was engaged to be married to Ashlene. So much had been packed into such a short life.

Now people asked themselves what they could do. Could they take a team in their local club? Maybe they could spend more time at home with their own family. They focused on the small efforts they could make to improve the world they lived in, just like Cormac did. In time his death would promote greater awareness around Sudden Adult Death Syndrome and the pressing need for access to defibrillators in public places and heart checks for young people. His death first drew the very best from people.

The Great Competitor, by Grantland Rice

Beyond the winning and the goal, beyond the glory
*   and the flame,*
He feels the flame within his soul, born of the spirit
*   of the game,*
And where the barriers may wait, built up by the
*   opposing Gods,*
He finds a thrill in bucking fate and riding down the
*   endless odds.*
Where others wither in the fire or fall below some
*   raw mishap,*
Where others lag behind or tire and break beneath
*   the handicap,*
He finds a new and deeper thrill to take him on an
*   uphill spin,*
Because the test is greater still, and something he can
*   revel in.*

There is never a day that I don't see him. There is never a day Cormac doesn't enter my thoughts. He and Paul McGirr reside in my daily prayers, their faces etched into my mind. They will never leave it.

When I think of Paul, I think of the wisecracks and his personality. With Cormac, it's different. I feel an energy inside me, the same energy he applied to everything he did. In five years I have visited his grave only once. I don't need to. He is in my mind, constantly there, probing and pushing me to be better. To attack every day like Anthony De Mello says. Cormac's application to everything was so complete it could blow your mind. Paul's death was the catalyst for everything that came for this generation of players. During that time, Cormac became the embodiment of the ethos we all created.

I still see him. A child, maybe 15 years old, in a circle of boys on the field in Eglish. He was about the fifth-best player on the under-16 team back then. Eglish sent him for minor trials with us a couple of years later; we still couldn't see the player Cormac would become over the next few years.

I reckoned he could be useful, but he was carrying some weight he would do well to shed. What he had, though, was determination. He was relentless. Once you instructed him on what you wanted him to do, he was tremendously effective. He wasn't the quickest in the world, but he was dogged. He coped with his limitations as a footballer, and exceeded everything anyone expected of him.

He was corner-back for his school team in 1996, but by 1997 he was already starting to improve. We settled him at centre-back with the minors. He was turning into a good reader of the game. He was losing the weight. We could tell he was a solid citizen. Perfect to hold the defence down.

In 1998 he went up another level, switched out to midfield as captain and assumed a whole new role within the team. He was lean now and developing into a wonderful athlete.

Players were looking to him. When they split into groups at a meeting after Paul died, they all wanted to be in Cormac's. It was his single-mindedness I liked. No task intimidated or worried him. If he received the odd knockback, he simply saw it as a chance to try again. I loved that.

He never said we couldn't do things any better. He was a man in constant evolution: testing, studying, learning, revising, reflecting, reviewing. He kept diaries of his performances in training and matches years before it ever became innovative.

He was a man for solutions. I always thought he listened with his eyes. If you were talking to him, his neck would be stretching out, making sure he was absorbing every syllable of information. His eyes were totally focused on you. If somebody ran between you while you spoke, he wouldn't even notice. It was total focus. Precise, intense focus.

He was always a good guy to bounce ideas against. He would never tell you what he thought you would want to hear. Back with the minors, I had installed a warm-up as part of our routine at a pitch along the way to the match. At a meeting one day, Cormac suggested that the warm-ups were taking too much energy out of us before a match. They weren't really doing anything for us. I thought about what he said, and dispensed with the whole idea. I have never done it since. There seems to no point to me in going out, tearing into a warm-up and coming off again before heading out to play. Cormac was right. A complete waste of energy.

As a player he was the epitome of John Wooden's mantra: things work out best for those who make the best of the way things work out. That was Cormac.

ONCE THE FUNERAL was over, life had to move on. We met as a group a few days later. Our approach this time was slightly different to how we dealt with losing Paul. We had been through this sadness before. Players had the basic coping skills, but we still needed to talk our way through this. Dr Seamus Cassidy again outlined the random nature of Cormac's death for us. We split into our groups to talk.

I was worried. We hadn't just lost an ordinary player. This was Cormac. For the first time, it crossed my mind that maybe this team mightn't survive this.

He was such a special influence on the whole team. It wasn't because he died that we were making this point either. He always lived to be the best he possibly could. He was an example to everyone. You didn't get leaders like Cormac at such a young age.

We weren't just losing a footballer. We were losing a reason to succeed. This would ask serious questions of all of us. If we failed, the result would be simple. Could this be the end of something special?

That's where we had to make a decision. Do we crumble, or do we use this to come back stronger? The key statement through that time came from Kevin Hughes. He had lost his brother and sister in car accidents and lived through the Paul McGirr tragedy. "This is bad," he said, "but life goes on." He had lost family and learned to keep living. It was a statement that allowed our boys to take the next step. It wasn't something you could find in any manual. Kevin had the bravery to say what we needed to hear, even if it hurt a little. It struck a deep chord with me. If Kevin Hughes can say that, why should the rest of us hold back?

We would move on, but never forget. I was spending a lot of time on the road, driving to appointments for work. My mind would drift back to Cormac. Sometimes Michaela might ring and ask how I was. I would always say "Okay," but she knew. The sadness was impossible to shake.

Myself and Marian would visit the McAnallens every month over the first few years. The conversations might start out at some point miles from football. Gradually, though, football would ease its way into the flow, and by the end we were reminiscing on Cormac, or discussing some pressing issue, wondering how Cormac might handle it. It was good for all of us.

It's easy to glorify people in death, and over the years Cormac has been rightly enshrined as an icon. But there was a human being in there too, with the flaws we all carry. He knew how to have fun. He wasn't a driven footballing machine 24 hours a day. On team holidays he might do his own thing some days, but he mucked in the same as everyone else.

There's a video at home of him after one of the under-21 finals, strutting up and down the aisle of the bus singing an old party song. His choice for the 2003 team CD – "Gold" by Spandau Ballet – drew more hoots of derision than any other. The only time I ever saw him under the weather was late into the night after the 1998 All-Ireland minor final. If ever there was a night to let himself go, though, that was the one.

We retired his jersey for the rest of the year and never used Cormac as a banner to march behind. Before every training session and match we would form a circle and take 30 seconds to remember him. We were moving on, but we weren't letting go. Cormac was always with us.

At the same time, though, we could never be sure if we were leaning on Cormac's death, or whether our season would unfold as it did anyway. Deep inside all of us, though, we knew we were being drained of fuel. We were already surviving as a team on adrenalin. We wondered if we had the energy to go all the way again. We spent an entire summer trying to figure that out.

◄○►

8 April 2009

I AM STANDING in front of a packed room in St Catherine's College, Armagh, the school where Cormac taught. There are students from the school and right across Armagh city of all creeds, colours and religions. The annual Cormac Leadership Lecture was inaugurated in 2005. The first four key speakers were Mary McAleese, Bertie Ahern, Adi Roche and Micheál Ó Muircheartaigh. This year, it's my turn.

I looked out into the audience and saw familiar faces. The McAnallens were there. My own family too. I thought of Cormac, put my faith in God, and the words flowed.

"A good leader should show appreciation of the achievements of his team members, praising their strengths," I said. "This will motivate them to strive for excellence. He should judge them on their efforts rather than perceived talent because without hard workers there cannot be finesse. Encourage people to leave their comfort zone and they will experience growth.

"Positive relationships must be built on mutual respect and a sincere, caring attitude. Seek solutions, not blame – even if blame is justified, it serves no constructive purpose. The art of good communication is vital. A good leader should learn to listen and listen to learn. He should become aware of the circumstances of his people in a bid to understand them better. Equally, he should ensure that they are aware of his expectations of them. Being open and truthful means that little issues can be addressed before they become major concerns. Furthermore, positive feedback endorses good practice.

"Focus on team success rather than personal glory. Much more can be accomplished if no one cares who gets the credit for it. Build for your team a feeling of oneness, of dependence upon one another and of strength to be derived from unity."

These were the principles I had learned over many years. It had taken Cormac barely 23 years to figure them out. When I spoke about the importance of selflessness, I recalled Cormac's willingness to switch to full-back in 2003. That sacrifice and application ultimately handed us an All-Ireland title, but also bequeathed us a legacy we have been able to build on ever since.

When I think of the efforts and the gifts Cormac left us, it reminds me of another piece of wisdom from John Wooden. "You cannot live a perfect day," he said, "without doing something for someone who will never be able to repay you."

Cormac left us a lifetime of them.

17

THE DISEASE OF ME

"When a successful organisation becomes infected with the Disease of Me, people who create 20 per cent of the results will begin believing they deserve 80 per cent of the rewards"

PAT RILEY

I CAME ACROSS PAT RILEY some time around 2003. I had heard of the LA Lakers and Magic Johnson, but not the man who created those teams. I had never followed basketball closely as a sport, but over the years I had found some marvellous parallels between the path I was following and that chosen by many basketball coaches.

John Wooden had always been a terrific influence. Same with Jerry Lynch These guys had achieved wonderful success as college coaches. Wooden, in particular, left a deep impression on me. His experience working with talented young players made him acutely aware of the link between good practice on court and off court. He sourced much of his value system from his rural upbringing in Indiana. He wrote once how his father gave him a piece of paper on the day of his graduation from grade school on which was written a creed for life. Wooden carried the piece of paper in his wallet for years until it turned into scraps.

Some of the lines reminded me of my upbringing: be true to yourself; make friendship a fine art; help others; pray for guidance; count and give thanks for your blessings every day. Others recalled new lessons I had been picking up ever since: make each day your masterpiece; drink deeply from good books; build a shelter against a rainy day. It was a design for life, and for coaching.

Riley is cut from a shinier, slicker cloth than Wooden, but his ideas about team building and approaching problems reside in the same ballpark. His book, *The Winner Within*, is filled with little nuggets I can identify with. He sees the links between the values we cherish in sport and how they can be applied to any sphere: business, social, personal. Like Wooden, he knows good people make good teams. None of it felt new to me. But knowing I wasn't alone in carrying these ideals reinforced my own convictions about what I was doing.

One chapter talks about dealing with success. People can work very hard to achieve something and then start believing they were the only reason why it happened. They can take on board the adulation that goes with that success. That can be difficult to deal with. We had different age groups and different personalities in our group. It only takes a few people to start indulging themselves to diminish your chances of making more progress. When you make a breakthrough like we did, how do you stretch yourself to reach for more? I couldn't just stop and say that's all there is. If you do that, that's all there will be.

In fact, a quotation at the very beginning of Riley's chapter on success pretty much summed up the challenge ahead for us all: "It takes a strong constitution to withstand repeated attacks of prosperity."

It's a virulent virus, though, and as that year went on, Riley's seven signs of the Disease of Me were starting to show up among certain elements of our group:

- *Inexperience in dealing with sudden success*
- *Chronic feelings of under-appreciation*
- *Paranoia over being cheated out of one's rightful share*
- *Resentment against the competence of partners*
- *Personal effort mustered solely to outshine a team-mate*
- *A leadership vacuum resulting from the formation of cliques and rivalries*
- *Feelings of frustration even when the team performs successfully*

Sometimes you don't notice these symptoms. I didn't think we were in any danger of contracting the virus. As 2004 took shape, though, it was clear something had changed.

Paddy Tally had been a terrific influence as trainer in 2003. His drills were cutting-edge. He identified with my fanatical devotion to training sessions, where the ball was king, and our relationship had blossomed.

The various roles in my management structure have always been clearly defined – the trainer trains the team, I pick it. Paddy seemed happy in that framework, but during the championship, I discovered he was talking to influential players outside of training sessions about certain team selections. That team selection falls to me. No one else. I stand and fall by those selections. Over the years I have always consulted Fr Gerard or Tony Donnelly, but the ultimate decision always lies with me. The team trainer never assumed the same position.

Paddy's role never prescribed any involvement in picking the team. He never had any say in those decisions. Now he was questioning them and our methods of play – how I was playing players and where I was positioning them.

I confronted Paddy. We decided to park the issue for the rest of the summer, but the relationship never felt the same. To me, it was a case of enduring that managerial structure for the rest of the year. As far as I was concerned, Paddy's time with us was over.

I didn't feel it would serve any purpose to change trainers in the middle of the championship, but the tension left a mark on our preparations. Paddy's quality as a coach was unquestioned, but I found myself taking a more direct, hands-on approach at training. I wasn't taking total charge but I became much more involved than I might have been in the past when Paddy ran the sessions from start to finish.

I grasped the nettle once the championship was over. I tried to contact Paddy in mid-September. I made two or three attempts to meet him in person. None of them suited him. As autumn loomed, I needed to get this sorted, so I finally broke the news on the phone.

Paddy was disappointed, perhaps taken aback. He should have realised the relationship wasn't the same as it was before. I knew I didn't feel the same way. I wasn't rude or hateful in breaking the news. Any management package needs to be tight. He was a young man. Maybe he didn't appreciate the full significance of his actions. I certainly did, and I couldn't live with that kind of uncertainty about my management team.

The players had enjoyed a good relationship with Paddy, and he had done a fine job for us in 2003, but they also knew enough about me to know that if I made a decision like this, I would have good reasons to stand over it. They knew Paddy for two years. Most of them had shared dressing-rooms with me over seven years. They appreciated I would never do these things lightly. Nobody needed to know the inside line on why it happened at the time. They just needed to know it was done.

I wasn't doing it to make some point about power. I was doing it for totally honourable reasons.

While that problem unfolded, we were busy trying to get back playing football. Even dealing with those challenges – how to reinvent ourselves after 2003, how to cope with success – didn't seem important to me any more. We had chased that All-Ireland with fervour, but now we had a new perspective on life to deal with. I used to think it was great to win an All-Ireland. The greatest feeling there can be. Then you think, is it that good? Is it that important? We always wanted to respect Cormac's memory by doing the best we could, and we managed some fine results that year, but putting a value on sport in 2004 was almost impossible. It saddened me to say that, but at the time I couldn't say anything else. It was hard to put the required energy, drive and enthusiasm into football.

I had high hopes for that group, and especially for Cormac. The third historic All-Ireland as captain had been within his reach. I had cherished this vision where I could walk up to Cormac one day and say: I told you so. I felt the most difficult legs of the trilogy had already been accomplished too. Like the day I stood in a hospital room with the McGirrs looking at their son lying on a bed still wearing his Tyrone kit, words couldn't capture the emotions churning through me at that time. Football didn't seem important in light of Cormac's death, but it was Cormac's death that could make it important again. Football was part of our healing process. It still is.

WE RETURNED TO FOOTBALL against Mayo. A memorial Mass was held in Ballintubber Abbey the night before, which highlighted the significance of the weekend. This was about playing again. Everybody wanted to see what life would be like for us after Cormac, which placed the spotlight on us too. We had to deal with that, as well as the feelings running through us as we stood out on the field.

We verbalised everything. Everyone would have their own feelings at that moment. That was okay. All we could do was our best. When we arrived in the dressing-room, there was a good luck card from the McAnallens on the table. That was important and hugely appreciated. They knew we had to move on. That day, as we stood out on the field and the national anthem played, the entire team and staff lined out in the shape of a figure three. He was still with us.

Then we went and hammered Mayo.

We kept moving forward through the spring and made a league semi-final against Galway. Everyone was still dealing with our loss, but nothing about our performances reflected that grief. The match against Galway was a classic example.

It was a game that bristled with intensity. We went 1-3 up inside the first few minutes. Ryan McMenamin cracked a shot off the crossbar. It was game over if we nailed that goal. We paid a heavy price.

The atmosphere along the side-line was as fraught as on the pitch. At one point I spotted Galway manager John O'Mahony in the linesman's ear. He was complaining about something Kevin Hughes had allegedly done. If they didn't see any incident, it wasn't my business or John's to be telling them. I had watched Padraic Joyce commit three or four offences that warranted yellow cards under the experimental rules in place for that league. I never said a word about it. But once John started complaining about one of my players, I made my feelings known. Next thing I knew I was involved in a face-off. It was more of a confrontation than I would ever want to be involved in again.

The game crackled along. We were still a point up with a minute to go when Mark Harte lobbed a free over the bar. Next thing the Galway players are around the referee. He blows his whistle, deems Mark had taken too many steps before kicking the ball and cancels the point. Galway went downfield and earned a free of their own. Padraic Joyce took just as many steps and put the ball over. John O'Mahony was punching the air, celebrating in our faces. Draw. We were disgusted.

Afterwards, I made my points about Padraic Joyce and the Galway players surrounding the referee to the waiting media. John launched an impassioned defence of Joyce in response. I could see what was happening. This was a useful opportunity for him to forge a better relationship with Joyce. That was fine. I didn't let his comments get to me. Getting involved was probably an error on my part anyway. I felt I was protecting Kevin Hughes, but did it matter? I was distracting myself from the game by getting involved. I was frustrated. Stephen O'Neill had been sent off three times in two months during that league. It was the inconsistency of the decision-making and the kind of player getting sent off that was bugging me. Stephen O'Neill doesn't get involved in red card type play. It was all irritating me.

Maybe a lot of conflicting emotions were still in my system after Cormac's death too. This was a league final slipping away. Winning that match would have been hugely significant. Instead we had to traipse down to Salthill for a replay.

We battled hard and helped turn the game into another classic. In the end, though, Galway got through. After the match I visited the Galway dressing-room. I congratulated them, and made the point that my comments weren't necessarily directed in a personal way at Padraic Joyce, but at the rules that prevailed at the time. It was the inconsistent decision-making I was attacking, not Joyce. I have met John O'Mahony many times since, and the tension created in those few weeks has long since evaporated. We had Derry in the championship in a fortnight. Time to move on.

ONE OF THE INNOVATIONS I wanted to carry into 2004 was Bart McEnroe. Bart had played a fantastic role in helping me work through the psychological challenge of getting the team ready for the previous year's All-Ireland final. I wanted to integrate him more deeply into the scene. I wanted the players to have direct access to him. I knew what he had done for me. He could do the same for them.

His view was that, as players, they needed to develop an observing self, allowing them to step back and solve problems more creatively and objectively. When dealing with the players, Bart's approach was direct and unflinching. He asked questions about their emotional state. How were they feeling? How was training? Their form? The idea of the barrage of questions was to dig deep to find ways of improving their outlook on the game, to get them thinking more deeply about their role and how they could improve.

This approach to preparing players' minds and enhancing their confidence made sense to me, but Bart's approach didn't seem to be hitting the right notes with them. He tried to open players up using the sort of direct questioning that fazed some, annoyed others and didn't knock a feather from another few. Over time, though, it became clear the players felt they were under constant observation. They worried that every single move they made was being scrutinised. We were overanalysing. Even a few people chatting in the dressing-room were concerned they were being assessed. It came to a head at a weekend away, when the players asked for Bart's influence to be scaled back.

It was a hard call for me to make. Bart had been good for me, but this formula simply wasn't working for the group. I still keep in touch with him and have always valued the insights he has helped me find. Just because it didn't work for the group didn't mean they haven't indirectly fed off Bart's knowledge over the years.

The week before we played Derry, I didn't feel Kevin Hughes's head was in the right place either. With Owen Mulligan, Peter Canavan, Gerald Cavlan and Stephen O'Neill all missing through injury, we would need Kevin's presence, but he didn't seem focused in. I planned to start him against Derry but when I announced the team, his name was missing. I wanted to inflict the feeling of being denied a starting place without actually being left off. It's an experiment that's worth running sometimes. Getting that second chance can really act like a surge of energy for some players.

Out in the public domain, some symptoms of the Disease of Me were getting an airing. Some players were still partying, apparently. The team was on edge. I paid little heed to any of it. If we're in the business of empowering our players, then their behaviour off the field isn't something I need to be investigating. It's like Owen Mulligan running the London Marathon this year just before the start of the championship. I wasn't thrilled about it, but it was something Mugsy wanted to do, and ultimately it didn't impinge on his form. You simply can't have a team of clones. If you get distracted trying to force everyone into the same shaped holes, you'll miss out on getting the best from them. That's the ultimate goal.

If results were any guide for the condition of our panel, the Derry match provided some good news. Derry have always been our fiercest rivals but we drew their sting early this time. Kevin Hughes responded well to the shock of losing his place to score a goal. We ran out winners by 14 points. We beat Fermanagh by four points in a battle, but we were happy to be getting by. With so many players missing from our attack, it was a time for others to step forward. Few did as much as Mark Harte.

It had never been easy for Mark being his father's son. It always seemed Mark's errors were accentuated by the public, while the great things he did went unnoticed. In a league match against Mayo in 2005, the abuse was particularly shrill. He was recovering that day from a groin operation and wasn't 100 per cent. I have to take some of the blame for starting Mark before he was fully recovered. These people don't take any notice of such detail. But I respect their ignorance.

Mark's record has always stood up well to scrutiny. He would end 2004 as our top scorer. He was also top scorer as a minor in 1997 and an under-21 in 2000. He wasn't big, but he had a huge amount of skill and was central to some of the key moments in this team's history. When Antrim went seven points ahead in the 1997 Ulster final, Mark stood up, scored 1-7 and gave a man-of-the-match performance.

Would Tyrone be enjoying this current era if Mark hadn't kicked the equalising score from a crazy angle in the All-Ireland minor semi-final against Kerry that year? Can we forget the 0-12 he scored in the replay?

In 2004 he was on top of his game. He created Kevin Hughes's goal against Derry and played a key role in every match. It just seemed typical that in the year Mark hit top form, Tyrone didn't hit the heights we had enjoyed in 2003.

We played Donegal in the Ulster semi-final. We had no reason to believe we couldn't get past them, too. When we didn't, the result left a mark. In retrospect, Donegal were in the perfect place. They had the memory of a serious drubbing in the McKenna Cup final. We knew they weren't that poor, but it was going to be hard to steel the players against some strain of complacency. The conditions in Clones were bad. Owen Mulligan got involved with one of the Donegal players, who ended up being sent off. It did us more harm than good. Colm McFadden got a goal for Donegal and we simply faded out of the game. We lost by five points. Hateful stuff.

We regrouped the following week for a meeting. Peter Canavan set the tone again. We weren't champions any more, he said. We couldn't keep living on past glories. We couldn't feed off the past if we wanted to nourish the future. Donegal had taken the glory. Suddenly we were one-hit-wonders. We could live the rest of our lives like this, or we could change the script. We had a second chance. If we wanted, we could take it. That was our starting point.

The training over the next few weeks had a savage intensity. I'm never sure about the value of imposing that approach in training as a reaction to defeat, but this energy was coming from the players. Recovering from a loss is about finding ways to do things better, which doesn't always equate to doing more work. It's about deciding what you need to do and identifying the right things that will generate the correct frame of mind for your players.

Players wanted more aggression in the games, more intensity in the drills. It left Brian Dooher with a black eye one night and Enda McGinley with a cracked skull, but we approached our first qualifier against Down in equally ruthless form.

It was a massive game for us. The same old questions that tormented me in 2003 were raised again before the game. Tyrone had no full-back. We had no midfield. Down echoed all those concerns by pelting our defence with high balls all day. They completely overplayed the high ball. Ryan McMenamin went back, lodged himself in front of our full-back line and gathered ball without ever having to look for it. Mark Harte kicked four points from play and we ran away from them in the end.

Winning was a huge result. A lot of questions needed to be answered, for the public and ourselves. The last few months had affected our confidence. We needed to quell the idea that we might never again be successful. This was a huge match, and a major win.

We continued to answer those questions over the following few weeks. We beat Galway and hammered Laois to make the All-Ireland quarter-finals. The mood had improved immeasurably. We were back at the stage we would have reached if we had won the Ulster title. It felt like we were breaking even. We were a step away from an All-Ireland semi-final. When Fermanagh beat Armagh before we played Mayo, that lightened our mood even more. Suddenly the All-Ireland semi-final seemed very winnable. That attitude made us soft, too.

Injuries hurt us against Mayo as well. Brian McGuigan wasn't there. Peter Canavan could only come on towards the end. At one stage the sun caught Conor Gormley's eyes, he was hit in the face by the ball and had to come off. On top of that, Mayo were having an incredible day.

Over the course of that game, Mayo had 22 scoring attempts. They hit just four wides. Two of those wides came from their first two shots as well. We hit the post four times. One of those shots hopped off one post before hitting the other, and still didn't go over.

Mayo were prolific. Players who never knew where the goals were before that day were hitting points. We were three points down after half time before Stephen O'Neill nailed a brilliant goal. I thought we might kick on. Instead we looked drained. Mayo went on to win by four points. Sickening.

We were devastated. We had plumbed unimaginable depths and built ourselves back up. To let all that work slip without putting up the kind of fight we expected to have within ourselves was heartbreaking.

Despite that disappointment, though, part of me was glad to let the year go. Everyone in Tyrone understood that our season hadn't been a bad effort in the circumstances, but we always aspired to more. It was murder to watch that final between Mayo and Kerry. You wondered where Mayo's form had gone. Kerry walked through them. I believed it would have been a far better final if we had made it. I'm not sure whether we had the mental energy to actually win the All-Ireland, but we could have kept Kerry more honest. As it was, we had to absorb the year, and move on.

EVERYTHING WAS CHANGING. Having taken a break from teaching after the 2003 All-Ireland final, I had started a new job with

Martin Shortt Auctioneers. My job was essentially to establish new contacts for Martin's business. If someone was looking to buy land or houses, I acted as a facilitator. I developed contacts all over the country. It was the height of the housing boom and I lived a life on the road.

Work took me everywhere: Tipperary, Wicklow, Waterford, Galway, Mayo, Sligo, Longford, Meath, Cavan. All over the north. I never knew where the week might take me, but I loved the road and I enjoyed the work.

Life was taking on a different complexion. After winning the All-Ireland in 2003, people looked at you differently. They were intrigued by the mystique surrounding the winning of your first All-Ireland. People wanted to hear the secrets. The business world was opening up to me. Companies saw connections between building good teams in sport and business. I started getting invitations to speak at seminars and conferences. In time, my experiences with the grief process through Cormac and Paul McGirr would open other doors to share knowledge.

That recognition was even filtering down to the children. Some of it was good. Some was bad. That summer Michaela was invited to enter the Ulster Rose of Tralee competition. She asked myself and Marian about it. As long as she entered to enjoy the experience without any great worries about the outcome, how bad could it be?

We headed to the function in Cavan. The interview included a few questions about me. At the end of the night, Michaela was announced the winner. Not everyone was delighted for her. At one stage a woman passed our table. "You worked that out well," she said to me. God help her wit, I thought. We were only there to support Michaela.

A tabloid newspaper picked up on the story the following week. Plenty of headlines about a Thorny Rose. All very imaginative. They rang looking for a comment. We weren't entertaining any of that. We headed to Tralee for the Rose competition proper and enjoyed a wonderful week. The Kerry people were wonderful. Michaela made some enduring friendships among the Roses, and a small summer diversion managed to lift us out of the year's gloom for a while.

Back home, I had work to do. Once I had severed my relationship with Paddy Tally, I needed to restock my backroom team. It was finally time to get Tony Donnelly in.

Even before he became selector, I always bounced ideas off Tony. Sometimes I would meet him in the corridors outside our dressing-room at half-time during a game, or have a quick chat at the wire. I had wanted him alongside myself and Fr Gerard from the beginning. Now that time had passed and the heat had evaporated from my appointment, it was easier for Tony to climb aboard.

I was delighted. Tony brought something special to the group. If the players saw me as the boss, Tony's gregarious personality made him more accessible to some players. He was the kind of fella who knew Brian McGuigan hated vegetables and made sure the waitress piled the greens onto his plate when he left it unattended for a minute at a meal on the way back from the 2005 All-Ireland final. Gavin Devlin nearly fainted when he saw Tony take a drink one night: because he was a friend of mine, he had assumed Tony was a pioneer too.

Tony also brought a unique brain for football. When he coached Augher back in the early eighties, their resources were tight. He specialised in shifting his team about to find the best mix for any given match. He could read the opposition and work out where his own team could hurt them. He believed in making teams flexible, just like I did. He believed in the idea of total football and creating total players with the capacity to adapt to any circumstance. This was the road we were on now. The team needed a change of tactics and style. It needed to live in a different mood. It needed some light after so much darkness. Tony helped bring that.

Next job was finding a new team trainer. Tony had the man. Fergal McCann had worked with Tony in Augher and taken over Tyholland in Monaghan in 2004. He hadn't much experience at the highest level, but Tony seemed sure about him. That was good enough for me.

We met at Tony's house. Fergal brought a file with him containing a record of every training session he had conducted over the previous 12 months. Every session was written out: his objectives for each session, how the session would unfold. Every one was numbered, dated and laminated. It was dedication to detail of the highest order. He seemed delighted to be even considered for the role. I knew if Tony had worked with him, he would do things well. I also knew if he got on well with Tony, chances were he would click with me. The coming year was already looking different.

Then, we were knocked back again. Brian McGuigan wanted to travel. His girlfriend was heading away along with another pair of friends. It seemed the ideal time for him. I was hugely disappointed.

At least Brian mentioned he could be back for the 2005 championship. That wasn't the case with Kevin Hughes. He had committed himself to 12 months away. Next stop New Zealand. I was worried about Kevin. If he took a year out of football now, I didn't know if he could come back after a year at the same level. It takes at least another year to regain that form. I impressed that on him when we spoke, but he was determined to go.

It was devastating. I searched for the positives but it was hard. I thought we would be building on our success, not crumbling because of it. You felt this whole package was falling apart. It was happening, and there seemed nothing you could do about it. I couldn't force players to stay if they wanted something else from life.

I continued to search for hope. To live and work in the same environment as 2004 wasn't a runner. I wouldn't want to be there. That had changed. We started trialling players in autumn 2004. Our policy has always been to gradually include more established players as the trials progress, eventually ending up with the handful of triallists mixed in with the main team. Fergal and Tony were there throughout. That helped blend them in. Players grew familiar with Fergal's warm-ups and his style of training. I liked what he was doing. I loved having Tony around again. 2005 was ahead.

It was time to leave the gloom behind.

18

MIRACLE MOMENTS

"Twelve months ago, pundits were proclaiming the death of football as we knew it. We are delighted that it took a Kerry team to restore the pride in Gaelic football. The return to a free-flowing game from the packed defence ·type game is welcomed by the thousands of supporters that travel to our games."

SEAN WALSH, *Kerry County Board chairman,*
7 *December 2004*

KERRY WON THE ALL-IRELAND final that year without breaking sweat, enjoyed their win and the arrows kept flying in our direction. Mikey Sheehy had always been an icon to me during the seventies as the archetypal classy corner-forward. Now he was describing my teams as negative. Sean Walsh was claiming Kerry had saved football from the northern hordes. I thought it was disingenuous to say the least. I remembered Sean calling for rule changes after we beat Kerry in 2003 as well. It was tantamount to saying "let's change rules because we're not winning".

As for saving football as a spectacle, the 2004 All-Ireland final was over after 12 minutes. Why would people come to watch matches like that? That final was a complete disappointment.

Football needs Kerry, but it needs Tyrone too. It thrives on variety and conflicting styles. It's not good simply to react to statements like that. You have to be proactive. I wouldn't be driven to prove people like Sean Walsh wrong, but I took those comments on board.

That winter I sat beside Jack O'Connor at the All Stars banquet. He told me our performance in the first half of the 2003 semi-final was among the best 30 minutes of football he had ever seen. I was glad someone acknowledged we had to have played some decent football to score nine points against Kerry in the first half. Turns out he had read my book, *Kicking Down Heaven's Door*, charting Tyrone's journey through the 2003 season as well. We had more in common than Sean Walsh might have imagined.

While Sean Walsh and Mikey Sheehy might have considered our approach to the game as some kind of threat, the coming year was about to justify every football principle I believed in. By the time we reached September, Tyrone had played the same number of matches it took Kerry to win two All-Irelands and three Munster titles back in the seventies.

We would win an All-Ireland in ten games, something no team has ever done. Two of those games would be classed among the greatest seen this decade. Owen Mulligan would hit one of the great goals Croke Park has ever witnessed. The popularity of our rivalry with Armagh would bring the Ulster final out of Clones and down to Croke Park.

We would meet ferocity against Cavan and tame them. We would face adversity against Armagh and overcome it. We would survive a shoot-out against Dublin. We would face Kerry on their terms fuelled by a confidence and belief never before carried by a Tyrone team in Croke Park. It was a summer filled with landmarks and defining moments. After so much tragedy in 2004, this year would colour the team's history a different shade. But like so many successes, it was built on the smallest quirks, the slightest edges that went in our favour. We played over 700 minutes of football to win an All-Ireland. Like Wayne Dyer once wrote: miracles come in moments. Four of those paved the way for the rest.

1. The Steal

IT STARTED IN a sopping wet dressing-room in Portlaoise. We stood in our circle in the half light, soaking. The mood was foul. Wexford had just beaten us in the league semi-final. This was unthinkable stuff. What was this match saying about us? We had been outfought. We were missing players. That wasn't relevant. We were flat. Why? Our circle has never accepted anything less than complete honesty. We would face the hardest truths here.

I spoke first. There were two ways we could go, I said. We could fade away and confirm what many people assumed would happen to us: win one All-Ireland and dine out on it for the rest of our lives. Or we could do something different. Results don't tell lies, I said. We had been beaten by Wexford. We had failed to make a league final. We needed to look at ourselves. Were we doing all we could?

Some players threw out a few ideas about our training methods. Fergal McCann had settled into his new role nicely from the beginning of the year, and as the discussion went on, it became clear the players realised the problems they were seeing at training had nothing to do with Fergal.

It was them.

Rather than looking out, we looked in and found some answers. Some players weren't fully adhering to their personal fitness programmes. The drills at training were fine, but the players needed to inject greater urgency into their work. I knew I needed to be more vocal. It wasn't about berating them, but encouraging them to do things better. It wasn't about rewriting our script, just improving the delivery.

We started a forward line against Wexford without Enda McGinley, Stephen O'Neill, Brian McGuigan, Brian Dooher, Peter Canavan or Owen Mulligan. We were recycling backs into forwards as we went along, but the excuses needed to stop. If we had applied ourselves better, missing all those forwards wouldn't have mattered. Were we still leaning on last year? If we truly wanted to leave 2004 behind, we had to stop creating escape hatches for ourselves. We also had to learn to drop this baggage. Life had been hard on us, but it was still in our hands to make our situation better. "Remember, boys," I said, "the darkest hour comes before the dawn."

The circle broke after ten minutes with our minds cleared.

A few days later Peter Canavan came back to training. With an ankle injury still troubling him, we were entering the last stages of Peter's career. I didn't think about getting Peter right for 70 minutes' football any more. It was about getting Peter in there for the right minutes.

After losing to Wexford, his return was a major moment, but he had questions for the group, too. At the beginning of the year he had been quoted in the papers about the players' reaction to defeat in 2004. They hadn't hurt enough, he said. Cormac's death had played a role in the team's decline, but he felt other cracks had started to show. I could see what he meant, but I couldn't be as definitive as Peter about the reasons for our failure in 2004.

It hadn't been a normal situation. With all the grief and emotional turmoil churning through our collective system, it was impossible for me to separate the impact that tragedy had on our form. Maybe that was being easy on the players, but I felt 2004 had assumed a life of its own. Having escaped that, we needed to create a new future for ourselves, starting after the Wexford game. Peter had asked those searching questions in January. The players had to answer them now.

Alongside the panel's renewed sense of determination, Peter's return to the panel was a huge moment. That spring he decided to opt out of the league and get some games with Errigal Ciarán. The rest of the country saw this as the final resting place for his career. They wondered about our relationship. Was I getting on all right with Peter? Had there been a personality clash? All the usual stuff.

I always knew I'd have him back for the championship. His retirement might have been coming down the line, but we were preparing ourselves and the team for life without him all the time. From a position where Tyrone once had a total dependency on Peter, we now had a good team built around him. It was a perfect situation that year: we still had Peter, but the team was also developing without him. People were learning to take up the responsibilities left by Peter, but we always had him in reserve if we needed him.

Our first championship match against Down was a classic example. The mood at training had improved immeasurably since the Wexford game. We knew we could beat Down in Omagh, but as the rain fell we got mired in a battle.

The game was level with 20 minutes left. I had hoped we could get through the game without using Peter, but we needed him. I looked back to Tony in the stand. Without saying a word, we both knew it was time.

Peter's impact was immediate. As a Down defender came out of defence, Peter anticipated his pass and managed to half-intercept it. He scrambled to get the ball, shook off a few defenders and managed to slip a pass to Stephen O'Neill, who linked with Martin Penrose. Martin was through on goal and slotted his shot past the keeper.

The crowd lifted. Peter took control. He played Stephen O'Neill through for a point. Then he set up Sean Cavanagh for another. He clipped a point for himself on the run. In eight minutes, Peter had put us out of sight and we eased home by seven points. It was magical stuff. The summer would offer us more vivid memories on bigger days as we went along, but the sight of Canavan sniping at a defender and stealing the ball has stayed with me. It was a crucial moment.

The living didn't get any easier in the Ulster semi-final against Cavan. Their approach was straightforward and brutal. They picked a team to stop us. They targeted Sean Cavanagh ruthlessly, and pulled every stroke in the book to knock him out of his stride. He was pulled and dragged, kicked and spat on. We didn't react well. Sean was distracted and we couldn't find our usual rhythm. We were ahead entering injury-time, but even that dragged on for eight minutes. In the end Cavan won a highly dubious free and earned the draw.

We needed to be different for the replay. We also knew we finally had some serious cards to play. Peter would start his first match in two years. Brian McGuigan had returned from Australia and was ready. Brian Dooher was fit again, too. We sat on the field in Clogher one night before the replay and talked out what had happened the previous Sunday. Cavan had made the pitch very small for us, Tony said. Dooher had a slightly different take, which reflected the way we needed to impose ourselves the following week. "Tony," he said, "we made the field very small for ourselves."

We addressed Cavan's tactics during the week, but the players knew themselves. They needed to rise above the dogfight. The referee wasn't going to save them. Playing our own game would.

We caught fire that day. We hit three goals in the first 15 minutes to knock the wind from them and didn't look back after that. We had made the Ulster final. The lessons from Portlaoise had been learned and applied.

Armagh had marched through the other side of the draw. Another showdown. Interest was so high that the Ulster final was moved to Croke Park. This was where our rivalry had brought us. For years Tyrone and Armagh had battled away in the Ulster championship away from view. Now the entire nation was watching.

Sometimes over the years people have wondered what Armagh might have won if Tyrone hadn't been around. Would Tyrone have dominated Ulster if Armagh hadn't been there? I prefer to think neither of us would have reached this peak without each other.

But there was room for only one at the top.

WHEN WE LOOKED at Armagh, we didn't find many alterations in style and content from the team we beat in the 2003 All-Ireland final. They had blown Wexford away in the league final on a dry day. Even though Wexford had beaten us, I could see that result coming if Armagh got the right conditions.

Although Armagh looked much the same, I felt we had changed as a team since 2003. We had confidence now. We were much more relaxed. All that translated into a much greater fluency in our play. The feeling at that stage in 2005 reminded me of coaching the minors and under-21s. The Cavan game was a release. We were playing with greater flair and abandon than we had for a long time. We weren't getting uptight about the opposition or overcomplicating our approach. Everyone was comfortable with our system. We were playing with an assurance that the pressure in 2003 didn't allow us.

We had mental barriers to break down in 2003 when we met Kerry and Armagh. Not now. We didn't buy into the mythology that Armagh were a physically superior team. We believed we could handle them. Bottom line: Tyrone expected to beat Armagh.

And we should have. Our approach was perfect. We always felt our legs were younger and fresher than Armagh's, and that's where we could hurt them. It was our energy and pace against

MIRACLE MOMENT: I'm not sure if Peter Canavan ever pointed a more crucial free for Tyrone. This finally beat Armagh, and sent us to the 2005 All-Ireland final.

(Photo © David Maher/Sportsfile)

THREE WISE MEN: Two great captains, Brian Dooher and Peter Canavan, share their wisdom with me before the 2005 All-Ireland final. Behind them, Gavin Devlin has already given so much to the weekend, and to our team for years before that.

(Photo © Kenny Curran)

NOT AN INCH: Conor Gormley challenges Kerry's Declan O'Sullivan during the 2005 All-Ireland final. Kerry expected a war that day, but we had other ideas.

(Photo © Jim Dunne)

FOR CORMAC: Looking to the heavens with Sam after the 2005 final.
One was never enough for us, or for Cormac. *(Photo © Jim Dunne)*

VISITING PARADISE: One sporting passion meets another as myself and Brian Dooher
bring Sam Maguire on to Celtic Park in autumn 2005. *(Photo © Kenny Curran)*

With my nephew and managing director of Carton House, Conor Mallaghan. Many years ago we started our All-Ireland weekends with his mum and dad, Mary and Lee. Now, we still avail of their hospitality on the outskirts of the capital when we bring the team to town.

FORGOTTEN TITLE: Sean Cavanagh and Brian Dooher with the Anglo-Celt Cup after the 2007 victory over Monaghan. It didn't feel like cause for huge celebration then. After defeat to Meath in the All-Ireland quarter-final, it was almost totally forgotten.

(Photo © Jim Dunne)

THE FAMILY HARTE: At Mark's wedding in March 2007. From left, Michaela, myself, Mark, his wife Sinead, Michael, Marian and Matthew.

(Photo © Cormac McAleer)

STEVIE'S BACK: Stephen O'Neill was an incredible trump card to be able to play during the 2008 All-Ireland final. *(Photo © Kenny Curran)*

KERRY DENIED: People say Declan O'Sullivan missed a golden chance for Kerry to win the All-Ireland. Not me. Packie McConnell saved it. *(Photo © Brendan Moran/Sportsfile)*

THE PEAK: I lift the Sam Maguire Cup after the 2008 All-Ireland final, as Tony and Fergal look on. These are moments I could never have dreamt of.

(Photo © Kenny Curran)

THREE AMIGOS: Tony Donnelly and Fergal McCann have been key components in our success since the start of 2005, and great friends too. *(Photo © Kenny Curran)*

THE SPECIAL ONE: I'm surrounded by a fantastic backroom team, but as Jose Mourinho might say, there's only one Special One: our kitman Mickey Moynagh. *(Photo © Kenny Curran)*

LOSING OUR WAY: Stephen O'Neill struggles to hang onto the ball and his jersey against Cork's Anthony Lynch in the 2009 All-Ireland semi-final. We weren't helped by the referee, but Cork also played with an intensity we couldn't match.

(Photo © Jim Dunne)

Armagh's power and strength. It's the kind of contrast Sean Walsh mightn't like, but it makes for compelling matches.

We ran at them and avoided getting cornered by their swamping defence. We managed to isolate our forwards against their defenders and dominated the match. Stephen O'Neill was flying and took Francie Bellew for 0-10. At one point in the game Stevie kicked a point before shipping a heavy knock. He hit the ground and bounced straight back up. That was our mood during that game. Not one step back.

We were four points up and in good nick as the game entered the last few minutes. Then the sucker punch. High ball into the full-back line, Steven McDonnell juggled it around his neck and managed to slip the ball past Packie McConnell. Then Paul McGrane won a kickout and charged through the middle. Not good. He kicked his point and the game ended level.

Little scraps of luck went their way too. Oisin definitely scooped the ball off the ground for their first goal. Brian McGuigan got creased by Kieran McGeeney near the end but we didn't get the free. Then Mark Harte managed to hustle Paul Hearty over the line but we weren't awarded a 45. We had been in complete control and let it slip at the crucial time. We were disappointed, but we weren't damaged. This game was ours to take.

The replay simply defied all logic. Midway through the second half, Armagh were hanging on. We were four points up. Time for the crack troops. We had planned to bring Peter Canavan on first, then Owen Mulligan. Martin Penrose would make way for Peter, but just before he was due to come off he put a goal chance over the bar. Peter turned to us and suggested we hold off a few minutes. If we took Martin off now it might look like the miss was the reason for his withdrawal. We decided to wait. In the end, we sent Owen and Peter in together.

I could imagine the impact on Armagh, already struggling to stay in the game only to see Canavan and Mulligan running on, fresh and eager to play. As it turned out, I don't think Peter even got his hands on the ball before he was back on the bench again. Inside of a minute, a mêlée broke out. Peter was somewhere in the mix before he was yanked out by the jersey. Next thing, the referee flashes a red card. At Peter. I was stunned. Whoever was causing the trouble, it certainly wasn't Peter.

That was bad. Then it got worse. Stephen O'Neill was blown for a foul. The referee shows him a yellow card, followed by a red. I didn't realise it until after the game, but Stevie had never been shown an initial yellow card. Suddenly we had lost our two best forwards and were down to 13 men.

The game was spun on its head. Armagh charged on. We tried to regroup. We didn't score again. They hit six points and won by two. We had lost purely because of two appalling errors by the referee. Both cases were rescinded on appeal, but it was no consolation to us.

Armagh might feel they won that Ulster title fairly over two games. To me, it's a dubious one. There's a strong case to suggest we would have won that title if Peter and Stevie had stayed on the field. History will always say we lost and we have to accept that, but it hurt our players a lot. It wasn't the kind of hurt that breaks your spirit, but the kind that makes men rage. I knew we could recycle that into fuel for the rest of the year. And we knew we'd see Armagh again.

2. The Save

WE HAD ANOTHER PROBLEM. In the fallout from the mêlée that saw Peter Canavan sent off, the GAA's disciplinary committees decided to revisit another incident involving Ryan McMenamin and John McEntee. Ryan had landed with his knees on McEntee's chest. The referee had given a yellow card at the time, but on review it was upgraded to a red card. Although what Ryan did wasn't pretty, I felt the GAA were wrong to single him out. If Ryan had received a red card at the time, we would have to accept that, but much like the incidents during the league this spring, it seemed a dreadfully arbitrary way to apportion justice. If we revisit that incident, why not others in the game? We had to do what we could.

The appeals dragged on. We were due to meet Monaghan in the qualifiers but Ryan missed the game. Meanwhile the Armagh players who had been picked out of the video for further scrutiny along with Ryan had their cases heard, been cleared and were back to face Laois in the All-Ireland quarter-final. Crazy stuff.

This wasn't about condoning what Ryan did, but about the inconsistencies in the GAA's disciplinary procedures. People say I shouldn't get involved in this stuff, but I feel it's essential. When committees act poorly, they need to be confronted by their errors and live with the consequences. As it turned out, the Disputes Resolution Authority, the GAA's final appeals body, ruled in our favour. The committee had been shown to be wrong in revisiting those incidents. People might still feel that we exploited loopholes in the system, but surely there should be a system where the rules are watertight? This case was poorly handled by the GAA. Indeed, as the DRA's decision reflects, it should never have been brought in the first place.

I do what I think is right in these situations, and supporting my players is important. There are times when they step over the line, and we let them know when they do, but that shared loyalty to each other is useful when there are other battles to be won. It might look wrong in some people's eyes, but that's neither here nor there.

While we dragged our case through the appeals process, we tried to get our season back together. It almost looked a lost cause before our qualifier against Monaghan was even warm. Tommy Freeman was on fire that day, and Monaghan raced into a five-point lead. We needed to get a foothold in the game. Rory Woods got through our defence, looking for a goal. He slid his shot along the ground, but Packie McConnell got his fingers to the ball. The game was still within our grasp at 1-4 to 0-2. If that ball had slipped past Packie, we were finished. Instead, Packie saved our season.

We started to find our way into the game. Conor Gormley went to full-back and settled things down. Stephen O'Neill was tearing the Monaghan defence to pieces. Peter Canavan came in at half-time and we eventually pulled away. We were back in the All-Ireland quarter-final against Dublin. Back where we would have been if we had beaten Armagh. That pain was easing a little.

Although the matches were starting to pile up, I never doubted our ability to make progress that year. The vibe around the players was good. The volume of matches was starting to test Fergal's training schedule, but everything was holding up well. It was about recovery sessions during the week now. We shortened our training sessions and concentrated on more intense bursts of activity.

We spliced that with some tactical work and found a rhythm that suited us. Tony had his niche, too. While I concentrated on recycling the video analysis into useful pointers for the team and setting the tone before the players hit the field, Tony provided the tactical breakdown for the players.

The day we played Dublin, we needed all that. And more.

Dublin hit us where it really hurt that day. For years Gavin Devlin had been the key man in our system, but the Dubs were targeting him now. They put Alan Brogan on him. Gavin let Brogan wander. Then Brogan started doing damage. He needed marking, and proceeded to take Horse on a tour of the field. The only gap in Gavin's game was his lack of pace. Once he left the confines of defence, he was in trouble.

Dublin had been chipping away all day, but the killer score came before half-time. We allowed them 13 passes to set up a chance for Jason Sherlock. Packie saved the first shot well, but Tomás Quinn stuck the rebound in the net. The Dubs were five up. The Hill was getting noisier. We had to make changes.

Taking Gavin Devlin off felt like kicking out the foundation stone on a building, but we had no choice. Joe McMahon was introduced to centre-field to try and quell Ciaran Whelan. Philip Jordan went into the full-back line to allow Ryan McMenamin to attack Dublin from wing-back. Conor Gormley took over on Brogan. Owen Mulligan came on in attack and Enda McGinley went to midfield. It was another docket of gambles that could have bankrupted us for the year.

The pay-out was beyond anything we could have expected.

3. The Goal

IT HAD BEEN a battle with Owen Mulligan all year. He wasn't happy. He loves being in the thick of the action, but his form was poor. Nothing was running for him. He had lost interest, and wasn't helping himself either. He was missing training sessions. He wasn't calling to explain his absence. He was picking up niggling injuries and indulging them. We had given him plenty of starts in the league and early on the championship, but he was on the bench now. He wasn't in the groove, and was looking for a way out.

One evening in Carton House before a match he sat down with myself and Tony, and levelled with us. People in his club were asking questions. Why train with Tyrone to sit on the bench? They wanted him to leave us and concentrate on his club football. It seemed a decent idea to him.

I had to nip that in the bud. With a player like Mugsy, your job is to get him to a place where he's enjoying his football. He's a quieter, more reflective individual than his public persona might suggest. This wasn't a time for criticism and ultimatums. I wasn't pinning him to the ground and telling him to buck up. He needed understanding and an alternative escape to simply quitting.

"That's not the way to get out of this," I said. "Hang in there. You have a lot to offer us. The opportunity will come when you least expect it. That's what happens when you have quality and you persist."

It seemed to sit well with him. His mood improved. Things didn't seem so gloomy.

The Dubs finally gave him the stage he needed.

When we met them in the league, Mugsy had stitched a fine goal. Exactly six months to the day had passed since that goal. Six months of hardship. All that would change in 15 minutes.

Peter Canavan came on in the second half to add some more guile, and we were finding a way back into the game. Then Brian McGuigan made a partial block on a Dublin free to set us off on a counterattack. The next 30 seconds are imprinted into my memory. Davy Harte brought it out of defence. We worked the ball towards Stephen O'Neill. Stevie had to battle to get the ball but once he made the space, he chipped the ball into his hand in one flowing movement. Mugsy was racing towards him and took the ball outside the 45-metre line.

He tore towards goal. Sold one outrageous dummy to Stephen O'Shaughnessy. Ran on. Soloed once. Sold another dummy to Paul Casey. He was through. Stephen Cluxton set himself, but Mugsy gave him no chance. Six months of frustration and bad vibes were unleashed in one stinging shot that smashed into the roof of the net. We were level. Mugsy had his groove back.

When people remember that goal they are always drawn to the dummies and the finish. It's the detail I love. John Wooden always said it takes ten hands to score a basket, and he's right. Mugsy's finish was fantastic, but so was Brian McGuigan's conviction to stretch and block a free. Stephen O'Neill could have let the Dublin defenders take a 50/50 ball. Instead, he fought for it. We got a draw that day. For the replay, I knew we'd be a different team.

We picked up where we left off. So did Mugsy. We got eight points ahead in the first half but Dublin were picking away at the deficit, gradually reducing it to three. Then Sean Cavanagh nicked a kick out and charged at the Hill. As he bore down on goal he was tackled and tumbled to the ground, but managed to get a pass to Mugsy. It was a tiny moment that defined the match. The hit came in, but Mugsy rolled the defender like a tacklebag – classic training ground stuff. He slid the ball under Stephen Cluxton, and we were six up again. At that second Mugsy stopped in front of Hill 16 and looked up at a silent crowd. For a moment everything seemed to stop. That gaze was worth more than a thousand words.

We would return to Croke Park to meet Armagh. Eight games down and a world of learning discovered. Our motto that year was condensed into one simple acronym: LINAO.

Losing Is Not An Option.

For a month, that chimed louder with us than ever before.

4. The Comeback

DESPITE ALL THE MATCHES, we reached the All-Ireland semi-final in good fettle. We thought a lot about how to deal with any fatigue-related issues, and decided the best way to deal with fatigue was to stop thinking about it. We were careful about the language we used. I spoke to the players about how much we were enjoying this year. The games were flying at us. Training was short, sharp and class. This was a good place to be, not a place that made us ache with tiredness. We were fresh;

competitively fresh. We weren't training to build up a store of fitness. We were training to play. No team in the country was as battle-hardened as we were. That counted for a lot.

The players responded superbly. Plus, we were meeting the right kind of opposition. We didn't need to press many buttons to rouse ourselves to play Armagh. We had a debt to settle.

This game wasn't simply an All-Ireland semi-final. This was about righting the wrongs that had denied us an Ulster title and handed Armagh a win. This was the team that had happily benefited from our misfortune. A year's football had hardened our team. Losing that Ulster title had sharpened our minds. There was a fury in the players before that game. We didn't need to stoke the fire. It was already raging.

Our drawn game against Dublin was already being lauded as an exhibition of football. This match would sit alongside it. It was intense stuff from the beginning, but amid the collisions and bone-juddering hits, we were playing some good football. Like the Ulster finals, we felt we were in control for most of the match. Both matches and the drawn game against Dublin suggested we were struggling to close out games, and Armagh were hanging in there again, but we were ready to attack the last 15 minutes this time.

We still had to negotiate some sickening knockbacks, though. One fumble handed them a goal to level the game. Then, with ten minutes left, a free from Paddy McKeever was collected by Steven McDonnell close to goal. Initially, everything seemed okay. Conor Gormley seemed to have McDonnell covered, and Packie had his angles right. Yet the ball slithered into the net. We had led all day. Now we were a point down.

Our reaction now promised to define us. If we lost that game, it would murder us as a team. We had let these leads slip from our grasp all summer. We knew we were stronger than that, yet people were asking questions. We had to answer. Once and for all.

Our response took us closer to history. Sean Cavanagh broke down a kick-out, collected the ball when he returned to earth and drove through the middle to narrow the gap to a point. By then, Kieran McGeeney had been taken off. People questioned Joe Kernan's wisdom in removing McGeeney but I could see what Joe was thinking.

Enda McNulty had come on instead of McGeeney and picked up Peter Canavan. Joe reckoned if Armagh could stop Peter, they could hang on till the end. Plus, Armagh were set up to attack us. They didn't lean against their defensive system. They tried to push up and attack their lead. If they had won, Joe's switch would have been a masterstroke.

The equaliser was a strange creature itself, but relayed what our team was about now. Peter managed to flick a pass to Shane Sweeney, a corner-back racing forward to support the attack. Shane launched a kick off his left boot that dropped over the bar.

The ending was almost poetic. First Stephen O'Neill is fouled by Ciaran McKeever; Stephen O'Neill, who received a false red card in the Ulster final minutes after Ciaran McKeever had yanked Peter Canavan out of a bunch of players. Now Canavan was standing over a free to win the game. It was too ironic for words.

I have often thought about Peter's mindset that day. Owen Mulligan might have had the ball, ready to kick the free, but only Peter could take that kick. He would have coped with the kick best, whatever the result. Mugsy had too much of his career ahead of him to carry the burden if he missed the kick. Peter had been converting these and making dreams come true his entire life. What's another kick?

The ball sailed over the bar. We hung on for the final few moments. Our ghosts had been exorcised.

We wouldn't meet Armagh again until 2009's Ulster championship with two different teams in entirely different places. That rivalry defined so much about both teams, and despite the hurt of losing that Ulster title, I'd be happy to think we won enough battles through the years to ultimately claim the war.

From 2002 to the present day, Armagh have received great credit for their achievements, but I would feel Tyrone have accomplished more. Would Armagh swap their All-Ireland and five Ulster titles for three All-Irelands and two Ulster titles? I think they would. Our development between 2003 and 2005 was the key. We loved the wide open spaces in Croke Park. Sometimes they stretched Armagh. We managed to effect a better transition of players across our team. Armagh's core group stayed together a long time. Only five Tyrone players started both the 2003 and 2005 All-Ireland finals. We had exactly the same turnover between the finals in 2005 and 2008. Essentially, we had ten different starters in two All-Ireland finals. That turnover wasn't happening with Armagh. In the end, that caught up with them.

The first thing we needed to remember before the final was history. Meath had played ten games to reach an All-Ireland final in 1991 and lost. It was Rick Pitino's mantra writ large again. Success is not a divine right. It's a choice. We could celebrate beating Armagh but we couldn't see it as an ending. The challenge ahead was even greater.

19

HISTORY

A FEW WEEKS BEFORE the All-Ireland final we gathered our players together for a meeting, split them into their groups, and asked them a question: why would Kerry want to beat Tyrone?

We filtered through the answers.

- The ambush of 2003 would still be raw for them.
- We hadn't allowed them to play football.
- Pat Spillane's comments about puke football implied we were plying a nasty trade.
- Kerry might have won the All-Ireland in 2004, but apparently they didn't receive any credit for it. The general consensus was that they whipped Mayo, and hadn't beaten us or Armagh along the way.
- They needed to beat us or Armagh to win a credible title.

Essentially, Kerry were out to redress the balance. Victory in 2005 would right all the wrongs we had perpetrated in 2003. We wanted the players to think about their incentives. At the end, Leo Meenan added one more. His clubmate Eoghan Bradley had been part of the TG4 team put together in a reality TV show that had beaten Kerry the previous December.

"Revenge for the Underdogs!"

It broke the mood again and reflected where we were at for this game. This was different from 2003. Our players were totally relaxed. On the Saturday morning before the final, we boarded the bus in Ballygawley to head for Dublin. Peter Canavan was delayed recording a final interview with Adrian Logan for UTV. Once we were all on, the boys gestured to the bus driver. Take off. Let's go. Cue Peter sprinting behind the bus as a few hundred Tyrone supporters wondered what in the name of God was going on.

That was how it was. The tension had evaporated, replaced by a new confidence. Kerry expected another war in the All-Ireland final. We had a completely different mindset now. We weren't the underdogs any more. We felt we were almost on a level footing with Kerry. We had won the All-Ireland in 2003, given a good account of ourselves in difficult circumstances in 2004 and we had made this final by scaling the harshest cliff-face of the championship. This final was about claiming our rightful place as legitimate, enduring champions. Other Ulster teams, aside from Down, had only managed to win one All-Ireland: Donegal, Derry, Armagh. We didn't want to be the fourth team in that group.

We had to show that 2003 wasn't a freak accident. Staging an ambush to catch Kerry might have been part of the process, but we didn't see ourselves as an ambush team. We were a team of quality. We had to convince the wider world of that.

The wonderful thing was, we never feared those challenges. We thrived within that context. I wanted the players to realise that these opportunities come only once. You don't want to say, "This is just another game." Your players need to make a mark.

Winning the first title was brilliant, but you have to create something of substance. It's too easy to become a one-off.

It was during those few weeks when Cormac McAnallen's voice returned to the panel. His words echoed through us all. We didn't want to be a one-win wonder. This wasn't about one great expression of excellence. We wanted the players to reach those heights at every opportunity.

They were in the perfect frame of mind to make it happen. Owen Mulligan was buzzing. Stephen O'Neill was already Footballer of the Year. Joe McMahon was doing a tidy job at full-back. Davy Harte had emerged in 2005 as a solid wing-back. Since then he has matured into the Brian Dooher of the defence. On the other wing, Philip Jordan was powering through a remarkable amount of work in every game. Since making his debut for Tyrone in 2002, Philip hasn't missed one championship match. That amounts to almost 50 consecutive championship matches to date. Simply phenomenal.

Even those struggling to make the team were outdoing themselves to contribute something. Gavin Devlin had lost his place on the team after playing Dublin, but not within the soul of the group. He still spoke strongly in meetings and on the training field about what he saw. He talked about marking Eoin Brosnan, what to watch, where to follow him. At a meeting the night before the final, Horse spoke on behalf of his group about why we would dearly wish to win this All-Ireland. He began in that impassioned way of his, gesturing to Peter Canavan and Chris Lawn, apologising before he even began. "I'm sorry, boys," he said, "and I don't want you to take this the wrong way, but tomorrow could be the last time these boys ever play for Tyrone." Canavan smiled. "Funny you should say that, Horse," he replied. "We've the same thing written down here about you!"

Gavin had reacted magnificently to losing his place, but it was typical of the man. He knew the game was moving in a particular direction. His brilliance at reading the game, his positional sense and his organisational ability on the field had served us over the years, but as football sped up, his lack of pace was overshadowing everything else. We were picking horses for courses to win an All-Ireland. Sadly, this Horse wasn't for this course any more.

We needed the same sense of perspective from Peter Canavan. His ankle was still a problem. He had tapered his year well, opting out of the league and easing himself through the summer. We had used him sparingly in matches, and it seemed inevitable we were going to have to conjure something to get the best from him in the All-Ireland final again.

I wanted to start him as we did in 2003, give him a break, and reintroduce him again. Unlike 2003, he wasn't as comfortable with the idea this time. I spoke to him about the need to have him on the field at both ends of the game. He wanted to start. I questioned the full extent of his effectiveness over 70 minutes. I reckoned he needed that extended break at half-time. We agreed that he would start the game, but he wasn't entirely convinced about the rest of the plan.

WHEN I LOOKED AT KERRY, I figured out a few things we could be certain about. After letting us build a serious lead in 2003 from the start, I knew they would seek to make a statement early on. Their selector Ger O'Keeffe had even reflected on the 2003 semi-final and wondered if Kerry had kept the gap lower, what would Tyrone have done next?

That had to inform their thinking this time. We knew they would take the game to us. When you expect that, there's nothing there to shock you. And it didn't.

We reckoned they would avoid coming through the centre of our defence, try and get the ball into their full-forward line at different angles, skirt around the flanks looking for space. True

enough, a couple of their opening scores came from the wings –
Eoin Brosnan's first point appeared to be covered out on the
wing but he still hung it over the bar.

The confidence we now carried meant we approached all
these challenges in a totally different way to 2003. We had
players that could stare Kerry in the eye. We could rely on our
system of play and the relentless work rate that supports the
entire structure. Back in 2003 we won an All-Ireland relying
largely on 16 players. Now we had developed a more rounded
panel.

Take Ryan Mellon. He had missed out on 2003 and suffered
a debilitating virus in 2004. He wasn't even staking a claim in
early 2005, but the season was so long he gradually got his game
together.

Around the time of the Ulster final replay he truly started to
hit form. He's not a tall player, but he has a terrific leap. He's
mobile and possesses a lot of ability, even if sometimes he doesn't
quite deliver that consistently.

In the run-up to the 2005 final, though, he was catching fire.
It was like watching Kevin Hughes before the 2008 final;
sometimes you just know when a player is right. That was the
case with Ryan Mellon in 2005.

The weekend of the match passed off smoothly. We convened
for our final meeting the night before the game. We ran through
some footage of Kerry, talked a little about the following day.
Gavin Devlin made us laugh and the mood was good. Then, at
the very end, Philip Jordan said it.

"Let's do it for Cormac."

It was the first time in almost two years we had mentioned
his name like that. It had always been there in us. It had
remained an unwritten motto all season. Now it had been said
and made real. At that moment, it felt like it needed to be said.
It was good. It was positive. It didn't knock people back or make

them scared. There was a sense it was the right time to say that. We had played our cards as well as we could.

It was time to show our hand.

IT STARTED AS WE IMAGINED. Kerry won a few kick-outs and pushed us back. After Eoin Brosnan's point, Colm Cooper got the ball and set off on a mazy run. Their second point.

Then a goal.

Whatever about points, conceding goals always hurt me. It was a well-created goal. Gooch held the ball up well. Dara Ó Cinnéide made a good run and finished it smartly. This was a shocker. What made it worse was that, although Kerry had started strongly, they weren't coming at us in waves. We had our share of the play. Suddenly, they had a cushion.

This was a test for both teams. How would they react? We knew Kerry would start like this. Once they had established a lead, what did Kerry now expect from us? The goal would surely allay their fears of the 2003 scenario where we raced into a serious lead early on. It could also land them into a comfort zone. This was their script as I saw it: get ahead early on, rattle Tyrone. A Tyrone comeback was one twist in the plot they didn't see.

We chipped away. Ryan Mellon was delivering one of those special All-Ireland final performances. Declan O'Sullivan was miles away from centre-forward for Kerry, deep into his own half. We were happy to let his marker Conor Gormley sweep across our defence. Owen Mulligan was looking dangerous. Peter was buzzing. Brian Dooher's engine was warming up too. At one stage in the first half he took a ball outside his own 45-metre line and set off. He drove at the Kerry defence. Drove on. And on. He was inside their 45-metre line when he finally launched a mighty kick from beneath the roof of the Cusack Stand. It dropped over the bar. The Tyrone crowd lifted. We all did. That effort meant more than a point. The message to Kerry was simple. You're not away yet.

By the half hour, we were ahead. Gooch levelled it. A few moments later, Owen Mulligan won a high ball in front of goal and slipped it to Peter. His finish was sublime. We were a goal up. We had turned the tide. Brian McGuigan hoisted another point. Four up. Class.

Then, Kerry delivered a message to us. Instead of falling away, Darragh Ó Sé took a ball and drove over a point. I was annoyed. 1-8 to 1-4 was a good half-time score. A three-point lead left us vulnerable.

But I had to mask that. We needed to be positive. We had forced a six-point swing in 25 minutes. We had weathered the storm. If Kerry thought we would struggle to respond to their surge, they now needed to find something extra.

I talked to Peter. At best, I was planning to keep him on until half-time. I proposed it was time for a break. He looked at the ankle and agreed. There was one last act left for him.

We also knew if the game drained into the final 15 minutes without a definite winner, the hard yards we had scrambled for over nine matches would count for everything. There was no way Kerry could be as prepared for that final battle as we were. We told the boys that at half-time. Call on all those days when we went to the edge and hung in there. If it's another battle to the edge, we will survive. The Sam Maguire was 35 minutes away, I told them. This wasn't about losing a match now. It was about staking everything. We were fighting for our credibility.

The players responded. They dominated the third quarter, built a five-point lead and looked comfortable. Things were looking bright, but you knew it wasn't over. Kerry had vast experience, quality, pride and a huge amount to play for. All they needed was a break.

They got it. Gooch went for a point. Someone got a hand to it. The ball fell to Eoin Brosnan. Conor Gormley and Ryan McMenamin dived on the ball. After starting the attack, the ball fell at Tomás Ó Sé's feet. He rifled the ball to the net. It was 1-12 to 2-8. Another massive test.

Then something crucial happened. Darragh Ó Sé drove upfield again. Last time he had pegged us back and left a slight moment of doubt with us before half-time. Now he could level it. We had already managed a six-point swing. Kerry were about to get close to the same mark. What impact might that have?

His shot headed towards the posts. Then it started to fade away. Wide. A wave of relief swept over me. Kerry's period of dominance hadn't been confirmed. In fact, it might even be over.

I immediately looked to Peter. There were 15 minutes left. Enough for him to help us win an All-Ireland.

His first act will endure among the most crucial of his career. He collected a ball near the end-line and angled over a point. We were two up again. The sting had been drawn from the Kerry goal.

A free from the Gooch made the match a one-point game, but we were where we wanted to be. The last five minutes in a battle. Kerry's best chance to rattle us was the first 20 minutes. After four months of football through almost ten games, this was our best chance to finish them.

Brian McGuigan kicked a point. Philip Jordan stormed forward and kicked another. One for Cormac. Moments later, the whistle came. 1-16 to 2-10. Job done.

It was an incredible sensation. It wasn't euphoria or delirium, just a warm, reassuring sense of satisfaction. Back in January, Ger Loughnane had been invited as a guest to the Errigal Ciarán dinner dance. I could remember his words now. "The second All-Ireland is fulfilment," he said. "There was so much more added value to a second All-Ireland."

I could see what he meant now.

This victory represented an endorsement of so many important things. This proved the value of the players' own belief in themselves. Five months after we stood in a sodden changing room in Portlaoise, having lost to Wexford, questioning everything we ever stood for, it told them the season and their efforts had been worth it. They had answered every question emphatically.

There had been setbacks and kicks along the way, but we had survived. We overcame everything and made the All-Ireland final. When that match took us down to the wire, there was no fear. We had won.

We had left our past as a footballing county behind forever. Two All-Irelands meant that we could aspire to great things every year. So could the generations that came after us. We had laid the foundation for a new era in our history. We had set ourselves apart. The little records that stuck in my head over the summer were now ours to keep. We were the first team to win an All-Ireland over ten games. We were the first team in a long time to win two All-Irelands in three seasons. We had moved ahead of the other Ulster counties with one All-Ireland. Pat Spillane's old after-dinner line about not recognising one-in-a-rows wouldn't run so smoothly in Tyrone now.

Matthew and Michaela were there. Brian Dooher too. We hugged and cried. Those tears were for the year we had lived through and for the man whose place Brian was taking. It was more than an All-Ireland. It was satisfying so many things for us all.

WINNING THAT ALL-IRELAND title also brought a sense of closure. If we hadn't won that All-Ireland title, Cormac's statement could have turned from a mantra into a millstone. One Is Not Enough. If the years had gone on without delivering the second All-Ireland, we would have started to wonder about ourselves. Now we were released. We had kept our side of the bargain to him. Anything that came after that now felt like a bonus.

The dressing-room crackled with joy. In one corner, though, Peter Canavan was announcing his retirement. On one level it was the perfect ending for a wonderful story. Canavan's skill deserved the tribute of an All-Ireland medal to end his career. People might have criticised him for a tackle on the Gooch and holding him down late in the game, but that was the burning competitor in Canavan. If you had walked the same path in his shoes, with victory so close, you wouldn't flinch from that challenge for a second.

Although I had known the day was near when Peter would finally retire, I was surprised he made his announcement at that moment. It was a pity. Maybe he could have savoured the occasion more and made his announcement later, but that was his way. I still wonder, if he had taken more time, maybe we might have got one more year from him. Take the league out of it, ease him into the team as the year went on. After 2005 worked so well, I thought we might be able to repeat the plan. But injuries were wearing him down, and now he was gone.

We have always got on well through the years. People might have speculated on our relationship, but there were never any battles between us. He wouldn't be the most talkative man. He always kept his counsel, but when we needed to talk about issues, we did.

We had an honourable respect for each other. We knew each other for so long in Glencull. He had commentated on home videos down at the Holm and starred in a few as he got older. He had brought something unique to my club as a player and blessed us all with his talent.

In 2003 I tried to match my experience as a manager with his playing quality and try to get the best from both of us. I needed to build a relationship and bind him into a generation of young players that saw him as a hero. Between us, I think we accomplished all that.

It was wonderful to be the manager of our first All-Ireland winning team. It was even more of a privilege to see a man from my own townland lift the cup as captain. This was the boy I had watched dinking and swerving his way through packs of imaginary defenders outside our local post office. He was the boy whose foot was pierced by the nail I'd never forgive that probably deprived the school of at least an Ulster title.

He was Peter, who hit the frees to calm us down in the 2003 final. He was Peter, who lobbed the ball over the bar against Armagh and took the wind from Kerry's sails with another point in the final. He was Peter, who trusted my plan to ensure Tyrone could cheer him on the field from the start of two All-Ireland finals and celebrate with him at the end. What he did in between was magic.

Always was.

THE FOLLOWING DAY, the team bus snaked its way home. We stopped in Castleblayney for a meal. While the rest of the boys ate, myself and Brian Dooher had a job to do.

Fr Shane McCaughey from Monaghan was waiting for us in a car. He would take us to Eglish.

A few days before the final, I had met Brian at a pre-All-Ireland function. Together we agreed we needed to do one job if we won the Cup. Before it ever arrived in Aughnacloy and the Tyrone public took ownership of the celebrations, we needed to go somewhere first. I organised for Fr Shane to drive us to Cormac's grave. When we got there, the cemetery was empty. It was silent. We brought the Cup to the graveside and said a few prayers. I don't think anyone else knew about our trip; just Brian and myself. When we were finished, we returned to the car and met the team bus on the road between Castleblayney and Monaghan. Someone handed Brian and myself a pair of dinners and the bus pulled away for Aughnacloy. We hadn't left Cormac behind. Our journey could now continue.

20

BREAKING GLASS

July 2009

BECAUSE WE WERE FACING Antrim in the Ulster final, people made their assumptions about us. Indeed, they assumed we'd make assumptions about Antrim. Some pundits suggested I had dropped my guard in the run-up to the game when I said I expected us to win. Ludicrous. I was saying exactly what I believed: if we played to our potential, we would win the game. I felt I needed to get that message across to our players.

Those were the facts. I wasn't going to patronise Antrim with some guff about 50/50 matches and so on. They had done well to reach an Ulster final and I fully acknowledged the performances they gave against Donegal and Cavan to get there. But the experience we had and the journey we had taken to reach this point over many years meant we should be winning this game. I'll never hide behind anything in terms of our team's capability. It wasn't said in arrogance, or to sound smug. It was based on the reality as I saw it. I'd only be bluffing if I said anything different.

To ensure it happened, though, we needed to safeguard against our players making those assumptions the public thought we would. People say success leaves clues. So does complacency. We had the magnifying glasses out all the way to Clones.

It was a process I needed to undertake myself, too. I tore into the videos of Antrim's previous matches and compiled the same kind of detailed dossiers on the Antrim players as I had for Armagh and Derry. Nothing was left unchecked. I could tell the players that Michael McCann would wear a midfielder's jersey and play full-forward. He was their go-to guy. I spotted a little solo dummy he always applies. Another little quirk to watch for.

Big Niall McKeever would be a regular target for kick-outs. Thomas McCann would run at us. Their inside backs didn't kick much ball, but they marked very tightly. Their half-back line was like ours. It loved to drive forward. Aodhan Gallagher was a good fielder and could kick scores. Terry O'Neill was their sweeper and had operated very well against Donegal and Cavan. We assumed they would retain that tactic, which suited us fine. We would push up on their sweeper and pin their half-back line back.

Little things tested our commitment. Carton House wasn't available for our usual pre-match weekend. Newcastle United were there. Didn't matter. We still took our weekend away in Dublin in the Citywest Hotel and trained at the Garda sports complex in Westmanstown.

We looked at what Antrim might be thinking. We asked the players the usual question: why did they think Antrim might believe they could win? The answers were edgy enough to focus them.

- Tyrone already have a lot of success
- Antrim have nothing to lose
- Antrim are young, we've been around the block
- Get at Tyrone early and shake them up
- Tyrone haven't been tested
- Tyrone aren't strong around the middle.

It all helped set the tone. That old chestnut that Tyrone didn't have a midfield pairing had been wafting about since 2003. We could reply emphatically against a tall, strong Antrim team. If Antrim reckoned they could shock us in the first quarter, we would be ready to shock them. The players' response to that probably won the game. Once we got nine points ahead early on, Antrim were destined to chase the match all day. They clawed the lead back to five a few times, and hit three points in a row to cut it to six at half-time.

That was probably as uncomfortable as it got. The mood in the dressing-room was sheepish. Myself and Tony didn't need to say much. The vibe from the players and the body language said enough. They knew themselves that wasn't good enough. Time to push on again.

We played some good passages of football without setting the world on fire. I found plenty of positives in the detail. PJ Quinn executed a perfect near-hand tackle, and completed the move by flicking it into his own path. Execute. Complete. Perfection.

We moved the ball at pace at times. The players were clearly tuned into each other. Antrim strangely abandoned their sweeper system and we enjoyed the space. Brian Dooher got a useful stint of game time into his legs. There was no jubilation at the end, just satisfaction. I took the Anglo Celt Cup up the road to Carrickmore to welcome home a group of charity walkers. The returning walkers got plenty more attention than the Cup. Such is life in Tyrone these days.

WE WERE BACK in Croke Park. Exactly where we wanted to be in August, but maybe not sure of precisely what part of the road we were on. If I had been told we would win an Ulster title beating Armagh and Derry, I'd have assumed the team would have proven itself by now. But it hadn't.

We knew the mood at training was intense. We also knew that could mean nothing in Croke Park. With everything running so smoothly, this felt like a unique scenario for us, but we had enough experience to piece together a similar set of circumstances.

This was 2007 again. The Ulster title meant nothing to anyone outside our circle, just as it was back then. After a ridiculous week of waiting around to see the draw, we got Kildare in the quarter-final. They were the new Meath. In 2007 we were flat and lifeless and got hunted out of the championship. We were in a different place now, but we still had to be aware of the parallels.

Even if the GAA's inability to make a quarter-final draw alongside the fourth round qualifier draw – so at least the provincial champions can narrow down their potential opponents from eight to two – meant we had little time to study Kildare, we were acutely aware of the need to right the wrongs from 2007.

Righting those wrongs proved just as difficult as we expected. Kildare pushed five ahead in the first half. We were giving too much ball away. We were struggling to match the intensity of Kildare's play. At half-time we recognised where we were at. I called on the memories of 2007 again. The choice was ours. Take this game or slink home again.

Our response was good. We hit six points in a row and missed four more. It reminded me of the comeback against Dublin in 2005, and how we left them for dead in the second half in 2008. Two points was a decent winning margin. Kildare had lifted us to another level. We knew Cork would demand the same in the semi-final. But we felt we were ready.

We were sure of it.

◄O►

July 2006

I WAS STANDING ON A PITCH in Portlaoise. The rain was pouring down as I waited to do a radio interview. A few minutes had passed since Laois quietly suffocated the life from our season. Over the

years we had become used to ending our seasons in Croke Park –
either in victory or defeat. Now here we were in a shadowy part of
the championship, far from the brightest lights and the biggest days.

I shuddered against the cold and the raindrops by the side-line.
I watched the crowd leaving – happy Laois people; sodden,
disappointed Tyrone supporters. Then I saw one Tyrone man break
from the line heading for the gates. He made straight for the
wire. Straight for me.

He let fly with a torrent of abuse, released all the frustration
of the defeat on me. It was vile stuff. For a second, I snapped.

"Tell me what you've won," I replied, "what teams you've
coached? How well have they done? If they stack up, then I'll
talk to you."

He spat out another mouth of abuse and marched off. We had
endured everything that year. The panel had been gutted by injuries.
We had fought battles in the corridors of Croke Park and even more
furious ones to simply try and stay alive in the championship. We
had started the year dreaming of history and ended up scrambling
to survive. Now here I was, being abused by one of my own with
an audience of locals looking on, slightly bemused by the notion
that barely a year had passed since I had helped my team win an All-
Ireland. As a quick snapshot of the mood that sometimes pervades
in Tyrone, it seemed to leave a mark.

My accuser might have thought it would leave one on me, but
he was wrong. Other people were probing for cracks too. A little
while after the Laois game I was down at a function in Ballymun
Kickhams GAA club in Dublin where Martin Shortt was sponsoring
a set of jerseys for the senior team. I chatted to a journalist as part
of the day's engagements and thought little about it. When nothing
appeared in the newspaper the following day, I did wonder what the
point of it all was, but didn't dwell too long on it.

A few weeks later I spotted another story in the same
newspaper. Apparently I had announced my intention to leave the

Tyrone job. I couldn't recall even having a chat with a journalist in the previous few days, never mind making such a life-altering decision. It was beyond maddening to see this. I called the newspaper. They said they trusted their reporter's version of events. Because I couldn't remember even doing this interview, the paper immediately cast doubt on my version. Then, it clicked.

The chat in Ballymun. Same reporter. Same paper.

Quitting wasn't even something that had entered my head. We might have put down a bad year, but doing this job still thrilled me. The challenge of patching the team together and starting again had already colonised my thoughts for the rest of the summer. While the paper refused to back down, I simply asked for the tape that contained these quotes. They refused. It annoyed me so much. 2006 couldn't be an end.

I had to make it a new beginning.

THE YEAR HAD STARTED out well. Kevin Hughes and Gerald Cavlan were back and looking eager. When we defended our first title in 2004 we had been faced with difficulties we could never imagine, but 2005 had helped us absorb that whole experience as part of our learning curve. If we could survive that and still find a way to success, what could stop us now?

We got together as usual before the season began. The mood was good. Chasing back-to-back All-Irelands energised us. Since no one had managed it since Cork in 1990, it was another little piece of history we wanted for ourselves. Putting that drive into players isn't something you can inject like a dose of vitamins at the start of every year, though. It must be wound into their psyches over time. It must gradually become part of who they are. These players were more mature now. They had two All-Ireland medals. You can't instruct people to want something. It's a decision they make themselves. By 2006, we knew the choice this group would make.

We also started the year without Peter Canavan for the first time. We talked about it. We knew we couldn't lean on Peter forever. His departure was inevitable, but we had enjoyed enough years with him that the residue of his influence would always stay with us. People could still relate to his ferocious will to win. When we were in difficult situations, it wasn't hard to imagine how Peter might deal with them and feed off that.

Since 2003 we had been slowly forced to wean ourselves off his influence anyway. We had used him sparingly in 2005 and seen players gradually grow into roles that helped compensate for his absence. It was never a case of replacing Peter Canavan, but developing other players into leaders who could share the same responsibilities.

When I looked back at the 2005 All-Ireland final, Brian McGuigan's role was central to everything positive we did. He would carry some of the burden. This was going to be a big year for Owen Mulligan, Stephen O'Neill, Sean Cavanagh and Enda McGinley. These were the players we needed to grow into new roles now. I always felt a combination of those people would cover any deficits left by Peter's departure. More importantly, though, our system of play always depended on trust. People who played for Tyrone played for each other. Work hard, and we'd cope.

The signs were good. We knew teams would hit us hard as All-Ireland champions but the players weren't taking a step back. We met Donegal in the McKenna Cup. After taking a battering in the first half we upped our tempo and ran out winners. Like everything else involving ourselves and Armagh around then, our McKenna Cup semi-final took on a life of its own. Over 20,000 people turned out on a glassy, sunny January day in Casement Park. We had maybe half our All-Ireland team, they had nine or ten of the team from the All-Ireland semi-final. Didn't matter to the public, though. The jerseys were enough.

It turned into a battle. The hits didn't seem that hard but the referee still flashed five yellow cards in the first 20 minutes. People certainly weren't standing around admiring each other. It was flat-out stuff for January and to win was an important blow to strike. If people had memories of how we were after winning our All-Ireland in 2003, our job was to erase those. Laying down markers isn't an all-consuming thing, but beating Armagh was vital at that point. This was a statement of intent. We were saying we can cope. We can manage winning an All-Ireland and come back with the same edge and desire we had 12 months ago. We turned into the National League feeling that confidence, nurturing that edge. Turns out other teams were noticing that, too.

OVER THE YEARS our games with Dublin had run the gamut of description. In the 2004 league game, Paddy Russell booked ten players, Brian Dooher shipped some savage punishment and Dublin toughed it out by a point. In 2005 we won in Omagh where some of their management got entangled with a steward and Ciaran Whelan was sent off. Owen Mulligan also cracked a superb goal that leapt back to mind in Croke Park six months later.

This time we expected a good game. Our pair of games in the championship in 2005 showed the Dubs had some good footballers, though much of the talk that followed them into the new year was about the need for them to bulk up. This was obviously a useful game for them to measure their progress. They hadn't been far away from us in the drawn game that year. Continuing that approach to beating us seemed the likely approach from them. We certainly didn't expect a physical statement. We expected a game of ball.

Instead, Dublin hit us hard from the start. Very hard. Raymond Mulgrew was a new kid on the block for us that day, and Dublin were keenly aware of him. He got cleaned out a good few times early on. Some of our other players were being hit hard too. The challenges were hefty enough that they set the tone for the rest of the day for us.

Then it started to escalate. There was one scuffle during the first half, but even by half-time it didn't feel like that behaviour was going to dominate the day. We got the players in, told them these were the challenges they needed to expect as champions. We weren't going to be able to play our usual game. We had to accept that and deal with it.

But there still didn't seem any need to tone things down. The game was rough, but it wasn't uncontrollable. Then problems started to arise. Our doctor, Seamus Cassidy, exchanged words with Alan Brogan as he left the field, having received a second yellow card. A few players got involved and a scuffle began. Colin Holmes jumped in to pull a few players apart and got red-carded. The game rumbled like an angry Vesuvius from then on without ever fully erupting. Stephen O'Neill and Denis Bastick followed Brogan later on as the game started to fall apart. It was hard and mean-spirited stuff, but deep down it didn't seem to warrant the reaction that followed.

Still, as I stood in the dressing-room after the game, I could sense what was coming next. You knew you were in the middle of something that wasn't going to be good. You needed to brace yourself. We never set out to create that environment on the day – that kind of encounter pretty much negated every advantage we would have had as a team anyway – but it happened. There was no way of trying to put the incidents in context just now, but equally there was no point in pontificating about the wrongs of the whole affair either. There was no black and white at Omagh that day, just lots of grey.

The frenzy began the following day. The newspapers called it the Battle of Omagh. I took serious issue with that description for a start. Where was the evidence for that? There were no broken jaws or cuts and bruises. The worst picture any newspaper could find was one of Peadar Andrews with his Dublin jersey ripped down the front.

I wouldn't condone anything that went on that day. It wasn't pretty and none of the incidents constitute the kind of behaviour we want to see on a football field, but this rush to turn the match into a bloodbath bothered me. As the days went on, the hype continued to inflate the match into something it wasn't. In the interests of trying to figure out the best censures and action to take, we needed context and a proper, unbiased disciplinary process.

The suspensions echoed all that mania instead. Seven players – including Kevin Hughes, Owen Mulligan and Mickey McGee – received bans totalling 52 weeks. There were warnings for others and fines for the county boards. It seemed excessive. I truly believed we weren't the instigators of the worst episodes. I knew for a fact some of our players were taken out of it from behind. Their opponents didn't even face them up. A number of our players tried to calm things but got dragged into scuffles by others. These players had been charged with discrediting the association, yet they had gone in to try and cool things down. These players hadn't tried to bring the game into disrepute. That charge bugged me. I looked at the video again. Was there something for us to defend here? I thought there was.

The match in Omagh had caused us a problem. It had taken us away from playing football and creating a spectacle that people wanted to see, rather than something they wanted to disown. That wasn't what we were about. At the same time, you can't always legislate for things that will happen on a football field. Sometimes things escalate in ways you can't anticipate. After Omagh, people started labelling us as cynical. In the history of my time with Tyrone, it's the only occasion I can remember a game exploding like that. That doesn't make it right, but it needs context. We played a lot of good football before that day and after it. When you place all that on the scales, they come down heavily in favour of us. Like the event itself, our reputation deserved to be contextualised, but all that was lost in the acres of newsprint and airtime devoted to the subject.

I wore the road down to Croke Park for the appeals process. As they pursued their appeals, we'd meet the Dubs in the same corridors. The relationship was cordial, even warm at times. In many ways, we were in this together now. We weren't going to sling mud at each other.

I spoke to Paul Caffrey regularly around the same time without a cross word. It had no impact on the relationship between the players afterwards either. In the end all the players were released on a technicality – members of the original committee that viewed the video and issued recommendations for suspension on the basis of the footage were asked to clarify some issues for the hearing committee. Allowing one committee to consult with another was a breach of GAA rules. It was a small loophole, but it was enough.

It might sound callous to some people, but I felt justice had ultimately been done. The suspensions might have fallen because of a technical loophole in the law, but if the GAA officials themselves weren't versed in the letter of their own laws back in 2006, that tells us something about the weaknesses that have damaged the GAA's entire disciplinary system.

The media coverage had been wildly excessive. The GAA's reaction had been coloured by that. Because it was on television, did that make the incidents worse? It brings me back to the events of spring 2009, when Ryan McMenamin and Tommy McGuigan were pulled up for incidents caught on camera and deemed worthy of more severe punishment after the referee had dealt with them. It mightn't have looked pretty on television, but did that add to the seriousness of it? I would accept that rigour if the same standards were applied to every inter-county game, but they're not. Were those the only two incidents that required review during the entire league? I know I could show incidents numbering well into double figures that deserved equal review. Not one person has said why that didn't happen. It's as though the GAA is saying "we're doing everything equitably across the board". That's not happening. It's arbitrary. It's random. It's wrong.

Meanwhile, the league continued. Suddenly we had some serious issues to address. Aside from the incidents in the game, we had reacted badly to the disruptions. We only scored one point in the second half and allowed Dublin to escape with a win. Thinking back to the events of the replayed Ulster final, and how Armagh pulled away after the spat in the second half, it was obvious these incidents didn't serve us well.

I was sure any bad vibes from the Dublin game had been cleared out, though results were patchy. We faced Kerry needing something to keep away from relegation trouble, trailed by four points at half time and pulled it round to win. By the time we played Mayo in our final game, we even had a shot of making the league semi-finals. Long before Stephen O'Neill missed a free in the last few moments to win the game though, little things were turning against us. Stevie took a terrible punch on the chin during the game and didn't even get a free. Mayo took their breaks and a draw was the best we could muster. It was the first time we had missed the league semi-finals in my time with Tyrone. That gnawed at me a little, but a turbulent spring hadn't knocked us off our stride. We were ready for the summer.

AS THAT YEAR went along, an old story I first read in a book by Phil Jackson seemed to take on even greater relevance. It concerned an encounter between an American psychiatrist at a Laotian forest monastery and an old master, Achaan Chah. "You see this goblet?" Chah says, holding up a glass. "This glass is already broken. I enjoy it. I drink out of it. But when I put this glass on a shelf and the wind knocks it over or my elbow brushes it from the table and it shatters, I say, 'Of course'. When I understand this glass is already broken, every moment with it is precious."

If we didn't have the right players to compensate, I could have ascribed those sentiments to losing Peter Canavan, but in May 2006 our panel seemed as strong as we could hope. Inside of one weekend, though, the glass was starting to crack.

With club matches on in Tyrone, I fulfilled an engagement with the Sam Maguire Cup in Wales. It was the first time the Cup had visited a Welsh club and promised to be a special weekend. That Sunday evening I was in my hotel room when I got a phone call from Gavin Devlin in Ardboe. He didn't sound good.

"It's wee Brian," he said. "He's got a bad break in his leg. It's awful."

Wee Brian was his pet name for Brian McGuigan. For a moment I was shaken. Horse is an expressive, emotional man, and I knew from his voice that Brian was in terrible trouble. It sounded so bad, I already sensed he might be gone for the season.

Once I landed in Belfast airport, I headed straight for the hospital in Derry. Brian was still awaiting further assessments. His leg wasn't bandaged or in a cage just yet. It was a terrible sight. He was disappointed and disgusted. Brian's health came first, but I knew how much this would hurt the team. Peter Canavan was gone. Brian McGuigan had a major contribution to make that year. Of all people to lose, it couldn't get any worse. I left for home that night, despondent. I just thought, "Where do you go now?" Without Peter we needed Brian to pull the strings and make things happen. Now we didn't have either of them.

The bad news kept coming. Owen Mulligan, Gerald Cavlan, Mickey McGee and Stephen O'Neill all bit the dust in one round of club matches. Martin Penrose twisted his ankle. Enda McGinley was struggling with an injury. That Sunday, I stared at my phone, praying it wouldn't ring any more. A week before we played Derry in the first round of the Ulster championship, I couldn't count our injuries on one hand. One picture from the day showed Brian Dooher, Stevie and Brian McGuigan sitting together in the stand. You just thought: what a bench that could be, never mind a forward line.

Then, when we played Derry, things somehow got worse. We were missing six of the team that had started the 2005 All-Ireland final. Only Conor Gormley was left from the central spine of that team. We had a new midfield pairing. Our half-back line was the only part of the team left untouched.

We needed so much to click. From the beginning, though, the match turned against us. Before the game was even 20 minutes old, Kevin Hughes was sent off for a needless punch. It wasn't the most vicious belt in the world, but he was caught and gave the referee no choice. Losing Kevin deprived us of a crucial source of possession around midfield, and played directly into Derry's hands.

Derry also came with a well-honed plan to stop us. They let nothing move. It was all legitimate confrontation – or as close as you'll get. They moved their foulers around, ensuring they could disrupt our rhythm without gathering a collection of cards. They had a blockade mentality. With our problems in attack, they knew a big score wouldn't be required to win this match. The only thing they wanted was a result.

On the day, we didn't score a single point from play. We were winning plenty of ball out the field but the return wasn't coming. Meanwhile Derry chipped away, adding point after point. The half-time scoreboard was an image burned into our minds for good: Derry 0-6, Tyrone 0-0.

Our plans weren't working. We wanted to try and get past Derry down the flanks. We expected them to clog up their defence with extra numbers, so we carried the ball at them to draw them out. We were looking to force them into tackles and concede fouls. We figured we needed to be closer to goal than usual because we were lacking finishers, which made it hard for us to open things up. We were workmanlike and committed, but we lacked the class to finish off all that hard work.

We had got it back to a five-point gap when Owen Mulligan, who had just regained fitness for the game, slid a shot past the post. Even now I wonder what might have happened if that goal had gone in. Having played all the football, Derry would have suddenly found themselves under pressure. Might they have cracked?

Instead, Enda Muldoon knocked in a goal and they smothered us for the rest of the game. They enjoyed their moment while we endured one of the hardest losses we've ever had to take. Even during the build-up, it felt like Derry saw this as their All-Ireland final. As things turned out, it effectively was.

We had to regroup and find the positives. I have never gone into a game thinking my team can't win, and that was the case against Derry. We had faced adversity before. Losing these players simply meant other people had to raise themselves to new levels. In 2008, we proved it could be done. If it happened then, it could have happened at any time. Even without that proof at the time, I still believed we could make something of 2006.

After the Derry game, Kevin Hughes apologised for getting himself sent off. It was the right thing to do, and reflected the kind of responsibility the players needed to take for their own performance for the rest of the year. Drawing Louth in the qualifiers got our heads up. We respected them as Division Two champions and for beating Donegal, but we felt we could handle them.

Everything was in hand during the first half. Owen Mulligan hit 2-2 from four shots. Louth were struggling to live with our intensity. It was good. I liked what I saw. We were edging back towards a good place.

Then Louth started to knock over a few scores and gain some confidence. Gerald Cavlan had made it back but suffered a groin strain taking a free kick. We were losing concentration. Maybe the players felt as good as I did about the first half and Louth were now taking advantage. They pushed us into extra-time but we had chances to win again. Dermot Carlin drove through the middle at the end but saw his shot for goal fade wide. A draw, but at least we had them back in Omagh.

Before the replay I had asked Colm McCullagh back into the panel to strengthen our options in attack. His decision to pursue a soccer career with Newry City had pretty much precluded him from our plans before that, but now there was no clash. Newry weren't pleased. We were just glad to have him.

He made an immediate impact, kicking a useful handful of points in the first half. Once again we started strongly and looked to have the game tidied up before half-time. Then, players started dropping like flies again. First Colin Holmes came down with a high ball and badly damaged his knee ligaments. Then someone crashed into Conor Gormley. Stretchered off. I stood on the side-line asking myself a depressingly familiar question: what's going on here? We held on to win comfortably in the end, but with more losses to contend with.

People were looking for solutions in places where none could be found. The evening we were beaten by Derry, talk was already gathering about the possibility of Peter Canavan returning. It never crossed my mind for a second. He had made a very public decision to retire at the pinnacle of his career. There was no way he could come back. Either way, if he had returned it would have been almost impossible to recreate such a fitting departure. It would have been wrong for me to try and get him to return and risk that ending stained by a defeat on a miserable day on a ground miles from the joy and majesty of Croke Park on All-Ireland final day. Peter's story with Tyrone had received the ending it deserved. I couldn't risk spoiling that.

Our own narrative was still twisting and turning through some dark places. One night before the next round of qualifiers, Brian Dooher and Ciaran Gourley collided with each other in training. Dooher's kneecap was broken. Another kick in the guts. We had tried to infuse our sessions with more energy in those weeks but even there, in the cocoon of our own training ground, we couldn't catch a break.

I had lived the previous decade chasing All-Irelands with Tyrone. For the first time I had to redraw the limits of my ambition. We were surviving. Hanging on. It was the most distressing playing season I had ever known with Tyrone. We were stumbling from one crisis to another. Players were disappearing and we were still expected to compete with the best. You weren't entering games wondering how well players would perform, but hoping all the players would come out the other side. You were almost worried about them going too hard in training now.

It was hard to say we could win an All-Ireland at that stage. Every step forward made it a more acceptable season, but it was impossible to see us lasting till September. The players were going down with serious injuries, not tweaks and strains. Whole seasons were being wiped out.

But we also needed to push on as a group. This couldn't be treated as a crisis point. We knew where we were. No one was trying to pretend this was great. We had lost a lot of players but we refused to lean on it in public. If we did, it would indirectly compromise the trust we had placed in the players who were there. We talked about taking responsibility, self-improvement. We asked those who were there to stretch themselves to new heights. By the time we played our next round in the qualifiers, we had already used 27 different players for three championship games. That was almost unsustainable, but I needed to think of John Wooden again, of Cormac: things work out best for those who make the very best of the way things work out.

From now on, we just needed to be whatever we could be.

The draw for the second round knocked us back too. Laois in Portlaoise. First of all, they weren't the type of team we needed to meet at that stage. Secondly, we were on the road again. Then, when we arrived in Portlaoise, the rain was milling down. This was typical of the entire year. Another bunch of short straws.

We battled hard for the first half into a driving wind and ended up just three points down. At half time I watched Mick O'Dwyer storm out to the referee and walk him down the tunnel, raging at him as he went. It didn't seem to do Laois any harm in the second half, but I said nothing. Maybe in the past I might have tracked Micko and got my say in, but I couldn't do it then and certainly wouldn't see myself doing it now.

At that stage we were still in the game, though not for long. Although we started the second half with the breeze, Laois seemed to be playing better against it. They drove on. We got worse. In the end they ground out a win, 0-9 to 0-6. We were left beaten and broken.

It was a terrible defeat. Just awful. Even with everything that had gone on, we still felt we should have got past them. When I looked at the teams Laois met after that – Meath, Offaly and Mayo – I saw at least a chance to get back to Croke Park. Even though we had a mixed team out, we had a decent forward line at last and should still have had enough quality on the day to compete, but we failed to deliver. After all the injuries and setbacks, that was the most sickening thing of all. We failed to deliver.

That evening I stood there, shipping mouthfuls of abuse from a Tyrone supporter, trying to do a radio interview and keep calm. Someone asked me about the referee. I thought of Micko's rant, and said nothing. The referee hadn't beaten us today, I replied. We didn't play enough football. The following week I received a letter from an official in Croke Park thanking me for resisting the temptation to criticise the referee. It wasn't a big deal for me. Just the right thing to do at the time.

It wasn't the time for wallowing in self-pity either. The week after defeat to Laois I pulled the players together for a meeting. We needed to get people looking forward. I didn't want players to start letting our disappointment percolate around their system for a month.

That's life, I told them. We had an awful season behind us, and thank God for that. We could start looking at new opportunities now. We would have fewer injuries and a host of new challenges. I found an optimistic take on things, and sold it as vigorously as I could. At the end of that evening, I left 2006 behind.

Myself and Tony went to club games and looked around for new players. Things would get better. Brian McGuigan's recovery was progressing at a fantastic rate. The other injuries were healing too. A few months later we started to organise trials.

One evening in October I hared up from Oldcastle, Meath, to the pitch in Omagh for an evening's football. When I got there, the gates were locked. No entry. We waited around for an hour and tried to get something sorted. No joy.

I stood there in the car park with 40 players waiting for a shot at the big time. Their chance was delayed. So was ours.

The winter couldn't pass quickly enough.

21

FIGHTING THE TIDE

WHAT MADE 2006 SO HARD wasn't the injuries. It was us. We had endured a lot of setbacks that year, but none of them explained why we had performed so poorly. The disappointment I felt that winter wasn't about failing to win an All-Ireland. It was about failing to perform to the levels we should have reached. An All-Ireland title never represents our final destination, but a signpost about where we are at. In 2007, we were lost.

For the first time during my tenure with this group of players, I had been forced to face the fact, in 2006, that we weren't capable of winning an All-Ireland. Even in 2007, when we started to make some progress by winning an Ulster title and getting back to Croke Park, I never felt fully comfortable with how the team was shaping up. My mental bar was now set much lower than it was in 2005. My expectations were now being influenced by outside forces. As you think, so you shall be? Something wasn't right.

We all needed time to adjust to the new situation in which we found ourselves. It comes back to that concept of awareness. You need to realise the need for change to progress, but sometimes you don't notice these things as you go along. You begin accepting a level of performance that conforms to your new idea of acceptability instead of demanding the level you want to reach. As 2007 began, we had 17 players who were either joining the panel for the first time or returning from a long absence. With Brian McGuigan and Stephen O'Neill battling with injuries, we hadn't been able to move on properly from the loss of Peter Canavan. We missed Chris Lawn too. Their calm and experience would have been priceless that year. The likes of Tommy McGuigan, Colm Cavanagh and Martin Penrose were making their first impact on the scene. They needed time to adapt to their new surroundings. We were developing a new team and that would take time. The greatest challenge now was patience, but that was a drain too.

When I look back now, my own energy levels needed renewal. I wasn't consciously saying, "I don't have the energy for this," but I needed to find a new take on our situation. I had fallen into the trap of accepting a decent season as a good one. A worrying trend had been established. In 2006 we had been beaten by Laois and felt we should have gone further. When we met Meath in Croke Park in 2007, we still believed we could beat them. No question. Once we got past them, we reckoned we would improve. An All-Ireland semi-final and sight of a final would lift us to another level. We reckoned we could make that climb.

Instead, we got stranded somewhere on the mountain.

THE BATTLES BEGAN from the outset of the year. The McKenna Cup has always been a crucial competition for us. Back in 2003 we attacked it like no other team before us. It laid the foundations for the winning mentality that we have built on since. Because we don't play challenge matches, the McKenna Cup is an important opportunity for us to assess our panel. But in 2007, we encountered a major difficulty.

The third-level colleges had been part of the competition without too much fuss, but a new rule stipulating that players eligible to play for their college and county in the McKenna Cup were obliged to choose the college caused us a problem.

I refused to abide by that. It seemed a ridiculous rule in so many ways. Firstly, how could one grouping within the GAA dictate to the wider association? There was so much misrepresentation around this issue. People said the influx of colleges rejuvenated the McKenna Cup. I believed it was the fact that we started taking the competition seriously. Tyrone and Armagh drew 20,000 to Casement Park in 2006. There was a record attendance at the 2004 final between Tyrone and Donegal. The arrival of the college teams offered another dimension to the competition, but they didn't arrive like the cavalry to save the McKenna Cup. They were driven by their own requirements.

January was a time when challenge matches against county teams in preparation for the Sigerson Cup were once easy to find. Now the McKenna Cup was consuming our attentions. They kept their heads down for the first few years, then suddenly the colleges seemed to be able to dictate the rules of engagement. Tyrone were made out as a sore loser in all of this, but I didn't think the policy was right or fair. I remember one college expressing their relief that they didn't reach the semi-final stages because it would have interfered with their Sigerson Cup preparations. Why should teams like that get worried about their playing personnel for a competition they don't even want to win?

I have no issue with the colleges being in the McKenna Cup, but they must agree that the McKenna Cup is a competition instigated by the Ulster Council for county teams. They have to accept the counties are the priority in this competition. If counties decide to release players to them, that's fine. I have always allowed my established players to line out with their colleges, and been particularly aware of the situation in St Mary's teacher training college, where playing numbers can be low. Yet we have always been viewed as the bad boys in this argument.

In 2007, we held tough. So did the Ulster Council. We won the McKenna Cup fielding a team that included allegedly ineligible players according to this rule. We were initially stripped of the title before being restored as champions. If that U-turn doesn't confirm the craziness of that rule, I don't know what else does.

Outside of that hassle, the clouds appeared to be clearing as the year began. Brian McGuigan was making terrific progress and looked close to returning as the league began. We were honoured with meeting Dublin for the first round of games to mark the inaugural use of the new floodlights at Croke Park. That night had the atmosphere of an All-Ireland final. I looked up over the Cusack Stand at one point during the match and saw a full moon nestling in a pitch-black sky, shining down on a packed Croke Park, illuminated in the night like an emerald. A little shiver ran through me. This was a unique, fantastic place to be.

There was no hangover from our previous meeting in Omagh either, and our comeback to win from five points down was encouraging for all sorts of reasons. It showed we were ready to fight that year after shipping some tough blows in 2006. It also highlighted how far this team had travelled. In years gone by, Tyrone teams would have feared treading on that pitch. This team just wanted to be unleashed in Croke Park. They love Croke Park. Nothing about playing there fazes them. There is no awe. No nerves. It's now a natural thing for Tyrone players to be in Croke Park. It's something that should serve future generations in Tyrone well.

The other abiding memory I will always carry is of Raymond Mulgrew taking a solo, selling a dummy, and angling a shot over the bar from a tight angle. Raymie has always been a wonderful talent, even if he hasn't quite advanced his career in a way we might have anticipated. That's partly our fault. Once Peter

Canavan went, Raymie's promise as a minor player ensured he would enter conversations as the next great hope for Tyrone football. We probably didn't legislate for the reputation he already had, even as a teenager, coming into the team.

With so many injuries, we needed him to be an established senior player almost immediately. He didn't get the chance to bed into a team cosseted by players with experience and quality. He suffered an injury in 2008 after enjoying a decent year in 2007, but he needed the team to push on into the second half of that season to allow him to mature a little more.

Although it's been a fractured beginning to his career, his class means he will make it in time. He's probably too modest to realise how good he is. It is a mindset we need to work on. He would have undue concerns over certain parts of his game, focusing on things he can't do rather than all the attributes he has. It will take time to help him work through that, but as Clive Woodward said once, winning doesn't happen in straight lines. He's had setbacks. How he deals with them now will determine his own greatness. And with Raymond Mulgrew, we can talk about potential greatness.

Just when we seemed to be stabilising, though, we hit another bend in the road. We headed for a league match in Cork in decent fettle and got blown away. Losing was bad. Losing by eight points, 0-15 to 0-7, was worse. It represented my heaviest defeat as a Tyrone manager for a start, and told the thumbnail story of the worst performance I have ever encountered with this team.

We were wiped out. Cork took us apart. Losing never sits well with me, and this one tore my guts out. We were missing men again, but this performance went beyond all those losses. We were overrun. It was the weakest fight we had ever put up in a game. It was difficult being in that dressing-room, trying to pick the right words. I was hurting badly inside, but people don't want recriminations immediately after the match. Everyone's demeanour told the story. This wasn't us. This was awful.

At least we were facing these truths together. I always respected Cork as a quality side but this defeat was unacceptable. "This isn't our style," I said, "but it happened. We've got to learn from this. Take it on the chin."

We left the dressing-room together, but the road ahead seemed to go on forever.

We were booked into a hotel in Dundrum, near Thurles, that night. A wedding was in full swing as I headed to bed, leaving the players to pass the rest of the evening among themselves.

It was well after midnight when I was awoken by a phone call from the front desk, asking me to come down. There had been an altercation. A few of our players had wandered into the wedding reception. Apparently Owen Mulligan had been signing a few autographs, getting pictures taken. There were a few girls on the scene. A few boyfriends got involved. Next thing there was a scuffle.

I came down to find 19 or 20 of my panel in a room away from the reception. Glasses were broken on the floor. It wasn't pretty. People were trying to convey their version of what happened. I wasn't interested. All I wanted to do was get the players out of there and back to their rooms without any further trouble.

We were staying in chalets connected to the hotel. With the help of the staff, I managed to get the players out another door, across the grounds and into their rooms. That ended my night's sleep. I stayed up to make sure there was no recurrence. When morning came, I had arranged for breakfast to be relocated to my chalet. I opened it up to the rest of our travelling party, then we boarded the bus and headed home. It was that kind of weekend.

I didn't spare anyone in the video analysis of the Cork game. It was time for some cold, hard facts.

There was a worrying lack of conviction about us. Maybe it was coming from our own perception of ourselves, that sense that we should be able to handle most teams. Either way, we weren't. We lacked a cutting edge, on the field and in our heads. We were playing the game hoping we would do well rather than making a decision to do well. We weren't 100 per cent committed to the task. We were losing too many one-on-one battles. Too many teams were outsmarting and outplaying us. We weren't coping with that and were spending too much time on the back foot. The challenge was to prevent that confidence from slipping away to the point where it becomes irretrievable.

Our next game against Donegal wasn't much better. Donegal were flying, playing with championship intensity in March. We had given them a good beating in the McKenna Cup. This was retribution. They won handsomely and enjoyed their win with glee. Their delight was evident in some of the exchanges on the pitch, and the shouts wafting down from the stand. I stored it all up. There's always another day.

Meanwhile, we tweaked our own approach in training. Traditionally we had always stayed faithful to one night's collective training a week before increasing that to two when the clocks went forward. This time we went to two nights a little earlier. Players were concerned that other teams had moved ahead of us with their fitness. They were playing with greater intensity and we couldn't keep pace.

It wasn't a criticism of Fergal's methods. The question the players were posing was directed more at themselves. Is there another way to inject more urgency into our approach? We all needed to be big enough to take responsibility for that.

I looked at my own contribution. I had always been happy to leave training to Fergal. Without impinging on his work, I needed to become more vocal. So did Tony. We needed to give the players the odd dart to push them on, not leaving all that energy-sapping work to Fergal. It was complacency on our part. When things are done well, you can get soft. We had to take on that responsibility and lift things to the required level again.

Results started to turn. We drew with Kerry in a scrap. That was significant. As the summer loomed we headed to Carton House for our annual pre-championship weekend away. Brian McGuigan had been progressing well. He was back playing with Ardboe and I reckoned it might be good for him to accompany us to Carton House. He wanted to play more football, though. Ardboe had a match that weekend. He felt the games would bring him on quicker than training. I didn't agree, but I understood his viewpoint. His club needed him too. He stayed behind to play, but something was nagging at me about that.

We got a call in Carton that Sunday evening. Another injury to Brian. This time it was his eye. You don't get news delivered like that about a trivial injury, but this was worse than we could ever have anticipated. Word continued to filter through. There had been an incident during the match. Brian was on his way to hospital in Derry. At that moment, he was blind in one eye.

When I got home, I made a few calls. We got the best surgeon we could find to work on Brian, but the prognosis was pessimistic from the beginning. It was hard to tell how much of his sight could be saved. At one point, it was estimated he could lose 80 per cent sight in that eye. You just thought about Brian's style as a footballer. His entire game was built around vision. It was beyond cruel.

He was devastated. Frustrated. Annoyed. I wondered how much it must have taken out of him mentally. He had just recovered from a dreadful broken leg. Now this. This recuperation process was even more harrowing than what he had endured the year before. After one operation to insert something to keep his retina in place, he was forced to lie absolutely still for a month. After the first operation he came home and lay face down on a physio's table for about a month. He could only move when he needed to eat or go to the bathroom. I can remember all sorts of things being improvised – television screens being placed underneath the table so he could see things. It was terrible.

We got all kinds of prayers said for him. Fr Gary Donegan from Holycross parish in the Ardoyne brought down a relic of St Charles from Belfast and blessed Brian. I kept in touch as much as possible. Football was nowhere now. This was about trying to get his eye healed to the point where he could resume some kind of normal life. In many ways, there was a point where you couldn't envisage Brian playing for Tyrone again. Coming back from the leg injury was tough enough on him. Even if he recovered completely, would he have the mental strength to push himself again? Would anyone in that situation? Plus, they were both career-threatening injuries. One of them would be enough to retire most people. What impact could both of them have?

Some people wondered about the wisdom of allowing our players play these club games so close to the championship. We had certainly lost a lot of players in 2006 and 2007 to them, but that's the nature of football. You need the goodwill of the clubs and they need their players. Give unto Caesar what is Caesar's, and unto God what it God's. Clubs get the players at the appropriate times. We get them when we need them too. There isn't any perfect solution, but that co-operation needs to be there.

WE STARTED THE CHAMPIONSHIP wrestling with a familiar problem: scoring power. With Brian gone again and Stephen O'Neill still struggling with injury, we had to take a few punts. Brian's brother Tommy came into the team to play Fermanagh in the first round. Sean Cavanagh's brother Colm was introduced. Niall Gormley made his debut. As it turned out, Niall and Tommy were outstanding and kicked the points that formed the core of our tally. Colm fell victim to injury, but we survived by a point.

It was a win, but it wasn't enough for people. Questions were being asked about the level of leadership within the group. Scoring just 0-13 didn't do much to remove those questions about our potency.

Some people were still talking about Peter Canavan. Martin McHugh again floated the view that Peter was the solution to our problems. This theory was now entering the realm of the ridiculous. How could anyone suggest that Peter could seriously return after two years away? How would that be a step forward for us, or him? If you asked him out of retirement, what message does that send to the likes of Tommy, Niall and Colm? It was such a crazy statement it didn't even annoy me. If I was to react to everybody's view I wouldn't know where I was. You do what you believe. Thinking back to Fr Vincent Travers' theory on treating criticism like gifts, I declined plenty of presents around that time.

Although many people had us buried for another year, I was sensing a slight change of mood among the players. Apart from Brian, we had a few players starting to return to the team. Our injuries were easing off. The distance between us and the debris of the previous year was starting to lengthen. After stitching their satisfaction into us after the league match, Donegal in the Ulster semi-final was the ideal draw. We were a game away from a final. It was slow work, but we were getting there.

Donegal were the perfect opponents for us. Their possession game always compelled us to increase our work rate and try to disrupt them. Michael Hegarty was pulling their strings in 2007 as well. If we could clamp down on him, we reckoned Donegal would struggle to generate much in attack.

We also needed to start pushing buttons among our own group. When I spoke to the group, I turned up the heat. We talked about the Tyrone jersey. What did it say to opponents now? It was a long time since our last All-Ireland title in 2005. What had we accomplished since? Nothing of real significance. Getting to an Ulster final would represent a redemption. This was a time we needed to stand up and redeem some status for ourselves. To make that jersey forbidding again.

That was the feeling in that dressing-room. Teams who struggled against us before were getting stronger. The jersey wasn't doing a lot to faze them. It was even encouraging some of them. This was the most important game we played since the 2005 final. We would make our stand here.

Although Donegal had pushed on to win the league, I sensed they might be vulnerable. It was a significant tag they had to carry. Donegal had never won a league title before. They would be expected to kick on from that and win Ulster. That generated confidence, but it brought pressure too. How would they respond to that? How would we respond to the league result?

Our answer was definitive. We pinned them back and let them have it. We committed plenty of errors too, but we dominated Donegal in a manner that covered all those cracks.

The sweetest moment again featured Raymond Mulgrew. Stephen O'Neill was fit to play that day, and delivered one of his patented bullet passes to Owen Mulligan. It was precision engineering to land it into Mugsy's chest. When Raymie got on the ball he still had work to do, but he offered a classy dummy any Donegal defender within reach was happy to buy. The finish was immaculate. It was a beautiful moment.

We won comfortably in the end. Donegal were broken. Our players were energised. It brought me back to those strange conundrums sport can create. I remembered how that Ballygawley team were heavily beaten in the 1963 county semi-final to Omagh, but could turn them over a few months later. I coached an Errigal Ciarán juvenile team that lost a league match 4-11 to

0-4 to a combination team from around Edendork but beat them by a couple of points in the championship a few days later.

How you deal with that mental approach to playing a team you have already beaten well probably resembles how you deal with a deficit. If you're behind in a game, you take the deficit out of the equation. Park it somewhere out of sight. Forget the past and the future, deal with the present. Meeting teams isn't about history or incentives. It's about meeting the challenges of the day. If players accept that, they can progress. It's an attitude you learn during that innocent climb.

The players were happier. So were the public. I was still treading warily. The team was pointed in the right direction, but we weren't where I wanted us yet. We needed more tests. Monaghan in the Ulster final would be another useful gauge.

Monaghan hadn't left any doubt about their requirements that year. They were building an impressive sense of belief. They had gone a long time without a trophy. That stopped here. Clones would be a home venue for the final. Plus, they pulled a small stroke, just to get us thinking.

Back on a cold McKenna Cup night in Kingspan Breffni Park, we had travelled to play Monaghan. On arrival, we realised we had forgotten our change strip. I asked Seamus McEnaney if Monaghan had theirs. It turned out they had a set of blue jerseys. I asked if they'd mind wearing those. "Aye," replied Seamus, "when we're in the Ulster final you'll change."

I might have chuckled. I don't really recall. It was a throwaway line that didn't stick in my memory until the day of the Ulster final.

That day, both teams were due to turn out in their change strip – Tyrone in red, Monaghan in blue. Instead, Monaghan insisted on wearing their white jerseys. I was told I was within my rights to insist Tyrone wear white, and see what happens. I could see what was happening. I didn't reckon getting drawn into a confrontation before the match even started would do us any good. Monaghan might have benefited from an increase in temperature. We wouldn't.

There hadn't been any communication between ourselves and Monaghan about jerseys since that McKenna Cup match. It wasn't a major issue now, but it was something that could have become more than it did. If we could pour any frustrations we had over this little stroke into the first 20 minutes, I thought, that would hurt Monaghan a lot more.

Turns out it did. We blitzed them twice: from the start of the match, and once again early in the second half. Monaghan pulled us back before half-time, but when we pulled away again, we were looking good. Raymond Mulgrew had a chance for a point to stretch us nine points ahead but it drifted wide. Then Monaghan started chipping at the lead. We conceded a point or two. Ryan McMenamin fumbled a ball. Monaghan recycled that possession into a goal.

Suddenly we were on the back foot. A pair of goal chances slipped through their fingers and we won by two points, but the narrative of that match was fixed in people's heads. Monaghan had pushed us to the wire. In my mind, it was more ambiguous. If we had gone nine points ahead, we would probably have strolled home. Monaghan came out of the game with a lot of credit. No one remembered us opening up two huge gaps. The abiding memory for the public was Tyrone clinging on.

We certainly weren't pleased that we could compile those kinds of leads and lose them. It was camouflaged by the fact that we won, but I still felt we were further ahead of Monaghan than the score-line said. It was a decent victory and an Ulster title. The public reaction, though, told us everything we needed to know.

This was par for the course. We don't have enough Ulster titles as a county to diminish winning one, but the public didn't think much of it. There wasn't much delirium among the players that night either. I thought about that change in attitude. Would we have reacted that way in 2003? Another interesting signpost on the journey.

It was good to have that Ulster title, but our form was still troubling me. I couldn't honestly say we had convinced ourselves that we had the power to get all the way to an All-Ireland title. Even when we lost the first round in 2008, we still believed beyond debate that we could. Why was that? Maybe the players were a little more mature. A few others were staring at a ticking clock. Others took responsibility for new leadership roles. In 2007, we possibly decided subliminally that an Ulster title represented steady progress for this evolving team. We would push on, but we lacked that absolute belief that we could go the whole way.

I could have been responsible for that lack of conviction too. Maybe the players were. No one set out to think that way, but we allowed it to invade our thoughts. Before we met Meath in the quarter-final, we prepared as well as we could. I watched them mow Galway down in their last qualifier match. That rang a bell with me. Galway were always hard opponents for us.

I showed our players plenty of positive video footage featuring Meath. I took a lot of moments from their two matches that year against Dublin. The players could see how good Meath could be. Whether they really expected Meath to repeat that kind of form is open to debate. We had never played Meath before. Their recent record wasn't mind-boggling. They hadn't beaten Dublin for a long time. There were enough signals coming out suggesting Meath would be difficult opponents, but I never believed we wouldn't beat them.

On the day we generated enough opportunities to confirm that assumption. We were poor in the first half and lost Brian Dooher before half-time, but we pounded them for the duration of the second half.

Standing on the side-line that day, I could see all our old problems haunting us. I imagined what might happen if Peter Canavan or a fully fit Stephen O'Neill had been close to goal that day. We struggled for scores and inspiration. Joe McMahon went up-field from defence and tried a shot that landed in the Meath goalkeeper's hands. They broke. Joe was slow getting back. As a result, it was a two-against-two situation in defence as the ball headed towards Graham Geraghty. He palmed it over John Devine's head into the net, and Meath were through. Without that goal, we would have won the game.

It was an awful result but I had to forage for positives. The Ulster title was slightly devalued in our eyes, but history always treats those victories kindly. The players had matured a little more. They had gained some more experience. Out in Ardboe, Brian McGuigan was starting to make a remarkable recovery that would see him back with Tyrone in 2008. When we sat down with the players a few days after the Meath defeat, I could see they felt the same pain as we did. We were in this together. There was only one way out.

An All-Ireland.

That autumn I met Damien Taggart. He loved his boxing, had fought as an amateur and now fancied the idea of trying his hand as a professional. He had spent some time with Wayne McCullough in Las Vegas. Although Damien was carrying plenty of weight when he visited, McCullough saw something he liked. I knew Martin Donnelly was involved with Brian Peters, the boxing promoter. Brian agreed to meet Damien. He had a picture taken from an internet page of Damien with McCullough. Welterweights weigh in around 11 stones. Damien was tipping the scales closer to 16 stone back then. Could he make it? Peters gave him a chance.

I kept in touch with Damien from then on. He would tell me about his training. I texted him on any suitable little motivational phrases and lines. I got him reading Anthony Robbins, Pat Riley, Phil Jackson. I watched him train, started attending fight nights. I had never enjoyed more than a passing interest in boxing, but I saw things in the fighters that fascinated me.

I had never fully appreciated how tough boxing was. The demands were brutal. The gloves were smaller than amateur boxing. The professionals didn't wear any headgear. If fatigue hits a footballer you could lay a ball off or find a moment somewhere in the game to catch your breath. In boxing, there is no hiding place.

I was drawing lines back to my own team. A boxer's life is defined in three minutes. He must fight. He cannot retreat. If he stops, he is sunk. Finished. There are no escape hatches in the ring. There are people screaming advice and abuse outside those ropes who would never possess the courage to step into that ring. In that ring, your mind has to be freed from all that clutter. It needs to be aware and alive. It has to strip away all those distractions and find the essence of your task.

Being a boxer isn't simply about punching hard. If you don't find the right mental plateau within yourself, you won't produce your optimum performance. At the end of 2007, my journey with Tyrone had brought us a long way from where we had begun, but I felt a distance from where I wanted us to be.

But we were ready to walk. We talked and forged new bonds. We introduced new players. We trusted each other again. When the players found themselves on the ropes, they ducked out. They didn't retreat. They didn't stop. They fought.

They won.

EPILOGUE

"It is inevitable that some defeat will enter even the most victorious life. The human spirit is never finished when it is defeated . . . it is finished when it surrenders."

BEN STEIN

Monday, 7 September 2009, Kelly's Inn, Ballygawley

WE'RE ALL HERE. *Myself, Tony and Fergal. The players are arriving. We're here to talk and reflect. It strikes me that, for all the meetings we have, and the value we put on the need to communicate, this is one meeting we don't want to hold. We live to spend September on the training pitch, not in an empty function room.*

I watched the All-Ireland hurling final yesterday. Before the pleasure of the match came the dreadful pain of watching the preamble. I watched the managers walking the field. I saw the crowd rising to acclaim the teams during the parade. I watched the President meet the players. I recognised the scenes and remembered the sensations that accompany that weekend. In two weeks' time, Cork and Kerry will have the same experience. We won't. That hurt.

Tonight, though, we must end the year as we began. With honesty. With trust. With a renewed belief in what we're doing. There's a new perception out there about us after losing to Cork. Suddenly everything is turning sour. We're ageing. We've gone from All-Ireland champions-elect to a force in decline in the space of 70 minutes. What are the players thinking? All sorts of questions and theories can take flight after a defeat. We need to check those now. Bring some of them back down to earth, and learn from others. Defeats have never finished us before. They just take us on a different path. We start exploring our new route tonight.

I HAVE THOUGHT ABOUT the hours I spent looking at Cork, figuring them out. If you believed the hype, the shorthand synopsis of Cork's strengths was simple. They are bigger than Tyrone. They can pull ball down from the sky and physically dominate all over the field. Like a boxer, though, sometimes your strongest punch can mask your most effective one.

That was the case with Cork. Their strength wasn't entirely based on their size. Their goalkeeper, Alan Quirke, had an excellent kick-out strategy. Although Cork had two men standing at 6'5" at midfield, Quirke never ballooned his kick-outs into the air. He reduced the percentages. Instead of catching ball over their heads, Cork's tall men were catching ball at chest height. Quirke was spreading his kicks to the wings. That cleverness was their strength. That's where we wanted to attack them. Make them doubt.

The same criticism has often followed my Tyrone teams over the years. Too small. Not enough ball-winning ability. Rubbish. Over the years we were rarely cleaned out at midfield because we were too small. We worked hard and competed. If the opposition were bigger, we reduced the margins through hard work and pressurising them in possession.

By kicking the ball at chest height, Cork were automatically removing any height differential. We knew Quirke would kick to the wings. Ordinarily any midfielder will mark his man by standing by his inside shoulder, forcing him out towards the wing. This time, our midfielders could take a calculated gamble and stand outside their men. If they did, they had an extra millisecond to disrupt the kick-out.

We knew Cork's real strength was their running game. Paul Kerrigan had a terrific burst of speed at wing-forward. We needed to stop him before he got started. Their half-backs loved to come forward. They needed pinning back. Although Justin McMahon was named at centre-back to mark big Pearse O'Neill, we wanted Ryan McMenamin's mobility out there. When Cork had to kick out after conceding a score, they used the extra 20 metres to find O'Neill. For those kick-outs, Justin would come out from corner-back and pick him up. Otherwise, Ryan would run at them. Make O'Neill mark him.

When Ricey raced up-field to score our first point it seemed justification enough for that ploy. Then, the match changed. Alan Quirke's kick-outs were aimed at his midfielders' chests, but we weren't pressuring them as we planned. We were letting them run. They were catching ball unhindered. John Bannon was playing too much of a role. By half-time we had stabilised our own performance, but we had problems to deal with.

As the players took a breather in the dressing-room, I took Tony Donnelly and our trainer, Fergal McCann, into a side room. We looked at our half-time statistics. Forget the referee; we weren't coming up to the mark ourselves. We hadn't created many scoring chances. Our number of turnovers was too low. We were falling for Cork's kick-out strategy. After exhaustively highlighting the evidence over the previous few weeks, that was criminal.

Our routine at half-time is now well-rehearsed. Tony takes the team through the tactical alterations we need to make. I paint the bigger picture, but the scene was uncluttered and chillingly simple this time. We were on our own in this game.

Now it's September. We're still trying to find our way back.

I SPLIT THE BOYS *into small groups of five or six and set the tone. "We're here reflecting on a season that hasn't gone where we wanted it to go," I tell them. "But let's not think it's been a terrible season. We won an Ulster title. We made an All-Ireland semi-final. We must have done a lot of things right. Otherwise we wouldn't have been there.*

"What are we doing here? We're reflecting. We're at a meeting now instead of training in September. Remember that. Obviously we didn't do all we might have done. What else can we do? This isn't about finding fault. It's about examining our inner selves. Whenever you lose a game, it's easy to read a whole lot of things into it. Now we have to check whether these things are entirely accurate. If we can take learning from it for the season ahead, then that's the essence of what we're about. We can't fix what's gone but we can be different people for the future. Sometimes you only find these things out when you lose."

The players start to chat among themselves. Eventually they present their thoughts. We collate all their views and make a list. A pattern begins to emerge:

- *Were we in a comfort zone?*
- *Were we complacent?*
- *Fatigue from training?*
- *More work on set plays?*
- *Did the panel push each other enough?*
- *Can we communicate better?*

It's encouraging, candid stuff. Some of it we can deal with immediately. Fergal addresses the issue of fatigue. By the Cork game, we had done 61 collective training sessions in 2009. By the time we reached the All-Ireland semi-final in 2008, we had done 69 and played more games. The season might have stretched into December 2008 for some players with their clubs, making them feel psychologically stale as a result, and defeats in Croke Park always make your legs feel heavy. Physiologically and factually, though, there was nothing to support the fatigue argument.

There were other areas where we could all agree. Our kick-out strategies over the years had returned mixed results. Same again against Cork. It was a symptom of our need to refocus on our set plays. We needed greater rigour when dealing with prearranged moves and ploys for 2010. Our training sessions this year were blessed with a fantastic vibe. They were feel-good sessions. You could see the work being done. You could see players improving. You sensed the growing confidence and contentment coming from the players. Generating momentum from that positivity was a key component in 2009. That has to change for 2010.

You can come off feeling good knowing you've done the work, but a session leaning towards set plays mightn't necessarily give you the same kick. Tending the mechanics of your game is never as fun as pressing on the accelerator and hearing the engine roar. We have to accept the need for even more detailed work. That will also require us to change our view of what constitutes a good training session.

Did everyone push each other enough? Cork's desire and aggression levels reminded me of our team in 2003, when we came to Croke Park looking to break our own moulds. We needed to match that. We were an older team now, but we were better too. Last year the work the substitutes took on during the year pushed everyone to another level. Those sessions were still available to them, but the same intensity and attendance wasn't there.

When the opposition didn't come up to the mark we expected during the summer, did we allow ourselves to stay in a comfort zone? Were there signs of that during the year that we missed? Victories often mask those flaws. Even if we spotted them, how could we address them when we were still winning? Even when the team wasn't fully clicking, different individuals stood up every day and got us through. We need to figure out how to drive on as a team regardless of the challenge posed by the opposition. If the opposition are playing like a team ten points worse than us, then beat them by ten or more, not by five. Nail our performances. Get our confidence from delivering our best in combat, not the training ground. That's the very essence of these meetings. We can't fix what went wrong in 2009 now. The learning is all for the future.

IN THE PAST I would have let defeat to Cork eat at me for six months. Now I know I have a choice. We all do. If you want this to sicken you, you can allow this defeat to burden you for as long as you like. Or you can leave it behind.

We can listen to the criticism and take it on board. We can consider the perception that our team is finished. We can listen to one journalist suggest that John Bannon deserves an apology for being asked to reconsider the incident with Brian McGuigan that saw John Miskella spared a red card. What part of the high moral ground was that journalist inhabiting when two referees were asked to review two incidents involving Ryan McMenamin and Tommy McGuigan during the league in order to upgrade their punishments?

A month earlier we were the greatest team around, cruising to an All-Ireland title. Now, we're being told we're nowhere.

That's what Fr Vincent Travers, Wayne Dyer and Eckhart Tolle have shown me. Am I going to hand my wellbeing over to someone else? Or do I take charge of this situation myself? Criticism doesn't hurt me. It fuels me. Contrary to what some pundits appear to think, the team hasn't stood still since 2003. Even the core of the 1997/98 minor generation are in better shape now than a few years back.

Consider this. Kevin Hughes enjoyed his best season for many years. Owen Mulligan performed well. Stephen O'Neill was on fire. Philip Jordan will undergo surgery for an injury this winter, but has already committed to returning. Brian McGuigan is gradually coming back to himself. Whether he returns to the heights of 2005 is uncertain, but it's not impossible.

Ryan McMenamin will be there. Brian Dooher hasn't mentioned retirement. Martin Penrose followed up a good 2008 with a better 2009. PJ Quinn, Justin McMahon and Davy Harte are young but carrying plenty of experience now. Joe McMahon has years ahead of him too.

Before we played Kildare in the All-Ireland quarter-final, word filtered through from Owen Mulligan that Raymond Mulgrew was feeling unsettled. Having experienced some of the same expectation and frustration Raymie was feeling, Mugsy wanted to help his club-mate. But Mugsy wasn't finished helping yet.

One Sunday, myself and Tony arranged to meet and chat with Raymie. He was doing some gym work at the Glenavon Hotel near his home in Cookstown, but we agreed to follow him to his house to talk. This needed to be kept low-key.

Fat chance. As we got to the gates of the hotel heading for Raymie's house, I spotted a familiar sight: Mugsy in his van, hazard lights on, honking the horn as he led us into Cookstown. Raymie took a wee detour to shake our cheerleader off, but as he turned onto the road leading to his house, there was Mugsy again, still flashing lights, still honking.

It broke the mood brilliantly. Raymie didn't feel he was progressing the way he wanted, and wished to leave the panel. The day we won the 2008 All-Ireland final, I had told Raymie he would be on the field the next time Tyrone won an All-Ireland. He has the quality and talent to be great. He won't make it alone, though. He needed to stay with us. In the end, he did. Like many others, 2010 is a mighty challenge for him.

IT'S A CHALLENGE for us all. My own contribution will have to change. I can push myself harder. I can find new ways to inform our players. I can connect with them better. We will continue to seek difference. Our experience with Sean Cavanagh on the morning of the Cork game, and the way the team failed to counter Cork's kick-out tactic despite all our work, shows the need to continually improve our methods of communication with the players. Are they seeing the game as we do? Are we doing enough to understand their state of mind? The coming season is going to force us to monitor individuals more closely. If "positivity" was the key word that defined out preparations in 2009, "accountability" is the word for 2010. Players must prove themselves. It's about them. What they are doing. Why they should be considered serious contenders for a starting place. If that forces them to face some uncomfortable truths, then they must.

We have often spoken before about providing a much more detailed breakdown from game to game for each player to chart their form and inform our reasons why they're starting or struggling to get game time. That will finally be put in place fully in 2010. The feedback will be much more specific and consistent from game to game. It will pile a significant amount of work on the backroom staff, but we have told the players we will deliver that data. That is probably the next stage in terms of dealing with players: more one-on-one assessment. More detail in relation to their own personal performance and development. It's not enough to name 15 players and a set of subs any more. Players need to know precisely where they stand, and why.

I'm looking at six or seven minors from the 2008 All-Ireland winning team. They will be put on strength and conditioning programmes for the McKenna Cup. If they make it, that means a handful of current panellists are going to lose out. That sends its own message to everyone. We will retain a large panel for the start of the year, but prune it all the way to the championship. There will be no comfort zones. No hiding places. No excuses. We all have things to prove. Success costs. We start paying now.

FOR ME, THE SHOW will continue. I have one more year left with Tyrone and if it feels right I don't feel any need to step back. The only title I never won at home with Errigal Ciarán was an All-Ireland club title. The ambition nags at me sometimes, but not these days. Sometimes I think about the system of play and the ethos we have created among our players and wonder if it might work just as well somewhere else. Promoting a set of core values among my players was always central to creating a team, but it takes time and the ability to absorb victory and defeat in the same way. We have also been blessed in Tyrone with a marvellous generation of talent, but I still believe the basic principles of team-buildingtrust, loyalty, good practice, communication – can deliver results anywhere.

But I also know that if I left Tyrone now, I'd only try and fill the void with something else. Why leave this situation, when you're operating with the best?

Experience tells me I have known far worse than this. I think of 1997 so much. Sometimes I wonder if anything changed me as much as that year. Nothing influenced my sporting life like it, for sure. If we had won that All-Ireland minor final, where would I be now? I would have retired from management, no question. Would I have ever managed the Tyrone seniors? Would the same players have come through? Would the blend have been right for 2003?

Would I have followed the same journey and learned the lessons I have? Would my life have been illuminated by Wooden, Jackson, Zalucki, De Mello? By Owen Mulligan's charm and good humour? By Cormac McAnallen's rare humility and relentless ambition? By Peter Canavan and Stevie O'Neill's genius? By Gavin Devlin's personality? By Kevin Hughes' hats? By Tony Donnelly's friendship and wisdom, and the dedication of so many players and people in the background through the years? By the joy and excitement our adventures inspired for Marian and the children?

After losing Paul McGirr and seeing the All-Ireland slip away in 1997, I never thought any good could come from that. Instead, that year created a whole new life for us all. Defeat never meant the end to me again. It is a fresh beginning.

We are in a new place now, but still driven by the same convictions. We will never surrender. As you think, so you shall be.

Together, we move on.

MICKEY HARTE'S MANAGERIAL RECORD
WITH TYRONE SENIORS
January 2003 – September 2009

Record by Competition

	Pld	W	D	L
McKenna Cup	28	24	0	4
National League	54	30	6	18
Championship	46	31	7	8
TOTALS	128	85	13	30

MICKEY HARTE'S MANAGERIAL HONOURS
WITH TYRONE AND ERRIGAL CIARÁN

- 3 All-Ireland senior championships, 2003, 2005, 2008
- 2 All-Ireland under-21 championships, 2000, 2001
- 1 All-Ireland minor championship, 1998
- 1 National football league, 2003
- 2 All-Ireland vocational schools, 2001, 2002
- 3 Ulster senior championships, 2003, 2007, 2009
- 4 Dr McKenna Cups 2004, 2005, 2006, 2007
- 3 Ulster under-21 championships, 2000, 2001, 2002
- 3 Ulster minor championships, 1993, 1997, 1998

- 1 Ulster minor league, 1998
- 1 Ulster senior club championship, 2002
- 1 Tyrone senior football championship, 2002
- 1 Tyrone All-County league, 2002
- 1 Ulster SFC runner-up (replay), 2005
- 1 All-Ireland minor runner-up, 1997
- 1 Ulster minor runner-up, 1991
- Plus Tyrone and Ulster titles with St Ciaran's, Ballygawley, and reserve county titles with Errigal Ciarán

SFC Record and Results

Pld	W	D	L
46	31	7	8

2003

Tyrone 0-12	Derry 1-9
Tyrone 0-17	Derry 1-5
Tyrone 1-17	Antrim 1-9
Tyrone 1-17	Down 4-8
Tyrone 0-23	Down 1-5
Tyrone 1-21	Fermanagh 0-5
Tyrone 0-13	Kerry 0-6
Tyrone 0-12	Armagh 0-9

2004

Tyrone 1-17	Derry 1-6
Tyrone 1-13	Fermanagh 0-12
Tyrone 0-9	Donegal 1-11
Tyrone 1-15	Down 0-10
Tyrone 1-16	Galway 0-11
Tyrone 3-15	Laois 2-4
Tyrone 1-9	Mayo 0-16

2005

Tyrone 1-13	Down 1-6
Tyrone 0-10	Cavan 1-7
Tyrone 3-19	Cavan 0-7
Tyrone 0-14	Armagh 2-8
Tyrone 0-11	Armagh 0-13
Tyrone 2-14	Monaghan 1-7
Tyrone 1-14	Dublin 1-14
Tyrone 2-18	Dublin 1-14
Tyrone 1-13	Armagh 1-12
Tyrone 1-16	Kerry 2-10

2006

Tyrone 0-5	Derry 1-8
Tyrone 2-16	Louth 2-16
Tyrone 1-12	Louth 1-7
Tyrone 0-6	Laois 0-9

2007

Tyrone 0-13	Fermanagh 1-9
Tyrone 2-15	Donegal 1-7
Tyrone 1-15	Monaghan 1-13
Tyrone 2-8	Meath 1-13

2008

Tyrone 2-8	Down 2-8
Tyrone 0-21	Down 1-19
Tyrone 1-18	Louth 1-10
Tyrone 0-14	Westmeath 1-7
Tyrone 0-13	Mayo 1-9
Tyrone 3-14	Dublin 1-8
Tyrone 0-23	Wexford 1-14
Tyrone 1-15	Kerry 0-14

2009

Tyrone 2-10	Armagh 1-10
Tyrone 0-15	Derry 0-7
Tyrone 1-18	Antrim 0-15
Tyrone 0-16	Kildare 1-11
Tyrone 0-11	Cork 1-13

NFL Record and Results (2003–2009)

Pld	W	D	L
54	30	6	18

2003

Tyrone 0-10	Roscommon 0-11
Tyrone 1-13	Galway 0-11
Tyrone 0-11	Dublin 0-12
Tyrone 1-14	Donegal 0-10
Tyrone 1-9	Armagh 0-10
Tyrone 1-13	Kerry 0-14
Tyrone 1-17	Cork 0-14
Tyrone 4-11	Fermanagh 1-11
Tyrone 0-21	Laois 1-8

2004

Tyrone 0-8	Dublin 0-9
Tyrone 2-9	Fermanagh 0-10
Tyrone 3-15	Longford 0-9
Tyrone 2-11	Mayo 1-5
Tyrone 2-11	Westmeath 0-6
Tyrone 1-9	Cork 1-9
Tyrone 1-8	Kerry 1-7
Tyrone 1-16	Galway 1-16
Tyrone 1-19	Galway 2-18

2005

Tyrone 1-11	Donegal 0-10
Tyrone 1-10	Dublin 0-9
Tyrone 0-18	Offaly 0-9
Tyrone 1-12	Cork 0-13
Tyrone 1-11	Mayo 0-16
Tyrone 1-24	Westmeath 3-8
Tyrone 3-8	Kerry 2-17
Tyrone 1-7	Wexford 1-8

2006

Tyrone 1-6	Dublin 1-9
Tyrone 0-8	Fermanagh 0-9
Tyrone 0-12	Cork 0-8
Tyrone 2-15	Offaly 0-12
Tyrone 1-15	Monaghan 1-13
Tyrone 1-14	Kerry 1-12
Tyrone 0-11	Mayo 1-8

2007

Tyrone 0-11	Dublin 0-10
Tyrone 0-14	Fermanagh 0-8
Tyrone 0-7	Cork 0-15
Tyrone 1-8	Donegal 2-11

Tyrone 1-8	Limerick 0-9
Tyrone 0-9	Kerry 0-9
Tyrone 1-11	Mayo 4-7

2008

Tyrone 0-7	Kildare 1-4
Tyrone 0-9	Kerry 0-12
Tyrone 2-9	Galway 1-14
Tyrone 0-16	Laois 0-14
Tyrone 0-11	Donegal 0-9
Tyrone 0-10	Derry 0-14
Tyrone 0-15	Mayo 0-13

2009

Tyrone 1-18	Dublin 1-16
Tyrone 0-13	Kerry 2-10
Tyrone 0-8	Galway 0-10
Tyrone 1-15	Westmeath 2-10
Tyrone 0-9	Donegal 0-11
Tyrone 0-14	Derry 0-11
Tyrone 0-14	Mayo 1-11

McKenna Cup Results

Pld	W	D	L
28	24	0	4

2003

Tyrone 1-13   Fermanagh 1-11

Tyrone 3-16   Antrim 2-8

Tyrone 2-11   Cavan 0-10

Tyrone 0-12   Monaghan 1-12

2004

Tyrone 1-10   Derry 2-5

Tyrone 2-11   Antrim 1-2

Tyrone 1-12   UUJ 0-7

Tyrone 1-22   Donegal 0-7

2005

Tyrone 3-14   Cavan 0-7

Tyrone 0-18   UUJ 0-7

Tyrone 4-21   Antrim 1-10

Tyrone 3-14   Derry 1-10

2006

Tyrone 2-12	Down 0-11
Tyrone 4-9	St Mary's 1-9
Tyrone 0-11	Donegal 0-9
Tyrone 0-13	Armagh 0-11
Tyrone 1-15	Monaghan 0-8

2007

Tyrone 2-14	Queens 0-9
Tyrone 1-15	Derry 0-9
Tyrone 0-14	Cavan 0-10
Tyrone 2-16	Monaghan 0-8
Tyrone 2-09	Donegal 0-5

2008

Tyrone 0-9	UUJ 0-12
Tyrone 3-5	Down 1-7
Tyrone 0-11	Donegal 0-12

2009

Tyrone 0-9	Down 0-16
Tyrone 3-9	St Mary's 2-11
Tyrone 1-18	Monaghan 0-17

Senior record in Croke Park

- 2003 NFL semi-final: Tyrone 4-11   Fermanagh 1-11
- 2003 NFL final: Tyrone 0-21   Laois 1-8
- 2003 SFC quarter-final: Tyrone 1-21   Fermanagh 0-5
- 2003 SFC semi-final: Tyrone 0-13   Kerry 0-6
- 2003 All-Ireland final: Tyrone 0-12   Armagh 0-9
- 2004 SFC qualifier: Tyrone 1-16   Galway 0-11
- 2004 SFC qualifier: Tyrone 3-15   Laois 2-4
- 2004 SFC quarter-final: Tyrone 1-9   Mayo 0-16
- 2005 Ulster final: Tyrone 0-14   Armagh 2-8
- 2005 Ulster final replay: Tyrone 0-11   Armagh 0-13
- 2005 SFC qualifier: Tyrone 2-14   Monaghan 1-7
- 2005 SFC quarter-final: Tyrone 1-14   Dublin 1-14
- 2005 SFC quarter-final replay: Tyrone 2-18   Dublin 1-14
- 2005 SFC semi-final: Tyrone 1-13   Armagh 1-12
- 2005 All-Ireland final: Tyrone 1-16   Kerry 2-10
- 2007 NFL round one: Tyrone 0-11   Dublin 0-10
- 2007 SFC quarter-final: Tyrone 2-8   Meath 1-13
- 2008 SFC qualifier: Tyrone 0-13   Mayo 1-9
- 2008 SFC quarter-final: Tyrone 3-14   Dublin 1-8
- 2008 SFC semi-final: Tyrone 0-23   Wexford 1-14
- 2008 All-Ireland final: Tyrone 1-15   Kerry 0-14
- 2009 NFL round one: Tyrone 1-18   Dublin 1-16
- 2009 SFC quarter-final: Tyrone 0-16   Kildare 1-11
- 2009 SFC semi-final: Tyrone 0-11   Cork 1-13

Pld	W	D	L
24	18	2	4

Record in Senior Finals

- 2003 McKenna Cup final: Tyrone 0-12   Monaghan 1-12
- 2003 National league final: Tyrone 0-21   Laois 1-8
- 2003 Ulster senior final: Tyrone 1-17   Down 4-8
- 2003 Ulster final replay: Tyrone 0-23   Down 1-5
- 2003 All-Ireland senior final: Tyrone 0-12   Armagh 0-9
- 2004 McKenna Cup final: Tyrone 1-22   Donegal 0-7
- 2005 McKenna Cup final: Tyrone 3-14   Derry 1-10
- 2005 Ulster senior final: Tyrone 0-14   Armagh 2-8
- 2005 Ulster final replay: Tyrone 0-11   Armagh 0-13
- 2005 All-Ireland senior final: Tyrone 1-16   Kerry 2-10
- 2006 McKenna Cup final: Tyrone 1-15   Monaghan 0-8
- 2007 McKenna Cup final: Tyrone 2-9   Donegal 0-5
- 2007 Ulster senior final: Tyrone 1-15   Monaghan 1-13
- 2008 All-Ireland final: Tyrone 1-15   Kerry 0-14
- 2009 Ulster senior final: Tyrone 1-18   Antrim 0-15

Pld	W	D	L
15	11	2	2

Record by Opponent

	Pld	W	D	L
Donegal	11	7	0	4
Derry	10	7	1	2
Kerry	10	6	1	3
Down	9	5	2	2
Dublin	9	5	1	3
Fermanagh	8	7	0	1
Mayo	8	3	2	3
Monaghan	7	6	0	1
Armagh	7	5	1	1
Galway	6	2	1	3
Cavan	5	4	1	0
Cork	6	3	1	2
Antrim	5	5	0	0
Westmeath	4	4	0	0
Laois	4	3	0	1
Louth	3	2	1	0
UUJ	3	2	0	1
Offaly	2	2	0	0
St Mary's	2	2	0	0
Wexford	2	1	0	1
Limerick	1	1	0	0
Longford	1	1	0	0
Queen's	1	1	0	0
Kildare	2	1	1	0
Roscommon	1	0	0	1
Meath	1	0	0	1